Sheffield Hallam University
Learning and IT Services
Adsetts Centre City Campus
Sheffield   S1 1WB

101 807 978 5

D0255636

ONE WEEK LOAN

Shelle
Rose Charvet

SHEFFIELD HALLAM UNIVERSITY
LEARNING CENTRE
WITHDRAWN FROM STOCK

KENDALL/HUNT PUBLISHING COMPANY
4050 Westmark Drive   Dubuque, Iowa 52002

To my sons, Jason and Sammy,
who give me much joy and keep on teaching me,
to my Mum, Betty Rose,
for always being there,
in memory of my Dad, Frank Rose,
who taught me about intellectual rigour and humour,
and in memory of my Grandma, Katie Rose,
who kept asking me: "Who told you?"

Copyright © 1995, 1997 by Shelle Rose Charvet, Success Strategies

Library of Congress Catalog Card Number: 97-70788

ISBN: 0-7872-3479-6

All rights reserved. No part of this publication may be reproduced, stored in a retrieval system, or transmitted, in any form or by any means, electronic, mechanical, photocopying, recording, or otherwise, without the prior written permission of the copyright owner.

Printed in the United States of America
10   9   8   7   6   5

SHEFFIELD HALLAM UNIV.
WL
302.2242
CH
ADSETTS LEARNING CENTRE
LS

"*Words That Change Minds* is full of interesting tools for anyone who truly values good communication. This book will teach you how to understand people and how to speak to them. I highly recommend this book."

—Peter Urs Bender, author of *Secrets of Power Presentations*

"*Words That Change Minds* is a great self-help book, that will help you understand yourself and the people you work with."

—Joe Gaetan
Director of People and Improvement, Monsanto Canada Inc.,
Mississauga, Ontario

"I had to laugh at the bookstore on Monday. Everyone that asked me if I knew any good books got an enthusiastic presentation on yours. I told them how much pain I would have avoided in personnel if only I had had your book nine months earlier."

—Gary E. Megel
Colorado Springs, Colorado

"Can you imagine your business profits increasing by 10–30%? That is what my company was able to immediately experience, as I used Ms. Rose Charvet's LAB Profile to make improved hiring decisions."

—Edward Lund,
Telecommunications Manager, California

"At last I got your book, and on the strength of its information I have my first decent commercial assignment helping a local employer do his own recruiting, as he is fed up with the standard of the local employment bureaux."

—Roger Phillip,
Personnel Trainer
Devon, United Kingdom

"*Words That Change Minds* provides a comprehensive overview of the fundamental differences in individual behavioral patterns, questions that reveal these patterns and the language most likely to influence people according to their dominant patterns."

—Joel P. Bowman, Professor
Haworth College of Business, Western Michigan University
Kalamazoo, Michigan

"The LAB Profile was a fascinating discovery, which impacted the way I communicate with others, and transformed my consulting practice."

—Léon Tanguay,
Human Resource Development Consultant,
Montréal, Québec

"The LAB Profile and the book *Words That Change Minds*, written by Shelle Rose Charvet, have proven to be invaluable tools in my evaluation and hiring process. Candidates have been screened in to positions and screened out, far more appropriately, through the proper use of these techniques. I highly recommend these additions to your array of behavioural interviewing tools."

—Gordon I. Brown,
Vice-President, Executive Search,
Corporate Consultants, Toronto, Ontario

"*Words That Change Minds* is a book of insight and inquiry. Shelle Rose Charvet offers a new way to think about relationships with ourselves and others. She provides a strategic language of influence to support lasting effective improvements in the building of our relationships. She describes the basic mental structures that we use to perceive, organize and act on our social world. Words That Change Minds is a unique reference framework for individual and family self-development. It is a landmark for leaders, executives and associates who are committed to improve, with integrity, the quality of life and the effectiveness of their enterprise."

—Dr. François Sauer,
Director Strategic Growth, Transquest,
Atlanta, Georgia

"*Words That Change Minds* gave me a level of awareness and precision in communication that I did not think was possible. I used to get frustrated when I worked with others who had different communication patterns than my own. Now, I get curious. What a breakthrough!"

—Clay Conner,
Strategic Planning Analyst, Idaho Power,
Boise, Idaho

"I pull out *Words That Change Minds* whenever I am facing a situation where I am not connecting with an individual. By using Shelle's techniques I can understand them better and then establish a much higher level of rapport. As a sales professional there are times when I have to present to key decision makers. Shelle's book has helped me understand how to communicate with people on their terms and that has increased sales."

—Karl Meema,
Prairie Regional Manager, Microsoft Canada Inc.,
Calgary, Alberta

"*Words That Change Minds* belongs on the must read list for everyone who interacts with other people. I have found it to be invaluable for understanding and communicating effectively with business associates, family and friends. It's the first book I have read that identifies various styles of communicating and outlines an easy-to-follow process to create an accurate exchange of information."

—Tom Dearth,
President, Spotlight Presentations,
Denver, Colorado

"Shelle's book, *Words That Change Minds*, is a helpful and practical reference tool and guide in preparation for management, negotiation, mediation or conflict resolution. Understanding and respecting people is at the core of good communications. I have found the LAB Profile to be a useful and insightful tool. It helps you progress towards your desired outcome, while respecting the needs and pace of those with whom you are working."

—Geneviève O'Sullivan,
Director General, Strategic & Corporate Relations,
Agriculture and Agri-food Canada, Ottawa, Ontario

"I read the book during a ski trip in New Zealand—it's easy reading, entertaining, and very practical. I've used the motivation traits questions to help a Malaysian friend clarify his career goals, a middle-age friend to build her résumé, and most interesting of all, a Chinese lady to decide whether or not she should buy a South Sea pearl necklace! And all the while, they didn't know I was using the standard questions because it was like natural conversation."

—Kenzie L. Kwong,
Director, Kenn & K Consulting Ltd.,
Hong Kong and Asia Pacific

"This book provides intriguing insights into what motivates people, how they make decisions and generally what makes them tick. I found this information very valuable."

—Juel Hogg
Marketing Program Manager,
Hewlett-Packard, (Canada) Ltd.,
Toronto, Ontario

"*Words That Change Minds* has greatly assisted our staff in honing their negotiating skills—I highly recommend this book to anyone who has to deal with high stakes communication."

—Harry Hynd
Director, District 6, United Steelworkers of America,
Toronto, Ontario

"Knowing the precise definitions of spoken or written words is not enough to understand the real intended meaning. The LAB Profile solves this for each unique relationship and provides the influencing words that are most effective for that particular relationship."

—Chuck Watson
Corporate Accounts Vice President, Coulter Corporation,
Miami, Florida

"Excellent book—would recommend this book to anyone wanting to use NLP in the business world. Written in a down-to-earth, extremely readable, interesting style with useful real-world examples . . . and with a great sense of humor!"

—David Kintler,
President, SalesWinners, Inc.
Coral Springs, Florida

"After reading Shelle's book, I asked her to train my management, customer service representatives, consultants and sales staff. Not only does it work in achieving bottom line results in business, she also taught my wife and I how to communicate at a new level. Shelle is the master of influential communication. I strongly urge all business leaders to read this book . . . it could change your life!"

—Richard A. Grehalva,
Vice President, CSC Health Care Systems,
Birmingham, Alabama

Contents

Part 3 Working Traits 91

Part **4** Applications   149

Appendices   193

Acknowledgments

I would like to thank all those people, too numerous to name, who helped make this book possible by developing the original ideas, giving me valuable learning experiences, sharing with me their expert opinions and feedback, and allowing me to work and play with them, in personal and professional relationships.

Thank you to Richard Bandler, John Grinder, Leslie Cameron-Bandler, and Judith Delozier for their development of Neuro-linguistic Programming. A BIG thank you to Rodger Bailey for his creation of the Language and Behaviour Profile, which is the basis of this book and much of my work. And thanks to all the other developers, teachers, and practitioners of NLP who have influenced my life and my work.

I would like particularly to thank Dr. Lorraine Bourque, from the Faculty of Education at the Université de Moncton in Moncton, New Brunswick, for her insight, feedback, and friendship. Micheline Sirois and Étienne Godin from the same university contributed their research abstracts to the second edition. Many thanks to Dr. David Rosenbloom, head of pharmaceutical services at Chedoke-McMaster Hospitals in Hamilton, Ontario, for his ability to see and realize the potential of new ideas; and Doug MacPherson, assistant to the director of District 6 of the United Steelworkers of America, for his feedback and support of my work. Thanks to Thelma Egerton of IBM Europe for being a great client and friend, as well as a great trainer, who has shared many laughs and a few tears with me over the years. And a big "Merci!" to Pierre Artigues (Señor), my former boss in Paris and always my friend, for teaching me more about intellectual rigour and helping me understand and adapt to living and working in France. Thanks to Stever Robbins and Joseph O'Connor for their help editing my clumsy prose in the second edition. Thanks also to the many readers who enthusiastically contacted me with ideas and suggestions, many of which have been included in the second edition.

Thanks to Ainslie Smith for reading what I wrote on her island paradise in Georgian Bay and saying it was great. Thanks to Stever and Jay Arthur for their excellent ideas for a book title, and to Michael Erdos for cover ideas.

Most of all I wish to thank my family: my brothers, Michael Rose (my computer guru) and Professor Jonathan Rose, for learning and using the material and encouraging me to write the book; my sister-in-law, award-winning writer Barbara Wade Rose, for her personal support and critical eye; my mother, Betty Rose, for helping out in many ways; my kids, Jason and Sammy, for being who they are. All my family for loving and encouraging me. I love you all.

Part 1

Introduction

$\mathcal{C}$ntroduction

Cheryl walked into my office for her appointment looking frustrated and angry. A well-dressed, elegant professional, she did not waste a second on the customary niceties of a first encounter.

"I need to find a new job right away," she said. "I can't stand my boss and I heard that you do career profiles." After some discussion about what she wanted and what was important to her, we agreed to do a career profile. About halfway though the feedback on the profile she called a halt to the whole process. "Oh my God," she said. "My boss and I are obstinate in exactly the same way! We are constantly arguing. Neither of us will budge from our positions. No wonder we haven't been getting along! Can you show me how to communicate with him?" I took a few minutes and taught her the exact language to use and avoid. Within two months she called to tell me of a major promotion she had just received. Today she is one of the highest-ranking women in her sector in the country.

Poor communication is today's number one problem at work, at home, and in the world at large. Discords among people are frequent, from small annoyances like twenty-minute phone mail messages, to lifelong parent-child resentments, to intractable conflicts between nations. Finding solutions to communication problems has been the focus of much study and the development of many models.

Many psychometric assessments have been created to explain the differences that cause communication problems between people. These assessments often require sophisticated computerized instruments to administer. Even then, many of them only allow a few very specialized applications, or worse, stick people in boxes with labels, like round pegs into square holes. Often they do not recognize people's inherent flexibility to shift thinking and behaviour as situations change. It is not surprising that a great many individuals, while fascinated by questionnaires, tend to discount the sweeping generalizations these instruments produce. People often prefer to rely solely on their intuition and gut feelings to make critical decisions such as hiring or choosing a spouse. I once told a CEO that if he hired his executive vice president because he *liked* the person, he would be in big trouble. The last thing he needed was to recruit someone who thought just like he did.

3

It is well known that people communicate through a set of filters shaped by history, sense of identity, beliefs about what is true, and values about what is right, as well as perceptions and interpretations of what is going on. When someone else communicates with us, we squeeze the message through our own personal filtering system to understand. Of course, people from the same ethnic, cultural, gender, national, or geographic grouping have some common history and beliefs. That makes communication within a group easier than between people who come from different backgrounds.

We are now beginning to grasp that, beyond these differences, each of us also has unique *ways* of thinking and processing. We pay attention to various aspects of reality, based on how we *individually* use our brains. Some of us think in detailed linear sequences, while others prefer to envision a larger whole. Some people are attracted to those things that are different and new, while others attend to what is the same or similar to what they already know.

But what if we *could* really understand what someone means when he or she talks to us? Even better, what if we could predict someone's behaviour based simply on what was said? Best of all—what if we could *influence* that behaviour by how we responded?

I investigated the field to find some answers to these complex questions of understanding, communicating, and influencing. I wanted to avoid facile solutions. Any good theory must be well founded and verifiable by personal experience. It must also be applicable for a wide range of human activities, respectful of individual people and their differences, and learnable without a doctorate or engineering degree. Above all, it had to improve communication between people.

In 1983, while teaching communication seminars in Europe, I started to hear about some interesting work that came from (wouldn't you know it) California. I began to explore this approach, called Neuro-linguistic Programming (NLP). In spite of its techno-babble name, it seemed to be designed to reach into people's minds and discover how specifically each person is unique. It was based on studying some of the great communicators and therapists of our time. It examined *how* they were able to accomplish what they did, without the usual investigation into the reasons *why* people have problems. It was about learning strategies that work, not about scrutinizing the failures that people experience.

I wanted to find out if these people were onto something. I took some in-depth courses and began to test their techniques in my work. The results were remarkable. I learned how to create rapport with anyone, to change beliefs that had been limiting me, and to help others do the same. Being a doubting Thomas, I liked the requirement that every intervention be tested for possible negative consequences prior to being completed with a person. If someone were actually to let go of the belief that rainy days make them sick, a practitioner would have to check first if getting sick on rainy days had some positive benefits that needed to be met in some other healthier way for the person, *before* helping him replace the belief.

In 1985 I encountered a specific tool developed from NLP that completely changed the way I communicate. It is both rigourous and flexible. It can be woven naturally into casual conversation. I have spent the years since then exploring its uses in a wide range of contexts. I have used it to:

- create powerful presentations for large groups of people
- redesign marketing and sales processes to help companies successfully reach their major customers
- attract and select only the right candidates for key executive positions
- help clients I coached or counselled
- create *irresistible* influencing language for teenagers, and
- help organizations dramatically improve their communication about change with their own people.

While this tool has been widely taught, it had been treated as an abstract theory about the differences between people. I kept finding new ways of applying it and getting dramatic results. I wondered why no one had written a book on all the things you could do with it, provided you took the time to master the skill. This book is the result of testing it out for myself and with my clients.

In 1995 and 1996 I assisted in the supervision of two Master of Education theses. One thesis succeeded in establishing the reliability of the tool, and the other investigated whether there were predictable patterns in people who were able to make career decisions, compared with people who found it difficult or impossible to decide on a career. I have included the research abstracts in the appendices.

The Language and Behaviour Profile (LAB Profile)

The tool is called the **Language and Behaviour Profile (LAB Profile)**. It is a way of thinking about people and groups that allows you to notice and respond to how they get motivated, process information, and make decisions.

It is a set of about a dozen questions that you can feed into casual conversation or use as a formal survey for groups. You pay attention to *how* people talk when they answer, rather than *what* they talk about. Even when a person does not answer the question directly, he will reveal his pattern by the manner in which he answers (or doesn't).

As you become familiar with the questions and the kind of responses people give, you will find that you can hear and pick up the patterns people use without having to actually ask the questions. You can immediately use the Influencing Language that is just right for the situation. People communicate with their particular patterns naturally as they speak, both in words and in their body language, and they respond immediately when you use *their* language.

Because the LAB Profile can be used informally in conversation, I have included in this book many sample conversations. To illustrate the kind of emphasis and inflection that we typically employ when we talk, I have made liberal use of **bold** and *italic* characters.

As you read this book, check it out with your own experience, relating it to the people you know, recognizing yourself and others. I hope you will find some solutions to the challenges you face as you communicate with people on a daily basis. Even if you do not have specific communication problems, this book will provide you with useful information to consider and a vocabulary for describing what you are already doing—perhaps unconsciously.

I keep discovering new insights and uses for this material both in my personal life and in my work. I invite you to join with me in exploring the possible applications of the LAB Profile.

$\mathcal{H}$istory of the LAB Profile

Words That Change Minds is built on the Language and Behaviour Profile, or LAB Profile, created by Rodger Bailey. The LAB Profile is a development based on specific applications from *Neuro-linguistic Programming*, a field developed by Richard Bandler, John Grinder, and others in the United States, beginning in the mid-70s. They created the original models of Neuro-linguistic Programming (or NLP) by examining and understanding the processes used by highly successful communicators.

The field of NLP has been expanding exponentially since then, and is now the subject of hundreds of books written around the world. This approach is being taught in several dozen countries on all five continents. For those of you unfamiliar with Neuro-linguistic Programming, here is my own brief definition of what it is.[1]

Let's start with Programming. Each person, through genetic makeup, environmental influences, and individual biochemistry, has managed to *program* herself or himself to be excellent at a certain number of things, mediocre at different things, and just awful in other areas.

If we observe and listen carefully to how a person behaves and communicates *linguistically*, we can glean an understanding of how, *neurologically*, a person puts his or her experience together to be excellent, mediocre, or awful at the things he or she does. Hence, this field is called Neuro-linguistic Programming.

The applications are enormous. It means if someone is highly skilled at something, a person trained in certain NLP protocols can *model* her. Modelling is finding out how it is possible for that person to do what she does. The modeller searches for the answers to questions such as: "What are the absolute essentials?" or "What is that person paying attention to or ignoring, sequentially and/or simultaneously, to be able to do it?" When the answers to these and other questions are found, then it becomes possible to teach that skill to other people, and even learn it oneself.

The Language and Behaviour Profile is a model created by Rodger Bailey, an avid developer in the field of NLP. He created the LAB Profile in the

---

1. For a very complete introduction to NLP, see **Introducing NLP**, by Joseph O'Connor and John Seymour, (London: HarperCollins, 1993).

early 1980s. It is based on set of patterns from NLP called, at the time they were developed, the *Meta Programs*. These Meta Programs are based on the filters that we use to make up our *model of the world*.

Creating Our Model of the World

Every person has a certain number of filters by which they let in certain parts of the real world. In Noam Chomsky's 1957 Ph.D. thesis, *Transformational Grammar*, he said there are three processes by which people create the filters of their individual Model of the World:

Deletion

The first process is called **deletion**. We delete lots of information from the environment around us and internally. In his 1956 paper entitled **Seven Plus or Minus Two**, George Miller, an American psychologist, said that our conscious minds can only handle seven plus-or-minus two bits of information at any one time, and that we delete the rest. That means on a good day we can deal with nine bits and on a bad day, maybe only five.

This explains why most telephone numbers are a maximum of seven digits. However, while I was living in Paris in the 1980s, they changed the phone numbers to eight digits. Everyone then had to decide whether to remember phone numbers by groups of two, or four, or to simply add the new Paris code, 4, onto the front of their old number. No one had an easy way of keeping eight digits in their head at once. Each person had to find their own way to break it down. People would give out their new phone numbers in their own peculiar manner. It created a great deal of confusion.

So seven plus or minus two bits of information is what we can be comfortably be aware of at one time. Using the process of deletion, we filter out lots of things without being aware of it or consciously choosing to do so.

Distortion

The second process is called **distortion**. We distort things. Have you ever moved to a new place and gone into the living room before you moved your things in and pictured what it was going to look like furnished? Well, you were hallucinating. Your furniture was not *actually* in the room, was it? So you were distorting Reality.

Two examples of distortion are hallucination and creativity. They are both similar in that the external information is changed to something else. That is what the process of distortion is all about.

Generalization

Chomsky's third mental filtering process is called **generalization**. It is the opposite of Cartesian Logic (where you can go from a general rule to specific examples but not the other way around). Generalization is where you take a few examples and then create a general principle. This is how learning occurs. A small child learns to open one or two, or possibly three, doors and then she knows how to open all doors. The child develops a Generalization about how to open doors. That is, until she has to enter a high-tech company and realizes that, to open the door, there is a magnetic card that has to be slid down a slot in a certain way. She has to relearn how to open doors to deal with those exceptions.

Generalization is about how we unconsciously generate rules, beliefs, and principles about what is true, untrue, possible, and impossible. Some women, for example, may have had several bad experiences with men and then come to the conclusion that men (i.e., *all* men) cannot be trusted. They develop the rule: *Never trust a man.* People have a certain number of experiences of a similar type and then make a rule or develop a belief.

With the three filters, Deletion, Distortion and Generalization, we each create our own model of the world.

$\mathcal{M}$eta Programs

What is the link between these three processes—NLP, The Meta Programs, and the LAB Profile? The co-originators of NLP used Chomsky's Deletion, Distortion and Generalization model to create a map for discovering and influencing a person's perceptions and interpretations of their experiences.[2]

Leslie Cameron-Bandler took Chomsky's work even further. She postulated that each person makes specific kinds of Deletions, Distortions and Generalizations, which then show up in a person's behaviour. From her work in therapeutic settings, she identified about sixty different patterns, which she called Meta Programs.

Meta Programs are the specific filters we use to interact with the world. They edit and shape what we allow to come in from the outside world. They also mould what comes from inside ourselves as we communicate and behave in the world.

Meta Programs are like a door through which we interact with the world. This door has a particular shape and has the power to let only certain things in or out. This may appear to be part of our individual nature, and therefore permanent; in fact, the door itself can shift in response to changes in ourselves and our surrounding environment.

Rodger Bailey, a student of Leslie's, adapted and used her work in business settings. He created the LAB Profile, which enables us to understand what people are communicating about their reality when they talk. He said that the Meta Programs are a status report on how a person responds to a given situation. Most people would agree that our behaviour is different when we are with different people, at work, or at home with our family. The Meta Programs are not, therefore, descriptions of our *personality* as such, but rather a picture of how we interact with different environments or contexts.

The Meta Programs simply describe the form of our door, what specifically we let in and out in a given situation. It is this recognition of our ability to change our behaviour that sets this tool apart from the psychometric profiles that make sweeping generalizations about our personality.

---

2. Their map is called **The Meta Model**. Please see **The Structure of Magic 1** by Richard Bandler and John Grinder (Science and Behaviour Books, 1975).

Language and Behaviour Patterns

When I first learned about Meta Programs, there were about sixty patterns. We had to talk to the people we were studying with and *guess* what their patterns were. I spent a year and a half trying to guess what everyone's Meta Programs were, and needless to say, I was not very good at it.

To make detecting and using these patterns simpler, Rodger Bailey had the foresight to reduce the number of patterns from sixty to fourteen. (Do you really need to know sixty things about yourself or another person?) He also developed a small set of specific questions by which, regardless of what people answer, their unconscious patterns are revealed *in the structure* of the language they use. You pay attention to *how* people answer, instead of *what* they say. In this way, after asking a few simple questions, you can determine what will *trigger and maintain* someone's motivation and how they internally process information.

He identified two separate kinds of Meta Programs when he developed the LAB Profile. He called the first set of categories **Motivation Traits**. These are the patterns that indicate what a person needs to get and stay motivated in a given Context, or conversely what will demotivate someone. Sometimes I call these the Motivation Triggers because they reveal what will *make* a person do something or *prevent* a person from acting in a certain way.

Rodger Bailey called the second set **Working Traits**. These categories describe the internal mental processing that a person uses in a specific situation. For example, we can determine if a person prefers an overview or sequential details, the environments in which she is most productive, whether a person attends to people or tasks, how she responds to stress, and the mechanics that lead her to becoming convinced about something.

And all this shows up in *how* a person talks.

Influencing Language

He also developed the *Influencing Language*. Once you know a person's patterns, you can then tailor your language so that it has *maximum impact* for that person.

Imagine for a moment that someone who did not master your mother tongue very well was attempting to get some ideas across to you. Chances are that you would spend a lot of energy translating it into terms that were more meaningful to you. When someone uses terms that you can *immediately* understand, none of your energy is lost in translating; the meaning just goes in. When you use the appropriate Influencing Language, the impact is powerful precisely because you are *speaking in someone's own personal style*.

You can choose exactly those **words that change minds**.

Reality

I need to make another point before we go on, just to avoid any confusion. From Noam Chomsky and many others, we know that people do not actually live in Reality. By deleting, distorting and generalizing, we inhabit our *perceptions* and *interpretations* of Reality. The LAB Profile patterns reflect a person's Model of the World.

Because of this, I will NOT generally be dealing with Reality in this book, but rather the way we *perceive and interpret* it. As John Lennon said: "Reality leaves a lot to the imagination." On the other hand, Woody Allen said: "Reality is the pits, but it's the only place you can get a good steak." Since we do need to eat, I will make reference to Reality from time to time; the occasional Reality Check, so to speak.

How the LAB Profile Works in Communication

Let's say a person has an experience. When that person talks about his experience, he only communicates a minute portion of the actual event. He has to edit out the vast majority of what was going on for him, just to be able to communicate it in a reasonable time frame. It means that in order for you to tell someone about reading this book, you will need to eliminate most of what you experienced. You might say, "It was good," and nod your head, perhaps leaving out all the things this book made you think about, not mentioning whether you were physically comfortable at the time you were reading. Think of all those times when you did not grasp what someone was talking about because they left out elements you needed to fully understand.

People transform their actual experience, their opinions, and so on, in ways that correspond to their own particular Deletions, Distortions, and Generalizations.

Leslie Cameron-Bandler and Rodger Bailey determined that people who use the *same language patterns* in their speech have the *same behaviours*. The Language and Behaviour Profile got its name from the connections between a person's language and how they behave.

The tools in this book will enable you to *understand, predict* and *influence* behaviour. The LAB Profile is a set of tools that can be learned as a skill. You will have the opportunity to train your eyes and ears to perceive certain things that you may not have paid attention to before. You will also learn some ways of describing and working with behaviour patterns you may have already noticed.

Because the LAB Profile is a set of skills, you will need to use it with rigour, paying attention to the shifts people make as they move from situation to situation. This is where the notion of Context comes in.

Context

The Context is the frame of reference a person puts around a situation. Since human beings are flexible by nature, they are able to behave differently at different times. Are we talking about you at work, in a couple relationship, with your kids, with your peers, when you are on holiday, or when you are buying a house? Simply because a person has a certain pattern (or habit) in a given place and time does not indicate that she will have that same pattern in another Context.

When I run seminars in this material, people ask me: "Am I always that way?" The answer is no. We move, we grow, and our response to significant events in our lives can change how we function. These changes show up in the LAB Profile patterns we use in conversation. Because our behaviour can vary in different situations, you will need to make sure when using the LAB Profile questions, that you have clearly and specifically identified the Context. What is the frame of reference (or Context) around the situation for the person you are speaking with? I will demonstrate how specifically to do this as we discuss each pattern.

If used with integrity and care, the LAB Profile will enable you to improve your communication dramatically in many Contexts. It will enable you to adapt what you do to fit any situation.

The tools in this book will not only aid you in thinking about how you communicate, but will actually help you become a better communicator. They will enable you to prevent and avoid problems that you might not otherwise have foreseen. You will save time as you move more quickly toward your goals. You will become aware of the results, and others are sure to notice the difference. These tools will help you progress in your growth, or totally change the things you want.

Think of what you'll achieve as you master those *Words That Change Minds*.

Part 2

Motivation Traits

$\mathcal{M}$otivation Traits

Questions	Categories	Patterns—Indicators
(no question for Level)	LEVEL	_____ **Proactive**—*action, do it, short, crisp sentences* _____ **Reactive**—*try, think about it, could, wait*
• What do you want in your (*work*)?	CRITERIA	
• Why is that (*criteria*) important? (ask up to 3 times)	DIRECTION	_____ **Toward**—*attain, gain, achieve, get, include* _____ **Away From**—*avoid, exclude, recognize problems*
• How do you know you have done a good job (*at . . .*) ?	SOURCE	_____ **Internal**—*knows within self* _____ **External**—*told by others, facts and figures*
• Why did you choose (*your current work*)?	REASON	_____ **Options**—*criteria, choice, possibilities, variety* _____ **Procedures**—*story, how, necessity, didn't choose*
• What is the relationship between (*your work this year and last year*)?	DECISION FACTORS	_____ **Sameness**—*same, no change* _____ **Sameness with Exception**—*more, better, comparisons* _____ **Difference**—*change, new, unique* _____ **Sameness with Exception & Difference**—*new and comparisons*

$\mathcal{M}$otivation Traits

The first six categories in the LAB Profile will show you how different people trigger their motivation and what language you will need to use to capture their interest. Each category is dealt with in a separate chapter.

For each category of patterns you will learn the questions to ask, how to detect the patterns in ordinary conversation, what each person needs to get interested or excited about something, and conversely, what would turn them off.

There are no good or bad patterns to have. You can judge the appropriateness of each pattern only in the Context of the activity that needs to be done. For each pattern I have included ways to take advantage of the strengths and qualities inherent in each one.

While each category represents behaviour on a *continuum* from one pattern to another, **each pattern is described in its pure form. Behaviour predictions are only valid in the same Context in which the subject was profiled**.

After the behaviour description for each pattern you will find a section entitled **Influencing Language**. Listed here are examples of the kind of language that has the greatest impact. For each category, the distribution of the patterns is shown. The figures are from the research that Rodger Bailey conducted, and refer only to the Context of work. They will give you an idea of how frequently you can expect to find certain patterns.

I will discuss the patterns in different situations, with lots of examples to provide insight and illustrate the fine points of using *Words That Change Minds*.

At the end of both the Motivation Traits and Working Traits sections are **summary worksheets**, which can be used when profiling people. At the end of the book are complete profiling worksheets.

ℂ𝒲aiting for Godot or Jumping at the Bit: Motivation Level

Does the person take the initiative or wait for others?

This category in the Motivation Traits is about what will get you going and what will make you think. What is your LEVEL of activity? There are two patterns:

Proactive

Proactive people initiate. They tend to act with little or no consideration, to jump into situations without thinking or analyzing. They may upset some people because they can bulldoze ahead with what they want to do. They are good at going out and getting the job done. They do not wait for others to initiate.

Reactive

Reactive people wait for others to initiate or wait until the situation is right before they act. They may consider and analyze without acting. They want to fully understand and assess the situation before they will act. They believe in chance and luck. They will spend a lot of time waiting. Some people may get upset with them because they do not *get started*. They will wait for others to initiate and then respond. In the extreme, they operate with extra caution and study situations endlessly. They make good analysts.

Distribution _____ %

(in the work Context, from Rodger Bailey)

Proactive	Equally Proactive & Reactive	Reactive
15–20%	60–65%	15–20%

Since about 60 to 65 percent of the population in the work Context have an equally Proactive and Reactive pattern, it is reasonable to assume that the person you are profiling is in the middle, unless they clearly demonstrate that they lean to one side or the other.

Pattern Recognition

Since there is no specific question to ask for this category, you can pay attention to the person's sentence structure and body language, as they will be giving you their pattern throughout your conversation.

Proactive—sentence structure
- short sentences: noun, active verb, tangible object
- speaks as if they are in control of their world
- crisp and clear sentence structure
- direct
- at the extreme, they "bulldoze"

Proactive—body language
- signs of impatience, speaking quickly, pencil tapping, lots of movement or inability to sit for long periods

Reactive—sentence structure
- incomplete sentences, subject or verb missing
- passive verbs or verbs transformed into nouns
- lots of infinitives
- speak as if the world controls them, things happen to them, believe in chance or luck
- long and convoluted sentences
- talks about thinking about, analyzing, understanding, or waiting, or the principle of the thing
- conditionals, would, could, might, may
- overly cautious, need to understand and analyze

Reactive—body language
- willingness to sit for long periods

Examples

Proactive:	"I meet with my team every week."
Mainly Proactive:	"I meet with my team if it seems like we need it."
Equally Proactive and Reactive:	"I meet with my team to go over the current files. It is important to stay informed."
Mainly Reactive:	"Even though you might wonder if it is necessary

to meet with the team every week, I do it because it is important that they feel they are being listened to."

Reactive: "Even though everybody might wonder if it is really necessary to meet each week, it is important to consider the needs people have of being listened to."

Influencing Language

Just use these words and phrases to get people to jump into action. If you think about it, matching someone's way of being is very important when communicating.

Proactive
- go for it; just do it; jump in; why wait; now; right away; get it done; you'll get to do; take the initiative; take charge; run away with it; right now; what are you waiting for; let's hurry

Reactive
- let's think about it; now that you have analyzed it; you'll get to really understand; this will tell you why; consider this; this will clarify it for you; think about your response; you might consider; could; the time is ripe; good luck is coming your way

Since most people have some Proactive and Reactive, you can use both sets of Influencing Language; considering and doing.

Hiring

People who have a Proactive pattern at work are suitable for those positions that require taking the initiative, going out and getting it done. They would work well in outside sales, in independent businesses, or the kind of work where having *chutzpah*[1] is an asset. If you are advertising for a highly Proactive person, ask the applicants to phone instead of sending in a résumé. (Reactive people will not phone.)

People who have a Reactive pattern in the work Context are well suited to jobs that allow them to respond to requests. Representatives on customer service desks tend to be more Reactive. Many research and analytical jobs need someone who can spend a lot of time analyzing data.

Most people and most positions require a mixture of the two patterns. When hiring, you will need to examine what proportion of the work to be done consists of Reactive or Proactive activities, to determine the kind of balance you need. It is appropriate to profile the others on the team to make sure you have a good balance.

---

1. A Yiddish word, meaning having a lot of nerve

There are some *key questions* to ask yourself regarding this category when profiling a position. To what degree will this person need to take the initiative? How much of the job consists of responding, analyzing, or depending on the actions of others? You might want to estimate the percentage of overall time in Proactive or Reactive activities.

Stepping on Toes: People Management

People who have a strong Proactive pattern at work will be impatient with bureaucratic delays or internal politics, and may even go outside of their bounds, stepping on others' toes to get things done. They jump into activities and may go very far very fast, before you or they, notice when they are on the wrong track. As the manager of Proactive employees, you will need to channel their energy in appropriate directions. If they do not have the opportunity to use their high level of energy, they will become frustrated or bored, and as a result may use their initiative in unproductive ways. You can motivate them by giving them a job to do and telling them to "Go for it." You may need to remind them to think before they jump.

Reactive people will generally not take the initiative and will feel stressed or anxious when asked to do so. At the extreme, they will want to consider, analyze, and *be given* an understanding of situations almost to the exclusion of deciding or doing anything. In a team setting, Reactive people can contribute to the process by analyzing proposed solutions and slowing the process enough to consider ramifications and alternatives. You can motivate Reactive people by matching their pattern. "Now that you have had enough time to consider and think about this, I will need it on my desk by Monday at noon."

I recently discovered (by first-hand experience) how to drive Proactive people crazy. Put them in a situation that they dislike intensely, then make sure that they can do nothing about it.

Fate and Destiny

Reactive people do not believe that they control their world. Chances are that they will be waiting for someone else to solve problems or make improvements for them. Do you remember Vladimir and Estragon in Samuel Beckett's *Waiting for Godot*? They spent the entire play waiting for the mythical Godot to appear and solve all their problems.

Since most people at work are somewhere in the middle, they will need to think and do, respond and initiate. The best kinds of work for these people are tasks and responsibilities that allow enough of each. To motivate these people you would use both sets of Influencing Language. For example, "I would like you to think through what needs to be done and just go do it."

Sales and Marketing

Proactive people tend to buy when they get to do something right away. One day over coffee, I suggested doing a LAB Profile to help a prospective client decide on a career change. I told her that the profile would show her immediately what kinds of activities would trigger and maintain her motivation. She enthusiastically agreed and wanted to do it right then. As we were walking back to my office she said: "Can we run?" She has an off-the-scale Proactive pattern in that Context.

Reactive people will buy when the product or service allows them to gain understanding. They will often be waiting for something to happen before they will decide. I went to see the CEO of a company that sells mutual funds, to talk about sales training for his sales representatives. At our *third* meeting, he told me that the company was completing a merger and he was "waiting for the situation to be clarified." As a highly Proactive person, the voice in my head exploded and said, "What do you want, a message from God? *Who* is going to clarify the situation?" I managed to control the impulse and asked: "Oh, and when is this likely to happen?" I used that phrase to match his belief that things happen *to* him.

Reactive people will be more likely to buy if you suggest that this is what they have been waiting for, or "Haven't you waited long enough to get what you really want?" or "Once you have this, you'll understand why. . . . "

You will occasionally notice marketing campaigns that call to Proactive or Reactive people. These ads inadvertently may also be revealing aspects of the company's corporate culture. In 1993, a large Canadian bank had a slogan: "Get us working for you." My interpretation was that I, as a potential customer, was going to have to wake them up and make them do something for me. But perhaps that way of looking at it is a result of my propensity for being Proactive.

You may have noticed NIKE's slogan: "Just do it." It is a call to action for the Proactive sorts.

Golden Handshakes

During the early to mid-1990s, large corporations (and subsequently governments) decided they needed to shed large numbers of workers. In order to accomplish these large-scale layoffs, many organizations used the *Golden Handshake* approach, offering an attractive package to those who would take the money and leave.

Can you guess who took the money and jumped ship? Have you noticed that this period also coincided with the largest ever increase in home-based businesses?

Proactive people jump at the Golden Handshake as a chance to go out and set up their own operations. Organizations lost many of their most dynamic people. One friend told me that her boss said: "Oh, but we didn't want *you* to leave!" Too late, buddy.

My suggestion to organizations is to plan any necessary layoffs by first deciding *which roles to keep*. (Easier said than done, I know.) The roles will probably call for a mixture of Proactive and Reactive, as well as many of the other patterns described in this book. I then suggest that particular people be offered the buyout package: those who do not fit the desired profiles. Also, I believe it is important to offer counselling to those who will be leaving, to help them make decisions and set up their next steps.

Summary

Level

Question: There is no question for this category.

Proactive: Acts with little or no consideration. Motivated by doing.

Reactive: Motivated to wait, analyze, consider and react.

Distribution
at Work: Proactive 15–20%
          Equally 60–65%
          Reactive 15–20%

Influencing Language

Proactive: do it; jump in; get it done; don't wait; just do it; now

Reactive: understand; think about; wait; analyze; consider; wait; might; could; would

---

$\mathcal{P}$ushing Those Hot Buttons: Criteria

What are the words that will incite a physical and emotional response?

I asked Simone: "What do you want in your work?" She replied: "*A challenge,* something that allows me to *utilize my present skills* and *develop new ones, good remuneration* and *working with people.*"

Those are the things that are important to Simone in her work. Now what does this mean? Simone has given me her Criteria for work.

Criteria is the term we use to describe a person's way of making distinctions about what is good, bad, awful, wrong, right, and so on. They are personal labels. These words are the labels we give to our values.

A person's Criteria are those words that *incite a physical and emotional reaction:* **HOT BUTTONS.** The words themselves are associated, or stuck in our memory, to a series of emotionally similar events that we have experienced through our lives. So when a person hears one of her Criteria, *the word itself* will trigger the emotional response attached to it.

We each have our own definition for each Criterion. A single Criterion is composed of many elements, conscious and unconscious. You may never need to know a person's definition of her Criteria in those situations where you simply want to find out *how* she describes something she is excited about in a given Context.

In any family, each of you knows the others' negative hot buttons. The other members of your family know that if they say a particular word or phrase, you will explode. In my family, one son need only say to the other: "Nope, you're wrong!" to create an explosion of frustration, an emotional and physical reaction.

Many people took interpersonal communication courses in the 1970s and 80s and sometimes still today, where they learned Active Listening techniques, based on Carl Rogers' work. Active Listening consists of paraphrasing what the other person said, *in your own words,* in order to show him what you understood. We can now appreciate that if Simone says that she wants "a challenge" and I play back to her, "so you want something challenging," it does not *create* the same experience for her. When I paraphrase into my own words what you say, it has more to do with my reality than your reality, (and nothing whatever to do with Reality with a capital R). To solve this problem, we now teach participants in communication courses, that to show someone you have understood them, you will need to play back *their* key words, their Criteria.

Other questions to elicit Criteria:
- What do you want in . . . (a job, a home, a spouse, etc.)?
- What's important to you?
- What counts?
- What *has* to be there?
- What would you like to have, be or do?

What to Do with Criteria

Making Decisions: A Hierarchy of Criteria

Knowing how to uncover and work with Criteria can give you an infallible means of deciding what is more important and what is less important in a given Context. You can do this for yourself or with other people. I'll demonstrate with Simone. This technique is called making a **Hierarchy of Criteria**.

SRC:	Simone, you had a number of things that were important for you at work. Let's list them.
Simone:	A challenge, something that allows me to utilize my present skills and develop new ones, good remuneration, and working with people.

We have four Criteria here and we do not yet know which are essential, optional, or the most important for Simone. I, as the listener, may think one is more important than another for her, but that would be hallucinating.

SRC:	Simone, imagine for a moment that I have a couple of jobs that might fit your needs. In this hand over here (holding out my left hand, palm up), you will get a job with a *challenge*. And in this hand, (holding out my right hand, palm up, hands wide apart), this job allows you to *utilize your present skills and develop new ones*. Which one attracts you?
Simone:	A challenge.

If you observe carefully (which is *a challenge* to illustrate in a book) you can often see the choice being made before the person says anything. It is important to keep your hands wide apart so the person will perceive two *separate* choices. I do not know exactly how Simone is processing this choice, but by putting each option in a different hand, I am creating something more real or tangible for her.

How would I write down her choice if I were taking notes? An easy and quick way is to draw an arrow from *challenge* down to *allows me . . .* to indicate that "challenge" was chosen over "allows me."

SRC: In my right hand is a job that will offer you *a challenge*. In my left is one that has *good remuneration*. If you **had** to choose, which one would you want?

Simone: Hmmm. A challenge.

SRC: So challenge is the most important so far. OK, in my left hand is a job with a *challenge* and in my right hand is a job where you'll be *working with people*. Which one would you prefer? (I keep switching the hand I put *challenge* in so as not create an association with one hand.)

Simone: Still a challenge.

We now know that *a challenge* is the most important of these Criteria for Simone, in the Context of work. To complete the Hierarchy we will need to compare each of the other options to each other as we just did.

SRC: Simone, in my left hand is a job that allows you to *utilize your present skills and develop new ones*, and in my right hand is one with *good remuneration*. Which one would you like to take?

S: Good remuneration.

SRC: And in my left hand we have one with *good remuneration* and, in my right hand, one where you can be *working with people*?

S: Good remuneration.

SRC: And lastly, *working with people* in my left hand, and *allows you to utilize your present skills and develop new ones* in my right hand?

S: Working with people.

Now we have Simone's Criteria in order of importance to her:

1. A challenge
2. Good remuneration
3. Working with people
4. Allows me to utilize my present skills and develop new ones

For those of you who help people make decisions, as in sales, this is a very useful process to take your customers through. It can also be used when coaching employees or counselling clients. I also use it for career counselling, where I would also need to get the client to define what would constitute each Criterion.

The easiest way to get someone to define their Criteria is to ask: "Can you give me an example of something that was *a challenge?*" This works well because often people cannot give a straight definition of terms for something that is directly attached to a series of memories and emotions.

The Hierarchy of Criteria is also used to make some decision making processes much shorter. This is a way of helping people get their mind, soul, and body to decide. When you create a tangible, forced-choice situation, people will feel magnetically attracted to one option or the other.

Can't Make Up Your Mind?

Sometimes a person will have difficulty choosing between the two alternatives in your hands; you can confirm this by observing the vacillation in their body as they try to choose. What does this mean, and what do you do about it? There are five situations where this occurs that I have identified to date:

1. The person did not accept the idea that they *have* to choose between two things they want.
2. One Criterion is a component of the other one.
3. The person has two labels for the same set of experiences.
4. One Criterion causes the other to occur (a cause-effect relationship for the person).
5. The person has a conflict between two values or Criteria.

In the first case, if the person cannot or will not choose, you will need find a way to get them to play along. You can ask them to imagine that *if they **had** to choose*, knowing that in real life, they could actually have both, but if they *had* to choose, which one would attract them?

In teaching and working with the LAB Profile in different countries and cultures, I have noticed some cultural differences that may make it hard for some people to play along and choose which Criterion attracts them. In a culture where there is a belief that you *can* have anything you truly want (i.e., the United States), there is no problem in choosing.

Many cultures, however, do not maintain this belief. In fact, many people do not believe that life is *about* getting what you want. Life is about doing what you are *supposed* to do. The reason they cannot choose between Criteria is they believe that what they may want is irrelevant to what they are supposed to do. The weight of outside considerations is greater than their desires. When this is an issue in a group, we discuss what makes for good decisions. If a person can be unburdened from his cares and obligations and, *just for a moment,* considers what appeals to him, he gets the chance to sort out what is important to him. Then he can consider and negotiate with his external commitments.

Sometimes they cannot choose because one Criterion is a component of the other. In other words, one Criterion is *contained within* another Criterion. You can test for this by asking "Is *allows you to utilize your present skills and develop new ones* part of *a challenge* for you? Or the other way around?" In that case you can include the component within the larger Criterion and only use the larger one. "So when we're talking about *a challenge,* we know it includes *allows you to utilize your present skills and develop new ones.*"

Another possibility is that the person has two labels for the same set of experiences. If it means the same thing, he would have difficulty choosing between "it" and "itself." For example let's say a person cannot choose between *interesting* and *a challenge.* To test for this, you can simply ask: "Are *interesting* and *a challenge* really the same thing for you?" If the persons says: "Yes, it is always interesting when there's a challenge," you know that they are closely linked (in his mind anyway). In this case you might want to use both labels to stay in rapport with that person.

The fourth situation is when the person has the belief that one Criterion *causes* the other to occur in what is called a cause-effect relationship. You can check for this by asking: "For you, does having *a challenge* make you *utilize your present skills and develop new ones?*"

The fifth possibility for an unclear choice between two options presented in this manner is that the person has a conflict between two values or Criteria. They will waver back and forth and "yes, but" to themselves or out loud. You can predict, in this case, that the person will have difficulty making certain decisions in this Context and will feel in a "stuck" state. Remember Tevye in *Fiddler on the Roof,* "On one hand . . . on the other hand . . . ?"

Difficult to Satisfy?

What does it mean when you ask someone "What do you want?" or "What's important?" and the person lists fifteen or twenty things? It means that this person is difficult to satisfy. If she has fifteen or twenty Criteria and has no idea which ones are more important than the others, she will have a difficult time making decisions or even being able to find exactly what she wants. Can you imagine a woman finding the man of her dreams with fifteen Criteria?

What is a decision? Often making a decision consists of choosing between two or more alternatives. One of the biggest favours you can do for a person who has many undifferentiated Criteria is to take him through a Hierarchy of Criteria, and then have him create a bottom line cutoff point on what absolutely must be there and what is optional.

Uses for Criteria

If you are considering buying a product, for example, what *must* it have? If you are considering getting married, what are the most important things for you in the person and the relationship? Remember that, when you change Context, your Criteria may change. Many people do not want the same thing in a house that they want in a spouse.

In the process of goal-setting, you need to list the Criteria for success, and understand which are more important. We know that those people who have clearly defined Criteria for their goals are more likely to achieve them quickly. By defining your Criteria, you will have made them real and tangible to yourself.

One of the gentlemen I trained in this technique is a Real Estate broker. When he hires people he uses the Hierarchy of Criteria to find out whether the candidates have the priorities about work that he would like them to have. He asks them "What is important for you in your work?" He then casually asks: "If you *had* to choose between a job where you got to be a *team player* (putting out his left hand) and one where you could be *your own boss* (putting out his other hand), which one would you pick?"

If you are going to start a project with someone or select members of a team or task force, you might want to check out what is important to each prospective member. Do they have the values you are looking for? You can ask them these questions: What do you want from this project? What do you want in a company? What do you want in a team? What's more important to you? This (holding out one hand) or this? You will find that it is very easy to build this into ordinary conversation.

I was a member of the advisory board of the local YMCA. Our highest ranking woman staff member quit the Association because she had been told that there was no possibility of a full-time executive director position at one of the local branches. As a result of her leaving, there was a reshuffle and suddenly a full-time executive director position was established. As a board member I hit the roof because of the unfairness of this.

The next thing I knew, I was in charge of a Committee that was to examine whether our Association had systemic barriers which prevented some employees from having the same opportunities as others. We were to make recommendations on how we could become a better employer.

We set some goals, defined the methodology, and then had to give the Committee a name. Some members suggested "The Employment Equity Committee," named after recently adopted legislation. I mentioned that many people (especially white males) had felt very threatened by this legislation and that, should we identify ourselves with it, we would get very little co-operation from the staff of the Y.

We named ourselves "The Fairness in Employment Committee" and got an 85 percent response rate when we distributed employee questionnaires. My point to the Committee was that we needed to call ourselves something with positive connotations for all staff, and make sure that we avoided any negative hot buttons.

Influencing with Criteria:
A Powerful Sales and Marketing Tool

The gathering of Criteria is a necessary prerequisite for sales and any kind of influencing or persuading process. Unskilled sales people just *pitch their product* (usually using their own Criteria) without much regard to what their prospective customer actually wants. "Lady, this car has everything you want: good mileage, great handling, and flashy decals on the side!" This is what I call the "shot in the dark" approach. Who knows? They might actually hit something.

Many market researchers investigate people's Criteria so that the exact phrasing of an advertising campaign can match what is most important to the groups they wish to influence.

If you want to get and keep someone's interest you will need to link what you are proposing with their Criteria. Often when I am giving a speech I do a question-and-answer session before I begin the body of my talk. I will often ask an audience "What's important to you when you communicate?" Or "If you knew how to understand, predict, and influence behaviour, what would you want to use this ability for?" If someone tells me they want to "know how to present their proposals in a negotiation so that they will be accepted," then I make sure to link those Criteria with the points I am making.

Many people underestimate the power of matching someone's Criteria. Once, as a demonstration with a group, I told a woman about a job opportunity, using all her highly held Criteria. I did not tell her what the job *was*; I simply used her Criteria: "You'll really be needed, people will appreciate what you do for them, you'll be in charge of how you work, and the hours are regular." She said she would take the job, without even finding out what it was.

I know someone who moved from New England to California for a career opportunity that *matched* his Criteria, only to find that the work and the company did not at all meet his expectations. You will need to be careful to deliver what you promise when you use someone's Criteria to persuade them. Otherwise their disappointment and anger likely will be directed at you. Just ask the leaders of all the governments thrown out of office by disenchanted voters.

In Grade One, my son was having difficulties learning to read. We practised at home and the teachers signed him up for the "Reading Club." Parent volunteers take members of the reading club out of class to help them with their reading skills. By the end of Grade One, my son had made *some* progress. He summed up his experience to me: "Only the stupid kids have to go to the reading club."

I met with the teachers at the beginning of Grade Two because they wanted Jason to join the club again. I explained to them what the *meaning* of the reading club was to my son and said that I didn't want him to join. After much discussion, they agreed, and I agreed to continue working with him. Two weeks later he said to me: "They didn't put me in the reading club this year. That's because I'm good at reading. And I'm not stupid." His reading skills picked up exceedingly quickly over the next few weeks.

Criteria are verbal triggers that bring up emotions, both positive and negative. Remember, in order to influence with Criteria, you will need to state them *exactly* as the other person expressed them.

Summary

Criteria

A person's labels for things are important to them in a given Context. They are *hot buttons* because they are attached to emotions and memories.

Questions: What do you want in a . . . ? What is important to you?

Influencing Language

Use the person's Criteria to attract and maintain interest. When a person hears his own Criteria, he will immediately feel the emotions attached to those words.

⟨⟩he Carrot or the Stick: Motivation Direction

> What will trigger a person into action? In what direction
> do they move? Do they move toward an objective, or away
> from problems to be solved or prevented?

When you master this category, you will be able to prevent and avoid many problems, and know how to reach your goals more effectively.

There are two patterns in this category describing the *Direction* a person is moving in for a given Context. They are either moving **toward** a goal, or **away from** problems. Each pattern is first described in its pure form.

Toward

People with a Toward pattern in a given Context are focused on their goal. They think in terms of goals to be achieved. They are motivated to have, get, achieve, attain, and so on. Because of their concentration on goals to be accomplished, they tend to be good at managing priorities. Moreover, they are excited and energized by their goals.

They often have trouble either recognizing what should be avoided, or identifying problems. At the extreme, they are perceived as naive by others because they do not take potential obstacles into account.

Away From

People who have an Away From pattern notice what should be avoided and gotten rid of, and otherwise not happen. Their motivation is triggered when there is a problem to be solved or when there is something to move away from. They are energized by threats. A salesperson told me: "If I don't get out there and sell, I won't be able to pay my bills at the end of the month." Deadlines, for example, get these people into action. People with an Away From pattern in a given Context are good at troubleshooting, solving problems, and pinpointing possible obstacles during planning, because they automatically pick up on what is or could be going wrong.

They may have trouble maintaining focus on their goals because they are easily distracted by and compelled to respond to negative situations. This is the kind of person who will drop everything to fix something. At the extreme they forget what the priorities are and only concentrate on treating crises. If this person is at the top of a department or an organization, the *entire organization will be run by crisis management.* Away From people have some difficulty managing priorities because whatever is wrong will attract most of their attention. People who have a strong Away From orientation in a given Context are often perceived as jaded or cynical, particularly by Toward people.

Distribution _____ %

(*in the work Context, from Rodger Bailey*)

Toward	Equally Toward & Away From	Away From
40%	20%	40%

Most people will have a mainly Toward or mainly Away From pattern on this continuum, in a given Context.

Pattern Recognition

Questions

WHY IS HAVING THAT (THEIR CRITERIA) IMPORTANT?

or

WHAT WILL HAVING THAT (THEIR CRITERIA) DO FOR YOU?

Toward—sentence structure
- talks about what they gain, achieve, get, have etc.
- inclusion
- what they want, goals

Toward—body language
- pointing toward something, head nodding, gestures of inclusion

Away from—sentence structure
- will mention situations to be avoided, gotten rid of
- exclusion of unwanted situations, things
- problems

Away from—body language
- gestures of exclusion, shaking head, arms indicating that something is to be avoided, gotten rid of

Note: Listen to what a person says after the word **because**. It will either be a Toward or an Away From statement.

Examples

Toward:	"I would get personal satisfaction and a promotion."
Mainly Toward:	"I would get a promotion, personal satisfaction, make more money and not have to go on the road."
Equally Toward and Away From:	"I would get personal satisfaction and not have to go on the road."
Mainly Away From:	"I would not have all this routine work, or be away from my family often, plus I would get a promotion."
Away From:	"I would get away from this boring work, all the deadlines, and my boss who keeps looking over my shoulder."

You will need to ask the questions in a series or laddering approach, as follows:

SRC:	Adam, can you give me your Criteria for a job?
A:	Effective, more proficient, fun and taken seriously.
SRC:	All right, Adam, *why is having that important?*
A:	To help people.
SRC:	To help people. And why is that important?
A:	Because I get satisfaction from helping people.
SRC:	So why is satisfaction important?
A:	Well, *that's what I want* from a job.

Here's a different example:

SRC:	Joanne, what do you want in a job?
J:	I like to know what I have to do, and to be evaluated based on my own performance.
SRC:	Why is that important?
J:	It gives me a sense of calm.
SRC:	And why is *that* important?
J:	If I'm not calm with myself, I can't be calm with my kids.
SRC:	And why is that important?
J:	*It keeps me from hitting my kids.*

Joanne wanted to have her Criteria met in order to prevent a certain outcome, while Adam was motivated to attain his Criteria in order to achieve an outcome.

The reason we ask the Motivation Direction questions several times is to get a more accurate sense of where the person puts their energy: *toward goals* or *away from* problems. In my experience, when we ask the question only once, we often get a one-line Toward answer, regardless of the person's actual pattern. I believe that is because many of us have subscribed to the "Power of Positive Thinking," and so devalue the importance of recognizing problems.

There was an elderly gentleman who resided at a hotel. Every evening he shuffled gingerly to the front desk to get his keys and over to the elevator to go up to his room. One day he got his keys and went up the elevator as usual, only to immediately return to the front desk. He addressed the clerk: "Young lady, I have a problem." The bright young employee had been trained in customer service and the power of positive thinking, so she replied: "We don't have problems here, sir, we have challenges!" The gentleman snorted and said: "Harumph! I don't know if it's a problem or a challenge, but there is a woman in my room."

So we ask the questions about three times to find out what is behind the answer, or what is triggering the person into action in that Context.

Alternate Questions:
  What's the point?
  Why bother?
  What's important about X?
  What's in that for you?

So, Why *Did* You Leave Your Last Job?

Changes in Context

Why *did* you leave your last job? Because you couldn't stand it anymore? Or because there was something better on the burner? Why did you leave your last spouse? Because you were unhappy, or because there was someone else on the horizon? Why did you take your last vacation? Was it because you wanted a break from the grind or because you were interested in doing something in particular?

You may have a Toward pattern in one Context and an Away From pattern in another Context.

Can your Direction change over time? Yes, it can. Your response to a single significant event may change your pattern. Let's say someone has a Toward pattern and has all kinds of habits that probably are not good for his health. Then he has a heart attack and what happens? Because the heart attack was a very nasty yet compelling experience, he may change Direction and begin moving *away from* health problems. He might change his behaviour, quitting smoking, doing more exercise, changing his diet, and so on, because he *does not want* to have another heart attack. Some addiction treatment programs work on that basis.

Sometimes people do not make changes in their lives because they have not yet hit rock bottom. A helpful question to ask might be: "Do you *feel bad enough now* to make some changes or would you rather wait until you feel *even worse?*"

Influencing Language

Using the Influencing Language appropriately will get you a person's complete attention. That will prevent you from having to repeat things several times. The rapport that you establish will be deeper because you have matched how the person thinks; you will not have to spend a lot of time to get on the same wavelength. Because you have established rapport, you can avoid a lot of misunderstandings.

Here are some typical expressions to use:

Toward
- attain; obtain; have; get; include; achieve; enable you to; benefits; advantages; here's what you would accomplish

Away From
- won't have to; solve; prevent; avoid; fix; prevent; not have to deal with; get rid of; it's not perfect; let's find out what's wrong; there'll be no problems

What Would Make You Set and Attain Goals?

For many years people have been teaching and learning about the importance of setting goals. It has been proven many times that if you do not have goals, chances are you will not be able to find what you truly want. Was that last sentence a Toward statement or an Away From statement? It was Away From. You don't get anywhere if you don't have goals.

When we are discussing a person's Motivation Direction, we are talking about what will **trigger** her into doing something, such as setting goals. Why do I personally set goals in my business? Because if I didn't, I would be totally disorganized. I do set goals, and I have an Away From pattern at work. For me, this means that I can get distracted by whatever squeaks the loudest. In order to stay focused on what I am to achieve (and particularly so as *not* to become disorganized), about every two weeks I ask myself: "What business am I in?" This helps me recenter on what I really need to be doing. Another useful question for Away From people to ask themselves is: "How does this activity fit in with what I want to accomplish?"

Toward people need to ask themselves: Are my plans going to work? What else do I need to predict? What haven't I thought of yet that may go wrong? They may need the services of a devil's advocate in order to make sure they are being realistic.

While North American culture seems to have a bias against the Away From pattern, there is a need for a balance between Toward and Away From in many situations. A good equilibrium between Toward and Away From on a team will help ensure that goals are set, well-laid contingency plans are made, and focus is kept on priorities.

Is It Fear of Success or Motivation Direction?

Here's another consideration regarding Away From people and goal achievement. Let me give you an example. This happened to John Overdurf, a therapist I know. He had a client who came to see him and said: "I'm very upset. My life is really going down the tubes. I've been a millionaire four times." At first glance you might say, "You've been a millionaire four times. So what's the problem?" Let's think about it. If he has been a millionaire four times, that means he lost it three times. So let's look at what happened.

John asked him some questions and found out that he had an extreme Away From pattern about work. He was motivated *to move away from poverty.* Let's put this on a graph to understand his pattern. On the vertical axis, we have his amount of motivation, or how motivated he is, from "not very motivated" at the bottom to "very motivated" at the top. Let's put revenue on the horizontal axis, zero revenue to one million dollars. If he is highly motivated away from poverty, at zero revenue, how motivated is he? Very motivated. As he earns money, what happens? His interest level declines as his revenue increases. Once poverty was not an issue, he would not finish work on contracts, or he would forget to submit quotes to potential clients, or procrastinate and not follow up. When the big contract would come that could push him over the million-dollar point, he says "Ahh, I'll do it when I get around to it," whereas when he is threatened by poverty (whatever that means to him) he is highly motivated to do whatever it takes to generate revenue.

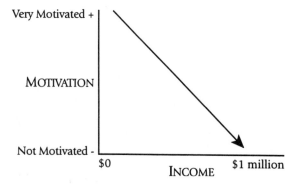

Although this is an extreme example, it explains why highly Away From people need to recenter at regular intervals on what they are trying to achieve.

Positive or Negative Thinking?

When first acquainted with these patterns, many people judge people with a Toward pattern as positive, while the Away From pattern is seen as negative. This judgment comes from a certain interpretation of the words "positive thinking." Remember that these patterns are simply triggers that will catapult someone into action.

Mother Teresa was quoted as saying that she started her work when "I discovered there was a Hitler in my heart." Her Motivation Direction is Away From. Many lobby groups, such as Greenpeace, the National Action Committee for the Status of Women (NAC), the anti-nuclear movement, Amnesty International, and so on, are essentially motivated to move away from certain practices with which they do not agree. You can therefore predict that these groups will notice what is insufficient or wrong with government legislation to protect the environment, rape victim protection laws, nuclear safety regulations, welfare reform, and so on. Many journalists also have this pattern.

Here is a statement by Nelson Mandela, on May 24, 1994, the day he became President of South Africa:

> "My government's commitment to create a people-centred society of liberty binds us to the pursuit of the goals of . . .

(at first glance this sounds pretty Toward, doesn't it?)

> freedom from hunger, freedom from deprivation, freedom from ignorance, freedom from suppression and freedom from fear."

If a person answers "freedom" in response to *Why is that important?*, do not assume that it is either Toward or Away From. Probe to find out if it is freedom *to* or freedom *from*.

Conflicts of Language in Labour Relations

In the Context of labour relations and negotiations, conflict arises not only because of the often contrary vested interests of labour and management. Conflict also arises because of the cultural differences between the two groups. If I can make a generalization for a moment, let's take top management as a culture. Is top management mainly Toward or Away From? Goals, business plans, objectives, and so on, are Toward activities. What is the primary reason for the existence of a union? To make another generalization, unions often exist to protect their members from disasters: poor pay, bad working conditions, lay offs, and the like.

Frequently management and labour do not speak the same language. Management tends to negotiate in terms of moving toward its objectives, while labour attempts to prevent certain things from occurring.

In 1995 the Canadian rail strike/lockout between the Canadian National Railway (CN) and the Canadian Pacific Railway (CP) on the one hand, and the Canadian Auto Workers (CAW) and the Brotherhood of Maintenance of Way Employees (BMWE) on the other, gave clear examples of these patterns at work. The principal issue was over employment security, a hard-won benefit that the unions were determined to *prevent* the railways from changing, particularly in the face of possible privatization of CN and massive layoffs. The railways were equally determined to modify the contract in order to *increase* their competitiveness with American railways and the trucking industry. In this example, each side was moving in a different Direction and, as is the case in labour disputes that escalate, operating out of different Criteria.

If labour and management could each learn to understand the patterns of the other side, and learn how to speak in their language, they would improve their chances of reaching agreement with less strife.[2] Of course, in Reality, not all unions have an Away From motivation, nor do all employers have a Toward pattern.

Professions Have Cultures

Some professions are inherently Toward or Away From. For example, medicine, as it is usually practised in the West, is highly Away From. As a culture (as distinct from individual patterns) medical practitioners tend to focus on what is wrong with their patients. They move *away from sickness and dying*. I recently completed profiling all the pharmacists in a hospital and found that, out of seventeen pharmacists, fourteen had a mainly or highly Away From pattern at work. The other three were only slightly on the Toward side of the equation. As a culture, the medical professions are so Away From, that when the idea occurred to them that holistic health might be something worth considering, they called it *Preventative Medicine*.

The Away From orientation is appropriate for treating and curing (getting rid of) disease. Can you imagine rushing in to your doctor about a medical emergency, and when you see her, she ignores your symptoms only to ask you about your health goals?

On the other hand, a number of medical practitioners work outside the traditional medical structures. I am willing to bet that many herbalists, iridologists, and others have a Toward pattern about their work and

---

2. For much more complete information on how to negotiate, please see Fischer and Ury's **Getting to Yes**, Ury's **Getting Beyond No**, and Fischer's **Beyond Machiavelli**.

do not feel comfortable with people who primarily seek out and destroy disease.

As you read about the different patterns, you may find that you can deduce the cultural patterns of different professions.

Hiring

If you are going to hire someone, it would be useful to know whether the day-to-day activities of the job consist mainly of troubleshooting and problem-solving or rather concentrating on the attainment of objectives. Although most organizations are now, at the very least, paying lip service to performance appraisals based on employee objectives, you will need to examine the day-to-day realities of the position more closely.

To assist a design and manufacturing firm in hiring a plant manager, I needed a list of responsibilities and tasks that this person would perform. The tasks included monitoring production reports and investigating causes of errors in production, shipping, and data entry; ensuring that shipments are properly done; quality control; government compliance; negotiating with suppliers and facility maintenance. With the possible exception of negotiating with suppliers, most of the activities needed to meet these responsibilities required looking for, preventing, and solving problems. A Toward Plant Manager would have missed many of the potential errors and omissions while charging ahead to meet production targets. (I have noticed that many people who have an Away From pattern call targets "deadlines.") I also profiled the senior management to ensure there would be a balance in the team, and someone would be looking out to make sure objectives were met.

If you want to hire someone motivated to perform the job at hand, it is important to determine whether the job is goal-oriented or is mainly troubleshooting. Do you need someone who is excited about working toward goals, or someone who delights in solving crises?

I will deal with how to write career advertisements to only attract the "right" candidates in the Applications section of the book.

People Management and Task Assignment: The Carrot or the Stick

Since most managers already have a team of existing employees, they would be well advised to discover what their strengths are, and to capitalize on those strengths instead of suffering from the weaknesses.

To get and keep Toward employees motivated, they will need tasks that allow them to attain goals. You can tell them the benefits of doing a certain task, such as *improving* efficiency, *increasing* departmental revenue, or *receiving a bonus*. In meetings they will want to stay focused on the objective and will have little patience for discussions about what might go or is going wrong. They will consider such talk as off-topic. You will need to explain to them the benefits of discussing potential problems and make sure you do

that in Toward terms: "If we discuss and plan for potential problems now we'll reach the objective that much sooner," is more appropriate than: "If we don't look at problems now, we'll be unprepared later."

Toward employees, particularly when they also have a Proactive pattern, if left to charge on to their goals, may get some nasty surprises later, due to inattention to potential hurdles or unforeseen negative consequences.

Away From employees will steer meetings into discussions of obstacles and what is wrong with proposals. To help them be most productive in meetings, explain to them (in Away From terms) why keeping the goal in mind will *prevent the group from losing focus*, which could be a major *waste of resources* and allot them time for *disaster prevention*. For tasks, give them problems to solve and things to fix. Impending disaster will energize them. "If this isn't out on time, they'll have our heads." The worst thing that you, as a manager, could do to an Away From employee is to take away all their problems. "Nothing's wrong, I'm worried." You, as a manager, also may not want to cope with the results of giving a Toward task to an Away From employee.

I also suggest that you do not ask a Toward employee to proofread a document. They will not pick out the errors. If you notice mistakes in text as if they jumped out of the page, then you have an Away From pattern in the Context of reading. I gave the first draft of this book to a friend to read over, having forgotten about her Toward pattern. Apart from adding a couple of commas, she said, "It's just great," and went on to tell me all the things she liked about it.

The Cure to Writers' Block

When you write letters, reports, articles, or books, do you ever suffer from Writer's Block? If this happens regularly, then you probably have an Away From pattern in this Context. It is much easier, and more motivating, for Away From people to correct mistakes than it is for them to remain focused on the goal of their text.

My philosophy is to work from my strengths, as opposed to suffering from my weaknesses. So, knowing about my Away From pattern, I decided to write this book by doing what I do best: fixing what's there. To do this, I had my audio tape series on the same topic transcribed and put onto diskette. Then I structured the book and imported sections of the transcript. Lastly, I did the fun part. I corrected the text, turning spoken language into written text, looking for errors and omissions, needed updates, and new examples.

I told my sister-in-law, who is a writer, that I was able to produce about twenty-two pages of text per day. She found this to be incredible until I explained that: "I wasn't writing twenty-two pages, I was correcting twenty-two pages and adding in what was missing."

My advice to those of you who suffer from Writer's Block is to get *anything* down on paper (or up on the screen), even if you have to ask someone

A very Toward dog!

else to draft a letter, for example. Then fix it. It will be much less tedious and you won't waste a lot of time wondering what to say.

Of course this trick would not help you if you *really* had nothing to say.

Sales and Marketing

Just out of curiosity, I phoned the local Automobile Association, and asked: "Why do people buy your service?" They told me that 90 percent of their members join the club to avoid problems such as having their car break down and paying a fortune for a tow. In the Context of travel by car, the vast majority of their members therefore have an Away From pattern.

I recently had the opportunity to work with the Automobile Association. To explain what I meant by Toward and Away From, I took the management down to the front desk to eavesdrop on what customers were saying. Person after person said that they *didn't want to have to deal with* breakdown problems, expensive alternatives, and so on. As a result we redesigned their marketing, sales, and customer service processes to use mainly Away From language: "Your one-stop worry-free travel agency," "You won't have to deal with . . . ," "You needn't worry about . . . ," "No-fee travellers cheques," "This will save you time," and the like.

Insurance is another Away From product. Most customers buy to avoid problems for themselves or their families. Investments, on the other hand, are inherently Toward. Imagine the difficulty insurance sales people must have had when insurance companies also began offering investment opportunities. They would have had to get their insurance customers into Toward thinking. Often they merely continued the pattern, pointing out the financial disasters inherent in not investing wisely.

I assisted the marketing department of a major pharmaceutical manufacturer in profiling its market. We also reviewed its print advertisements in light of our findings. One of their ads for a drug to prevent urinary incontinence had been particularly successful. It showed a smiling man in his sixties, swinging a golf club on a beautiful sunny day. The caption read: "18 holes and no accidents." Until we had diagnosed the Profile, they had assumed that the ad worked because of the positive scene in the picture. After they understood the nature of the product and the market in Away From terms, it was agreed that it was the caption that created the positive response.

As a salesperson or marketing director, there are several options you could take when planning your sales approach or marketing campaign. You can examine your product or service to discover if it is Toward or Away From by its very nature, and design your process to attract more of the appropriate market segment. Alternatively, especially if your product or service could be both, you could design your strategy to adapt to either, based on your individual customer's triggers. Another option is simply to find out who is already buying your product or service regardless of the characteristics of the product, and gear everything to increase your market share within that group. Or, if you have already saturated that group, you may judge it appropriate to go after the other pattern by using the correct Influencing Language.

Many books on sales will tell you that a person will buy either to *gain a benefit* or to *avoid a problem*. Once you have asked the question *Why is that important?*, to determine a Toward or Away From motivation, you can use the appropriate Influencing Language. If you want to sell a house to a Toward family, you might tell them (if it matches their Criteria) that this house *is close* to the schools, *has lots* of room, and *is near* public transport. For an Away From family, you could say that it *isn't far* from the schools, *isn't too small*, and you *don't have to walk miles* to get to public transport.

One real estate agent who studied and used the LAB Profile found that he only had to work two-thirds of the year to keep his income at the level he wanted, and this during a recessionary period when many agents had been forced to leave the business.

Culture

The LAB Profile is a tool that will enable you to understand cultures, corporate or national. One of the questions that has preoccupied Canadians for many years is: "How specifically are we different from Americans?" America, as a culture, is Toward. (Remember that *culture* is an umbrella; any given individual may or may not fall under that umbrella.) In Europe, Americans are perceived as extremely naive, because they just go ahead and do things, disregarding the possible negative implications. While I was living in France during the 1980s, I did some training and consulting for the OECD (The Organization for Economic Co-operation and Development) and UNESCO (The United Nations Educational, Scientific, and Cultural Organization). The criticism I heard many times about the Americans within those organizations was that "They always think that just because it's a good idea, we should go ahead and do it. They don't seem to understand that there is this political consideration and that possible problem, etc." You may recall that the American government withdrew from UNESCO.

Canadians, on the other hand, have a more Away From pattern, as a culture. We do not want to rock the boat or create waves. And look at my own Jewish culture. Any group that posts a slogan of "Never Again" and prescribes chicken soup because "it couldn't hurt" has to have an Away From pattern.

Summary

Direction

Question: Why is that (Criteria) important? [Ask 3 times]

Toward: Motivated to achieve or attain goals.
Away From: Motivated to solve or avoid problems.
Distribution: 40% mainly Away From
20% equally Toward and Away From
40% mainly Toward

Influencing Language

Toward: attain; obtain; have; get; include; achieve, etc.
Away From: avoid; prevent; eliminate; solve; get rid of, etc.

$\widehat{\bigcirc}$ he Margaret Thatchers of the World: Motivation Source

---

> *Where does the person find motivation? In external sources,*
> *or in internal standards and beliefs?*

This category deals with the source of motivation, or in other words, its location. Where are judgments made, inside a person's body or from outside? These patterns affect how you make judgments and decisions. As you try them out, you will be able to decide how best to use them, and others will notice your increased effectiveness.

Here are the two patterns:

Internal

People with an Internal pattern in a given context provide their own motivation from within themselves. They decide about the quality of their work. They have difficulty accepting other people's opinions and outside direction. When they get negative feedback on work they feel has been well done, they will question the opinion or judge the person giving the feedback.

They are motivated to *gather information* from outside sources and then *they decide* about it, based on internal standards. Because they *take orders as information,* they can be hard to supervise. "My boss wants this out by Tuesday? That's interesting."

Since they do not need external praise, they tend not to give much feedback as managers.

Internal people hold standards somewhere within themselves, for the things that are important to them. Their motivation is triggered when they get to gather information from the outside, process it against their own standards, and make judgments about it.

49

External

External people need other people's opinions, outside direction, and feedback from external sources to stay motivated. In the Context of work, if they do not get that feedback, they will not know how well they are doing. They take information as orders. "He said the green paper matches the decor. I'd better go get some."

They are motivated when someone else decides. They have trouble starting or continuing an activity without outside feedback or results of some kind.

External people do not hold standards within themselves. They gather them from the outside. In the absence of external feedback, they will experience something akin to sensory deprivation.

Distribution _____ %

(*in the work Context, from Rodger Bailey*)

Internal	Equally Internal & External	External
40%	20%	40%

Pattern Recognition

Question: HOW DO YOU KNOW THAT YOU HAVE DONE A GOOD JOB? (at work, at choosing a car, etc.)

Internal—sentence structure
- they decide or know themselves; "I know"
- they evaluate their own performance based on their own standards and Criteria
- they resist when someone tells them what to do, or decides for them
- outside instructions are taken as information

Internal—body language
- sitting upright, pointing to self, may pause before answering a judgment from someone else while they evaluate it, minimal gestures and facial expressions for their culture

External—sentence structure
- other people or external sources of information decide or judge for them
- need to compare their work to an external norm or standard i.e., a checklist or a quota
- outside information is taken as a decision or order

External—body language
- leaning forward, watching for your response, facial expressions indicating they want to know from you if it was all right

Examples

Internal:	"I know when I have done a good job."
Mainly Internal:	"I usually know. I appreciate it when my boss compliments me, but generally, I know when I have done well."
Equally Internal and External:	"Sometimes I know and sometimes my clients tell me."
Mainly External:	"Usually, when I meet the quotas set by my boss and my clients seem happy. And also I can tell when I am working well."
External:	"My clients are happy. My boss is happy. I met my quota."

Alternate Questions:

How would you react to regular feedback from peers in (a specific Context)?
Whom do you involve when you make a decision?
If you felt you had done good work and someone you respect criticized your work, how would you react? Listen if the person criticizes, judges, or attempts to persuade the other person (Internal), or if they question the value of their own work (External).

Questioning and testing:

Here are some examples to show you how to test if you are not sure from the answer to the first question:

SRC:	Can I ask you, Suzanne, how do you know you've done a good job at work?
S:	Feedback from other people plus knowing myself. (External & Internal)

This is an example of someone with both patterns. Because we know that only about 20 percent are right in the middle, I would like to test to see if Suzanne falls on one side or the other.

SRC:	Let's say you thought you did a good job on something and you didn't get good feedback from the other people. How would you react?
S:	Well, I'd still *think* I did a good job but . . . something would be missing. I'd have to go check what they didn't like.

Here are two more examples:

SRC:	Louise, how do you know you've done a good job at work?
L:	I feel good about it.
SRC:	What happens if you feel good about it and nobody else appreciated it?
L:	They probably didn't see what I saw in it (shrugging her shoulders).
SRC:	Robert, how do you know you've done a good job at work?
R:	I know I've done a good job when I get external feedback.
SRC:	What happens when there is no external feedback?
R:	I would feel, like, what's the point?

While Suzanne has both patterns at work, she has more External than Internal, because when push comes to shove, she needs the feedback to really know if it is good enough. Both Louise and Robert fall firmly in the Internal and External camps, respectively.

Where Do You Know That?

I recently discovered another question that will help you test in those cases where the answer to the first question is unclear. Ask: "*Where do you know that?*" An Internal person will point to a part of their body and an External person will either not understand the question or give a clear External answer.

Other Contexts

I have worked with many groups in which there are quite a few men with a highly Internal pattern. Often one of them will voice his conviction that he is always Internal because how else could one run one's life? I ask: "How do you know you bought the right house?" The answer frequently is: "Because my wife liked it."

Someone in a training group said to me, "Well it seems to me this External stuff is really immature. Obviously, when you grow up and gain a certain amount of maturity, you become more Internal." This is a typically Internal thing to say. Let's consider another possibility. Someone who has been highly Internal might define maturity as the ability to take other people seriously by responding to what they *say* they need, instead of *knowing* what is best for them. It depends on where you are coming from and what you are trying to achieve, whether it is more appropriate to be in an Internal mode or an External mode, or both.

Margaret Thatcher

When the Commonwealth countries were negotiating about whether to impose sanctions against South Africa during its long Apartheid period, the vote was forty-nine countries in favour of sanctions to one against. Who was the holdout? The United Kingdom. Who specifically? Margaret Thatcher. When the vote was announced, she declared: "I feel sorry for the other forty-nine." Margaret Thatcher has an *off-the-scale* Internal pattern.

Brian Mulroney, Michael Wilson, the GST, and Free Trade

I believe that the LAB Profile can help us understand what happened when the conservative government in Canada under Brian Mulroney brought in the very unpopular Goods and Services Tax (GST). Finance Minister Michael Wilson initiated the GST and originally announced in 1990 that it was to be levied at 9 percent. Who lowered it to 7 percent? The Prime Minister, Brian Mulroney. How could this happen? Wouldn't you suppose that when a finance minister announces a new tax, he has the support of the prime minister?

Michael Wilson has a strong Toward and Internal combination. He had calculated that in order to meet his goals he needed the GST to be set at 9 percent. The Canadian public vociferously rebelled at the thought of a new tax during a difficult economic period. And how did Michael Wilson respond? He expressed some regret that the public was upset but insisted that the 9 percent was needed to meet his targets.

When the fury escalated, Brian Mulroney intervened over Mr. Wilson's head and lowered the tax to 7 percent. Mr. Mulroney has a combination of Away From and External patterns, which means that he is motivated to respond to outside negative feedback. As Prime Minister he was well known for *governing by opinion poll,* jumping into action whenever specific groups yelled loud enough. (I suspect that President Clinton also has this pattern.)

This pattern combination also explains Mr. Mulroney's behaviour in the summer of 1992 regarding the negotiations on the Charlottetown Constitutional Accords. While Mr. Mulroney was away in Europe, the provincial premiers came to a preliminary agreement on a new federal system for the country, with former prime minister Joe Clark, who was representing the federal government. As a result of negative public reaction to the agreement, Brian Mulroney vetoed it upon his return to Canada.

Who oversaw the Canadian negotiations for the North American Free Trade Agreement (NAFTA)? Mr. Michael Wilson, who by this time had become the trade minister. With his combination of Internal and Toward, he neglected to foresee potential problems in the agreement, in spite of the warnings that came from both commentators and advocacy groups. An important omission in the final agreement was the creation of a fair and timely dispute resolution mechanism.

Since the agreement came into effect, there have been many long, drawn-out, high-level conflicts between Canadian and American producers of steel, softwood lumber, Durham wheat, and beer. I often wonder, if the Minister had been slightly less Internal and more Away From, whether some of these problems could have been avoided.

Making Criticism and Responding to Feedback

When an External person receives criticism or negative feedback, they question themselves. An Internal person in the same situation makes a judgment about the other person. "I must have done something wrong" (External) or "the customer is a jerk because he didn't appreciate what I did for him" (Internal).

If ten people say to a highly Internal person: "Boy, is your tie ugly!" he would say "Gee, isn't that funny? There are ten people walking around here with bad taste." An External person would go home and change.

I had the advantages of being External driven home to me recently. I bought a cheap bookcase, in a kit, which I had to assemble myself. As I was struggling to follow the instructions (my father used to say that if all else fails, read the instructions), I noticed that the top and bottom shelves did not fit properly onto the back board. "Cheap design," I grumbled to myself and I *made* it fit. When I set the bookcase up I noticed that I had assembled the top and bottom shelves backwards and the chipboard was showing! Had I been slightly more External, which is appropriate in Contexts one knows little about, I might have *questioned what I was doing* when I noticed the poor fit, instead of *criticizing the design.*

When following instructions, it may be more appropriate to be in an External mode. My twin brother confirmed this to me when we were discussing how the holes often seem to be in the wrong place in these sort of kits, that is, until you figure out that *you* made the mistake!

Recently when I returned to Paris to do some work, I went out to supper with a friend. She suggested a restaurant where she had liked both the food and the ambiance. "Although," she said," I've heard it's been taken over by new management, and that it's not nearly as good anymore." She then went on to insist that we go there anyway because she had to go see *for herself.* At the end of the evening she pronounced," Well, they were right; the service was poor and so was the food. But I had to check it out for myself." Because she was highly Internal, someone else's word was not good enough. It remained an unresolved issue for her until she could decide for herself.

Many women tell me that their husbands often do not believe them when they tell them that there is something wrong with the car. The husbands need to find out for themselves.

The easiest way to get an Internal person to listen and think about something is to phrase it as "information you might want to consider"; otherwise they may simply judge you or the way you said it.

Influencing Language

You might want to consider choosing your words carefully, based on the information you have gathered about someone. As the most skilled professional communicators can tell you, the impact will be enormous.

Internal
- only you can decide; you might consider; it's up to you; I suggest you think about; try it out and decide what you think; here's some information so you can decide; what do you think?; for all the information you need to decide, just call . . .

External
- you'll get good feedback; others will notice; it has been approved by; well-respected; you will make quite an impact; so-and-so thinks; I would strongly recommend; the experts say; give references; scientific studies show

What Self-Esteem Is Not

Someone asked me about these patterns. "Is it possible for a person to switch from Internal to External, or vice versa, depending on whether he or she receives positive or negative criticism?" As Rodger Bailey, the developer of the LAB Profile, said: The LAB Profile is a status report about how I (with my particular structural makeup) respond to Contexts." In a few of the profiles I have done, I noticed a pattern that corresponds to the question above. One person was highly Internal when she thought she had done a bad job (one Context) and highly External when she thought she had done something well (a different Context for her). Nothing anyone would say could convince her that she had done a good job when she had decided otherwise. However, when she thought she had done something well, she had to check with others to make sure it was all right. I suspect that this has to do with low self-esteem and self-confidence. I would this call it a self-handicapping strategy.

You should not, however, confuse an External pattern with low self-esteem. It is not the same thing. When I am presenting to a group, for example, where do I get my motivational energy? Do I get it because the participants are smiling at me, or because I know I prepared my presentation well? (In that Context, if my goal is to present well and meet the audience's needs, it is appropriate to do some of each.)

A friend of mine once asked me: "Do you think I'm too External?" She then realized what she had said and began to laugh. My response was: "Too

External for what?" I used to be influenced by peer pressure but my friends talked me out of it.

Educational Design

I was working with a large group of highschool principals in the province of New Brunswick and we were discussing the design of education programs. One of the participants made the comment that many of the new programs are structured to create an Internal pattern in the students. In my opinion, when you closely examine the structure and content of any educational program, you could probably do a LAB Profile of its creator. Most programs will favour one or the other pattern in each of the categories. The Principal's question was: "What about the kids who have an External pattern in school and therefore need outside feedback to stay motivated and to know if they are doing well?"

I believe that it is fine to teach and encourage self-evaluation. However, when you want to *trigger motivation and keep the students interested* (which is a separate Context), some people will need ongoing feedback or results to stay interested.

Hiring

Does the job need someone who must *provide their own motivation and judge for themselves* the quality of their work? Or does it need someone to *adapt what they are doing based on outside requirements*? Sales and reception positions, or any job where meeting someone else's needs is crucial, generally need someone with an External pattern. You would want to employ someone in these positions for whom feedback will determine what they do and how they behave. These people will need either to be closely supervised, or to have some external means of knowing if they are on track.

Many people-management positions require someone who has a mainly Internal pattern with some External. Managers make decisions and set standards. You would have to have standards inside your body somewhere to do that. Frequently people say, however, when their boss is extremely Internal, that he or she does not listen or respond to suggestions.

For sales or customer service positions, you would need someone with a good dose of External. In today's market, sales and customer service people must really care whether customers are happy. If a customer is not pleased with your product or service and your representative explains that it is because the customer is an idiot, it will not help you improve customer service. Customers have become much more Internal than they once were. They have high standards for value and service, and one bad experience is enough to turn them off.

One of the challenges that large Internal organizations now face is how to incorporate spontaneous customer feedback into improving product design and service. I often find myself making suggestions to the person behind the desk, who sighs and says he can't do anything about it.

However, one of the latest currents in sales concerns promoting the sales-person as a *long-term partner and consultant* to clients. If your sales representatives do consulting, that presupposes that they have some expertise to impart, for example, on technical issues and standards. The salesperson/consultant would therefore need to have some degree of Internal. You would not, however, want someone who has an overly Internal pattern, because ultimately their performance needs to be judged by the satisfaction of the client.

When you are profiling a job in preparation for hiring or selection, you will need to determine whether the person's success at the position is based on meeting their own standards or adapting to someone else's.

People Management

Internal people have trouble accepting being managed, and generally do not need praise to stay motivated. Their motivation comes from inside; they are self-starters. They need to make their own decisions and will do that even when they have not been given permission. They become demotivated when they do not get to decide anything. When you give them an instruction, they will consider that as a piece of information and then decide whether to follow it.

A friend recounted an intercultural incident between two people with an Internal pattern, an English manager and an American employee. The English boss told his employee: "I'd reconsider that if I were you," intending to communicate that he thought it was a bad idea and it should not be done. The American took him literally; he reconsidered, decided it *was* a good idea, and went ahead and did it, much to the annoyance of his boss.

When two or more Internal people are on a team, you can predict that they will have frequent arguments and conflicts because each will be operating from their own (usually unstated) internal standards (particularly if they also have an Away From pattern). They can work more successfully together when they first negotiate and explicitly agree upon the standards and measurements.

Employees with an Internal pattern work best with little supervision. You can assign them a task and give them "carte blanche" to see it through. Give them decisions to make and, in cases where you are not sure of their judgment, get agreement on the standards to be met first. Make sure you know their Criteria and attach them to the job to be done. "Here's a *challenge* for you."

When giving them instructions, preface them with "Only you can decide to . . . " or "Here is the information on this; the end goal is to achieve that. You get to decide the best way."

External employees will look to their manager for guidance and encouragement. You will need to be explicit about what you expect them to do, as they tend to interpret information as instructions. If you said to an External employee: "The order forms are now available," they would drop what they were doing and go get them.

In the absence of regular feedback, they will become demotivated and unsure of themselves. Where the manager is highly External, she may end up looking to the employees for approval. External employees need to have clear goals and some external means of knowing if they are on track, in the form of regular feedback sessions, checklists, quotas, or examples to follow.

Annual performance appraisals are insufficient feedback for people who have an External pattern. Many will work themselves into a lather before their performance appraisal, because they have no idea themselves of how well they have been performing.

When assigning a task to an External person, let them know how much it will be appreciated (if his or her Organization pattern is Person) or what the impact will be (if his or her Organization pattern is Thing).* "You will get lots of good feedback," or "This will make a noticeable difference to our work" are phrases you could use to get their interest. The tasks that will play to their strengths are those that demand that they adapt to and meet someone else's expectations, provided that those expectations are clear.

Irresistible Language: Managing Your Boss

Some people are extremely hard to influence or convince, *until you know how*. Let's take an example of someone, perhaps your boss, who has the following combination: Internal and Away From. Chances are that this person has been making your life miserable by only noticing what you do wrong, and disagreeing with every proposal. As Groucho Marx sang, "Whatever it is, I'm against it."

So you need some *irresistible* Influencing Language, tailor-made for this person. Let's imagine that one day you enter her office with the report she asked you for and you say: "I've drafted the proposal you asked for to deal with the issues. *It's not perfect. Would you take a look at it?*" Your boss will grab the paper from your hand, correct it to her liking, and accept it.

Selling in a Buyer's Market: Adapting to the Shift in Customers

As any business person will tell you, customers have become very difficult to deal with. They now demand products of perfect quality, resist complicated purchasing processes, and want anything that breaks to be fixed immediately at no cost to them. They quickly jump on any mistakes made, give customer service staff a very hard time, and even play one supplier off another to get the best deal. And they want more for less.

Guess what this means. The great customer shift has happened. Customers have become highly Internal to their suppliers. Suppliers beware!

---

*For more information on Organization, Person, and Thing, please refer to pages 123-128.

Spending time and money developing the best products and services for your clients may no longer be enough. You will also need to adapt your language and processes to meet the needs of people who take everything you say only as information to consider. Notice the skepticism with which clients scoff at your claims to be the best. "Prove it," they insist (to *their* satisfaction).

Canada Trust (a Canadian trust and mortgage company) seems to have responded to the change in the mortgage market. While once upon a time consumers would pay any interest rate just to get their mortgage accepted, since the early 1990s mortgage companies have had to beg people to choose them over the competition. The Canada Trust slogan was highly appropriate: "The best mortgage package in Canada? You be the judge."

When discussing sales and marketing, there are two axes to consider: promoting *who you are* (your organization's image or how you are perceived) and communicating to *the people you want to reach*. It is no secret that IBM, for example, has been struggling to be viewed as a more External company. They want to be perceived as giving the customer what the customer wants instead of what *they* have to offer. Their 1994 television commercial says it all: "We're trying to be more customer-focused." Trying?

You will need to decide what kind of image you want to convey. Are you the *experts* with the solutions or the company who will do whatever it takes to *meet your customers' needs*, or both?

Burger King has also been targeting Internals (and Proactives): "Your way. Right away." McDonald's, on the other hand, decides for you what you will have on your hamburger. If you do not believe me, try ordering a hamburger without mustard for your child at McDonald's.

The sales approach of a local career-counselling outfit consisted of booking an appointment with prospective clients, showing them the process they use, and then sending the person away to think about it and decide if they needed it. Upon questioning, it turned out that about 80 percent of their clients had an Internal pattern; so did the founder and majority of staff. When I suggested that they *might consider* using an approach for External people to attract more clients, the founder thought about it and decided against it. He felt that External clients would take up too much time in counselling sessions.

The national marketing director of a company that sells blood analysis equipment to hospitals spoke to me about a change in the buying process of their customers. Laboratory equipment used to be selected by the chief lab technician, who usually had a long-standing rapport with the sales representative. Now, all buying decisions are made centrally in the hospital purchasing department. The sales reps were finding themselves confronting highly Internal purchasing officers whose Criteria were about price and who did not understand the technical aspects of the equipment. They needed to change their sales approach by matching the price Criterion, giving only relevant information (one piece of which was the approval of the equipment by the chief lab technician), and asking the purchasing officer "to be the judge."

To sell to people who have an Internal pattern, you need to give them information and let them decide. I wrote an advertisement for a management training course geared to Internals with this statement at the bottom of the ad: "For all the information you need to decide, call. . . . " We had one person sign up over the phone without even bothering to find out what was in the course. We also had many calls for information that subsequently led to enrollments.

"I would like you to try it out and tell me what you think. The only way to know if this is the one for you is to test it out for yourself." That is why car dealerships insist that their sales people get the prospective buyer behind the wheel.

Doctors and Patients

In France I read a study that pronounced that 80 percent of patients do not finish taking their prescriptions. Doctors have told me that about the same percentage applies in North America. Many people simply forget to take their medicine when their symptoms disappear. We can use the LAB Profile to explain this. Many people have Internal and Away From patterns in the Context of bodily ailments. We tend to go to the doctor when we *feel* sick, not when someone else says we look unwell.

Doctors would therefore need to sell their patients on complying with their instructions. "*You need to decide* if you want to *get rid of this illness*. If you do, you will need to take all of this medicine, as prescribed" (Internal and Away From). Even though many people are External to doctors and other authority figures, once they get home they shift back into an Internal mode.

I believe that doctors need to recognize the implications of the fact that many of their patients shift into a highly External pattern in the doctor's office. Patients tend to believe whatever the doctor tells them because they have accepted the doctor as a knowledgeable authority figure. This means that doctors need to be very careful about what they say and imply.

My mother broke her wrist during an icy winter. I took her back to the hospital to have her cast replaced because the first one was too tight. The doctor fitted her new cast on and made a joke: "There, that'll keep you for *this time*." This time?! Right before my eyes I watched my mother nod to acknowledge the implicit presupposition that if he was talking about *this time*, there was going to be a *next time*! "No!" I shouted, "This is the last time!" But my mother does not have an External pattern to me; I am her daughter. Three months later, she tripped in her garden and broke the other wrist.

Just to contradict what I said above, there is also another trend in the doctor-patient relationship. Millions of people are now consulting practitioners of complementary medicine. When asked why, many say either that the doctor has not been able to cure a particular problem or that they do not believe the approach used by the doctor can help them. These people have developed Internal standards for what they want and don't want.

Selling in Other Contexts

The approach for getting patients to take their medicine could also work for Internals in other Contexts. "You need to decide if you really want (*customer's desired outcome*). If you do, then you'll need to try out *(our product or service)."*

External people need references. They need to know who else has bought. The advertisements where a famous person is flogging a product attract the attention of people who are External to that famous person, in that Context.

It can be easier selling to people provided you can get them to be External to you. This entails establishing credibility as well as rapport. One client of mine asked me: "Do you think I need it?" You can also do this by wearing clothes that are one notch more formal than your client's, showing credentials and references, and slipping in expressions such as "In my experience" or "If I were you, knowing what I know today . . . "

External people will also buy something for how it will make them look or the impact it will have on others. Why *do* people buy Jaguars? Because the leather seats are comfortable? A market researcher who worked on the Jaguar account told me that people today buy luxury cars more for the perceived value these cars offer than the status they confer. Then he stopped and thought. "Maybe," he snorted, "they are buying because they want to *be seen* as buying for value."

If you want to attract both groups, or if your client pays attention to both Internal standards and External feedback, use both patterns. For those cases where you are not sure, use one pattern and observe. If you do not get a positive response, try the other one.

Summary

Source

Question: How do you know that you have done a good job at . . . ?

Internal: They are motivated to decide based on their own internal standards.

External: They need outside feedback to know how well they are doing and to stay motivated.

Distribution: 40% mainly Internal
20% equally Internal and External
40% mainly External

Influencing Language

Internal: only you can decide; you might want to consider; it's up to you; what do you think?, etc.

External: others will notice; the feedback you'll get; results; give references; so-and-so thinks, etc.

Sometimes You Just Gotta Break the Rules: Motivation Reason

> *How does a person reason? Is there a continual quest to find alternatives, or is there a preference to follow established procedures?*

This category will lead you to unlimited possibilities and show you the right way to get there. There are two patterns:

Options

People with an Options pattern in a given Context are motivated by opportunities and possibilities to do something in a different way. There is always another better way to do things. They love to create procedures and systems but have great difficulty following them. If you give an Options person a guaranteed way to make a million dollars, he will try to improve it.

They are thrilled by unlimited possibilities and ideas. The thing that is irresistible to Options people is breaking or bending the rules.

Options people like to start a new idea or a new project. However, they do not necessarily feel compelled to finish it. They much prefer to do development and setup rather than maintenance activities. Sometimes they will have difficulty committing themselves because they believe this will reduce their options. At the extreme, they might avoid deciding anything (particularly if they also have a Reactive pattern). Alternatively, they can be totally committed to an idea or project, until the next new idea comes along.

Procedures

People with a Procedures pattern like to follow set ways. They believe there is a "right" way to do things. Once they have a procedure they can follow it over and over again. These are people who are interested in *how* to do things, not in *why* things are the way they are.

A procedure has a beginning and an end. It may have choice points at which you gather more information and make a decision. Without one, Procedures people feel lost or get stuck. When they commence a procedure, the most important thing for them is to get to the end of the procedure. They are the ones who will complete and finish what they start.

They can feel personally violated when it is suggested to them to break, or go around, the rules. Once they know the procedure to follow, they are happy doing that.

Distribution _____ **%**

(*in the work Context, from Rodger Bailey*)

	Equally	
Options	**Options & Procedures**	**Procedures**
40%	20%	40%

Pattern Recognition

Question: WHY DID YOU CHOOSE YOUR PRESENT JOB? (*or house, vacation, car, etc.*)

You may recall that in the introduction of this book we discussed Reality. In order for people to create their own models of reality, they use three processes called Deletion, Distortion, and Generalization. This category deals with Distortion. The question we ask for this pattern is: "Why did you choose . . . " and the rest refers to a particular Context.

For Options people, when they hear the question **Why did you choose?**, they hear the question **why** and give you a list of Criteria for their answer.

When Procedures people hear the question, they delete the word **why** and substitute **how did it come to be?** They answer the question: "How?" Sometimes, the first thing they will say is, "Well, I didn't choose." They will tell you a story or series of events that led them to getting the job. "I was working at my brother-in-law's and there was an opening in this other company at the time I finished a contract, so I took it."

Options
- list of Criteria
- opportunities, possibilities
- expanding options and choice

Procedures
- did not choose
- answers the question "why" by telling "how" it came to pass
- the facts, events leading to, a story

How you recognize someone who has an equally Options and Procedures pattern is interesting. They might tell you a story with Criteria imbedded in it. I happen to be quite in the middle on this pattern, and if someone asked me why I chose to set up my own company after I returned to Canada, I would say: "After I came back, I looked around for what to do, and became a partner in a small training company. After a while I became **dissatisfied**. And **being organized** is important to me. I realized that I could probably make **more money** in my own company, and **decrease expenses** and **be independent**. So I set up my company, Success Strategies." I have used both patterns in the answer.

Examples

Options:	"I thought it would be stimulating, interesting, and challenging."
Mainly Options:	"It was more interesting, and had more responsibility and better pay. A friend of mine told me about it."
Equally Options and Procedures:	"A friend told me about it and it looked more interesting."
Mainly Procedures:	"I had been with the same company ten years. A friend told me they were hiring in her company, so I applied and was hired. The job is more interesting and I make more money."
Procedures:	"I didn't really choose. I met my boss through my brother-in-law who worked with her. They needed a technician and I was just completing a contract."
Alternate Question:	What would your typical work day be like? (listen for Criteria or a set of procedures to be followed) Note: Make sure you ask *"Why* did you choose?" and not *"How* did you choose?"

Influencing Language

The possibilities are endless for finding the right thing to say.

Options
- opportunity; choice; break the rules just for you; another better way; unlimited possibilities; an alternative is; that's one way; here are the options; there has got to be a way; the sky's the limit

Procedures
- the right way; speak in procedures: first . . . then . . . after which . . . the

last step; tried and true; reliable; how to use this; just follow the procedure; the procedure is; proven methodology

Hiring

You can see that for hiring, the Options and Procedures patterns are quite important. In fact, this is one category where it really pays to get it right. When you profile a position, you will need to ask yourself whether the job mainly consists of *following procedures* or *creating and designing systems and procedures*? Is it setup and development, or maintenance? When you know what the balance is, you can write your advertisement to attract the right people and turn off the ones who would not fit. (See also the section on writing advertisements for jobs.)

You may have heard of some of the multilevel marketing companies or MLM's, such as NSA, Mary Kay, Nu Skin, and a number of other products. They have a real problem. Only one person in ten on average succeeds at making a full-time living at multilevel sales. I would say that this is very poor statistics for hiring, wouldn't you?

In my opinion, the reason is in how they promote themselves. The multilevel marketing companies try to recruit new distributors by telling them about *unlimited income possibilities*. This is Options language. Things with unlimited choice or possibilities, or no ceilings, or the sky's the limit, are *irresistible* to Options people.

However, when people actually become distributors they usually find that the companies have already worked out the procedures for selling the product. All you have to do is proactively and consistently follow the procedure to make your *sky's the limit* income, which most of them are incapable of doing. The irony is that if they used Procedures Influencing Language in their promotional packages, recruits would indeed make their unlimited income.

According to Rodger Bailey there has also been some research done on telemarketers, and this would apply to other kinds of salespeople. Telemarketers who have a Procedures pattern sell three times as much as the Options people. The reason for this is simple. Sales is basically a procedure. You contact prospective customers, establish rapport, do a needs analysis, present something that matches the needs, and lastly help the person make a decision. That's a procedure. If I am an Options person, this time I will do it one way; another time I will try another way. Options sales people tend to have an up-and-down performance, because occasionally they will get a brilliant idea and strike gold. They do not, however, hone their procedure until it works well. Procedures people will continue to follow the same process over and over again because it feels comfortable and right. This is ideal for sales (although in changing sales situations, they would need to be taught a new procedure).

Certain kinds of jobs are inherently Options or Procedures. Flying an airplane, for example, is quite clearly a procedure. Can you imagine a commercial airline pilot who has an Options pattern? "Let's go over the North

Pole this time." Anything to do with safety and security needs a Procedures person. Emergency procedures need to be memorized and followed to the letter. Someone who is Internal and Procedures would do very well at that kind of work. On the other hand, you would want an Options person to develop and test a safety procedure, preferably one who also has an Away From pattern to avoid mistakes.

Architecture would need someone with lots of Options and an understanding of Procedures. A building contractor would have a much heavier dose of Procedures to ensure compliance to regulations. You might want to test for this if you are going to do renovations.

Options people excel in situations where there is a need to develop creative solutions or alternatives to the present systems. Business process engineers, for example, would need a heavy dose of Options.

In a training company in France I worked closely with my boss, who has high Options and Internal patterns in his work. I learned much from him about creative seminar design. We frequently were asked to lead the same seminar several times over in the same large organizations. We would meet before each one to prepare and he would insist that we redesign each one. I would object: "But Pierre, it worked well last time, it was really good, and they liked it." He would say: "No, no, there has to be a better way to do this." I had the feeling we were constantly throwing the baby out with the bath water. You can see the conflict between Options and Procedures people.

In fact, to design training you need to develop Options, but in order to perfect the delivery of training you need to repeat enough Procedures to be able to reproduce processes that work. The best public speakers have well-honed routines, which necessitates doing both Options and Procedures.

For many years there has been a crisis in nursing; the media occasionally discuss examples from several European countries as well as North America. It is not solely attributed to low wages and abusive treatment by other medical professions. When I ask nurses: "Why did you choose to become a nurse?" the answer often is something like: "I want to help people," or "Once I got my certificate, I could travel." These are Criteria, Options answers. Many people attracted to nursing are interested because of the *possibilities* nursing has to offer. They are Options people. After they decide to become nurses, they go to nursing college. Who teaches in the nursing schools? People who did not find what they wanted in hospital work. So the nursing students get their certificates and go to work in the hospitals. What are hospitals all about? Procedures, and often very tight ones with little choice.

Now, in North America at least, where there is an increasing emphasis on home-based care, we have an expanding number of private nursing services. You can be a nurse, care for people, and do it your own way, getting a chance to develop alternatives. Hospitals themselves are also changing. One hospital I did some work for is well in advance of the trend in creating

A Little Variety

"Patient Care Teams," which include many of the medical professionals. This is a more Options approach to patient care.

To attract people who will perform well and be fulfilled by traditional hospital nursing, nursing educational institutions should be producing promotional materials that say: "Do you want to practice medicine the right way? Learn patient care from start to finish."

Culture Clashes at Work

One of the things I have noticed when participating in change operations in corporations is the internal culture clash between different departments. Let's take software design and marketing, for example. If you are a software designer, chances are you have a mainly Options pattern. You develop and design software. Marketing tends to be mainly Procedures because there are procedures to follow to take the product to market. The software designers develop some software and often they drop one project to work on another. They will keep changing it and adapting it and making it better and coming up with alternative solutions. The marketing department will be screaming at them: "Stop fixing it! Just give it to us so we can get it out on the market." Why are there so many upgrades to your favourite software package? A consultant friend summed up the software problem: "Not enough time to do it right once, but all the time in the world to fix it."

The same thing happens between the design engineers and the plant. What do design engineers do? They create systems and design products. What does the plant do? It makes them. Production managers get furious when engineering keeps changing the specs.

In order to work more effectively together and reduce the number of conflicts among Options and Procedures departments, each needs to understand the role of the other and how they function. Options people need to explore possibilities creatively in order to invent solutions. The Procedures people need to know that the fruit of these deliberations will actually arrive completed at the right time and place. Many companies would do well to have a person who handles Options and Procedures equally well to co-ordinate the work between these two departments.

Sales and Marketing

The means of choice for selling to an Options person is to get them to think of the possibilities. Give them lots of alternatives. They want to examine all the reasons *why* they should buy. I remember having a sales appointment with someone who was grappling with a problem. As I left, I inadvertently used an irresistible pattern. I said "There's gotta be a way to find what you're looking for." By the time I had returned to my office, the phone was ringing off the hook. She said: "You're right. There's gotta be a way. And you're the one who can help me." An Options person is motivated by unlimited choice. The more choice the better. To close the sale irresistibly, break with the normal procedure, just for them. My carpet cleaner told me: "The office says we have to charge $50 to clean the sofa, but since I'm already here, I can do that for you for $30."

If you want to know the right way to sell to a Procedures person, there are two keys. One is to get them started on a procedure because they are compelled to finish it, and the other one is to have them understand that this product or service is the tried and true, right way to do things. They will be more interested in *how* to buy it or use it than why they should buy it:

> *"The first step is, I'll show you the products. Then you can look at them. I will show you how to use them and you can try one out. You can then decide which one suits you best. After that, I'll tell you how the payment plan works and set it up for you to sign. Lastly, you can take your product home right away."*

You will have already started them on the first part of the procedure.

If the product meets their Criteria (and other factors do not interfere), they will complete the procedure. It is preferable to have the client going away happy with the product as the last step of the procedure, rather than paying the bill as the last step.

Certain kinds of stores naturally attract one or the other pattern. Some people (me, for example) are overwhelmed by the large amount of choice one has in music stores. Others are thrilled.

A well-known home furnishings chain that imports Far Eastern rattan furniture, cotton fabrics with Asian prints, and so on, ran an advertising campaign in magazines with an image on a grid pattern. A grid is a Procedures image. With this ad they increased their floor traffic by 20 percent. However, 75 percent of the people who walked in because of the ad, came into the store only once, and never came back. Why? It attracted Procedures people, but what does the store actually look like? It has clusters of stuff over here, clusters of stuff over there. It is very Options, lots of choice, all kinds of different materials, all kinds of gadgets, bricabrac, and so on. Bill Huckabee, a LAB Profile-trained market research consultant, looked at the results and designed a new advertisement. This time they laid out the ad in the same way the stores are laid out: clusters of images. They had another increase in store traffic, and a much higher percentage of the people who came in returned more than once.

Let's compare that chain to IKEA, the Swedish home furnishings put-it-together-yourself, store. When you walk into IKEA you cannot get out until you have gone through the entire store (short of pulling the fire alarm). I know; I have tried. They have a procedure for doing everything. They have procedures for walking through the store, measuring, deciding, ordering,

Terminal Options

The Latest Revision!

lining up, paying, parking, loading, and assembling the furniture once you get home.

Different Contexts create buying patterns among large groups of people. In the Context of buying cars, a large percentage of the population has an Options pattern concerning the car company and the model they choose. They might want a Ford Taurus or a Honda Civic, and they will tell you why. They are motivated by Criteria when they choose the make and model. Why did you choose your car? Because it has good fuel efficiency? Because it has great pick-up? Because there isn't another one like it on the road? Or some other Criteria? Probably not because you were walking along the street one day when you needed a car and happened to see one.

However, in the Context of choosing a dealership, most people have a Procedures pattern. This means they do not have Criteria about what dealership they choose. The first one they stumble on will do. For example, that is why all the Ford dealers in your region sponsor commercials together on local television stations. They know that which dealership you go to is of no importance, unless you experience very bad service and never want to go back there again.

Electronic marketing has grown by leaps and bounds over the last few years. There are many seminars that promote "exploring the sales opportunities of getting your company on the Internet" (Options language). Frankly, unless you have had your head in the sand since the mid-80s, you probably already know about the opportunities. I wish they would set up seminars to teach the step-by-step procedure for setting up web sites and so on.

Let's take fast-food chains again. When someone buys a McDonald's franchise, they find it is a turn-key operation. All the procedures are in place. The products are procedural as well. When you get a Big Mac it is always a Big Mac and it is always done the same way. The *right way.*

Compare them to Burger King one more time. Burger King's slogan in 1992 was: "Sometimes you just gotta break the rules." Now look at the Burger King products. You can have tomato or not, onions or not, relish and mustard or not, and so on. Options. Their 1993 slogan was: " Your way. Right Away." It is appealing to Proactive, Internal, Options people (in the Context of eating at fast-food places). I am willing to bet that their clientele has a different Profile from McDonald's. It has little to do with how their products taste. How different can one beef or chicken pattie be from another?

People Management

People with an Options pattern work best in situations where they get to develop or set up new systems and procedures. They will invariably find a way around standard operating procedures, so you will need to decide how best to harness their creativity. They will be motivated by tasks that involve creating something from scratch, particularly where the end result will increase options. To motivate them, you can tell them to think of the possibilities or to find an alternative to what we do now.

You can motivate Procedures people by telling them that this is the *right way* to do something. They feel comfortable doing the same thing over and over. Let them know how important the finished result is.

For staff who have both Options and Procedures patterns when at work, you will need to give them opportunities to both follow and develop or improve the procedures. You can use the Influencing Language for both patterns. "You will get to develop a better way to do this. Make sure it is right (Internal and Procedures), and then you can use it from now on." For someone who has an External pattern, you could substitute: "Check with me to make sure it is right. . . . "

Total Quality Management?

Many organizations have been preoccupied with introducing Total Quality Management, Continuous Improvement programs, and other forms of paradigm-shifting. They are aiming to get employees into new ways of thinking in order to respond to constantly changing environments. What are these programs designed to create? Options patterns. Basically the message is to tell workers that they ought to be Options people. You ought to be able to turn on a dime, totally change what you are doing, develop alternatives, and create new systems to anticipate and respond to changes.

What would actually happen to the corporate world, the helping professions, the education system, or any other sector, if no one finished or completed procedures? Imagine that for a moment. The new management practices have been designed to tell whole groups of people that what they do is no good, and yet if procedures were not completed, no money would be made.

I have found many biases against the idea of the Procedures pattern. My colleagues in France who teach the LAB profile found that they had to change the terminology. Instead of using the word *Procedures*, they changed it to *Process*. They found such a negative association with *being procedural* that people would not accept the term (and this in the country that invented the word *bureaucracy*).

I believe it is important to honour Procedures people for what they contribute, instead of pointing out to them how rigid this makes them. They get things done. We need Options people to think of new options, and we need Procedures people to see that they get done. Building a high-performance team depends on how well you use the different strengths in the team to accomplish what needs to be done.

Learning New Skills, or Why Some of Us Can't Understand Computer Nerds

Learning is a specific Context. People have different learning styles; knowing your Profile in that Context (or that of the people you are teaching) is useful for accelerating the speed at which new material can be integrated.

A few years ago I got my first computer. I had quite a few different packages of software with it. The person from whom I bought it was an experienced computer user, and he spent a lot of time teaching me. He would say, "I'd like you to *understand why* it's set up this way." I would say: "No, I don't want to understand why it's set up this way. Tell me *how* to turn it on." "Well," he would continue, "You need to *understand a few of the concepts* behind this particular program." "No I don't. I want to know *how you make* and *print* a document." Or he would say, in response to a how-to question: "There are *several ways* you can do this." And I would answer, feeling my blood pressure rise: "I don't want to know several ways. Just tell me *one way. The right way!*"

I needed the procedure to follow. It was only after I had mastered some needed procedures that I was the least bit interested in why things were set up the way they were. In that circumstance he could have matched my style by telling me: "I'm going to show you the *basic procedure* for making and printing a document. Once you've got that down, I'll explain *how it* works so that you can master the other things you'll need to do. Then *you will be able* to figure it out for yourself." An Options person would be motivated by all the possibilities the software has to offer. However, I suspect that many computer neophytes, and others learning new skills, simply want the procedure to follow.

Who writes the manuals for all your software and your computer? Options people, generally speaking. That is one possible explanation for why I, like many others, have difficulty understanding the manuals. The vocabulary is another problem. An exception is the very popular "For Dummies" series of manuals. They give you the step-by-step procedure and even warn you when they are about to give you some "technical drivel."

When you are learning or teaching something, it is useful to assess whether the need is to know the *why's* and *wherefore's*, or to simply know *how to.*

Working with Groups

When you are giving instructions to a group, if you give them options they will be paralyzed. You must be procedural when giving instructions to a group or they will not know what to do. I was giving an introductory workshop on the LAB Profile at a conference in Montreal and we did not finish all the patterns we wanted to do in the allotted time. The group seemed frustrated and wanted to continue. I said, "Okay, well there are some options. We could break for lunch now and come back early and do the last pattern, or we could keep going now and have lunch later, or we could just forget it. What would you prefer?" Everybody went um, ah, um. No answer.

I said "I have a suggestion. Let's break for lunch now. Those of you who want to, can come back a half an hour early and we'll meet in this room and we'll do it." They said great, and everyone left for lunch.

When explaining an exercise or assigning a task to a group, you need to give them explicitly the step-by-step procedure.

Coaching and Counselling

When we are coaching or counselling people, we often try to help them have more choice about what they do. If you have a Procedures person and you give him too many choices, you may inadvertently put him into sensory overload. Not deprivation, overload. Too much choice. What people with a Procedures pattern need is a procedure to enable them to discover what they want.

Summary

Reason

Question: Why did you choose your current work (or house, etc.)?

Options: Compelled to develop and create systems and procedures. Have difficulty following set procedures.

Procedures: Prefer to follow tried-and-true set ways. Get stumped when they have no procedures to follow.

Distribution: 40% mainly Options
20% equally Options and Procedures
40% mainly Procedures
in the Context of work, from Rodger Bailey

Influencing Language

Options: opportunities; variety; unlimited possibilities; lots of choice; options; break the rules just for them

Procedures: the right way; how to; tried and true; speak in procedures: first . . . then . . . lastly

---

ℭ𝒲hen the Bell Tolls: Motivation Decision Factors

> *How does a person react to change and what frequency of change is needed? Does the motivation come from a search for "difference" or "sameness"?*

The Decision Factors category is about your internal time clock and how often the *bell rings* for change. Are you motivated by evolution, revolution, both, or stability? There are four patterns:

Sameness

People with a Sameness pattern want their situation in a given Context to stay the same. They do not like change and may refuse to adapt. They may accept a major change once every ten years, but they will provoke change only once every *fifteen to twenty-five years.*

Sameness with Exception

Sameness with Exception people like a given Context to stay mainly the same, but will accept change once a year if the change is not too drastic. They prefer their situations to evolve slowly over time. They tend to resist major changes except when they are perceived to be progressive or gradual. They need major change once every *five to seven years.* This is by far the largest category in the work Context, and probably in many other Contexts.

Difference

People with a Difference pattern love change; they thrive on it and want it to be constant and major. They will resist static or stable situations. They need drastic change about every *one to two years,* and if they do not get it, they may leave. They like change to be revolutionary, dramatically different.

Sameness with Exception and Difference
(*the double pattern*)

People with this double pattern like change and revolutionary shifts but are also comfortable where things are evolving. They are happy with both revolution and evolution. They need major change every *three to four years*, on average.

Distribution _____ %

(*in the work Context, from Rodger Bailey*)

Sameness	Sameness with Exception	Difference	Sameness with Exception and Difference
5%	65%	20%	10%

Pattern Recognition

Question: WHAT IS THE RELATIONSHIP BETWEEN YOUR WORK THIS YEAR AND LAST YEAR? (vacation, this home and the last one, etc.)

or

WHAT IS THE RELATIONSHIP BETWEEN THIS JOB AND YOUR LAST ONE?

The question asks: "What is the relationship between . . . ?" In this situation, the word *relationship* has the connotation of similarity. People will either naturally understand the word and tell you how it is the same or similar, or alternatively they will not know what you mean, or reinterpret it to mean how is it *different*.

Sameness
- how they are the same, identical
- what they have in common
- how it has not changed

Sameness with Exception
- how it has evolved over time
- it is the same except more; less; better; worse; improving; etc. (comparisons on a sliding scale)
- focus on the trip more than arriving at the destination

Difference
- may not understand the word *relationship*
- will describe how it is completely different

- new, different, changed, transformed, revolutionary
- language points to an immediate switch
- focus on the destination, ignore the trip

Difference and Sameness with Exception
- use *both* Difference and Sameness with Exception responses

Examples

Sameness:	"It is exactly the *same*. I'm *still* crunching numbers."
Sameness with Exception:	"It's the *same but* I have *more* responsibility and *less* time."
Difference:	"It's *totally different*. Now I do outside sales."
Difference and Sameness with Exception:	"There have been *big changes* this year and my performance has *improved greatly*."

To test your diagnosis in the work Context, simply ask the person how often they changed what they were doing on the job. They may have had the same job title, but what we are looking for is *how often* they changed responsibilities. Their answers will usually match the change clocks for their pattern. In other Contexts you could check by asking how often they have moved homes, what they do for a vacation each year, whether they go to the same cottage or do different things, and so on.

You will need to be especially clear in identifying the Context when you ask the question, because people's patterns often change depending upon what they are talking about. I profiled a man in several Contexts. Regarding work, he said, "Well it's *basically the same*: I have *more* responsibility, I've got *more* people to supervise, and *more* accounts." Sameness with Exception. Then I said, "OK, what's the relationship between the last holiday you took and the holiday before that?" He said "Relationship! What do you mean by relationship?" Two minutes after answering the first *relationship* question he was suddenly unable to understand the word *relationship*, simply because we had switched Contexts.

Influencing Language

Here are some totally new ways to improve communication and maintain rapport.

- **Sameness:** same as; in common; as you always do; like before; unchanged; as you already know; maintaining; totally the same; exactly as before; identical
- **Sameness with Exception:** more; better; less; the same except; advanced; upgrade; progression; gradual improvement; similar but even better; moving up; growth; improvement

- **Difference:** new; totally different; unlike anything else; unique; one of a kind; completely changed; unrecognizable; shift; switch; a complete turn around; brand new; unheard of; the only one
- **Sameness with Exception & Difference:** use both Sameness with Exception and Difference vocabulary

Making Your Change Pattern Work for You

Since people may have different patterns from Context to Context, it is important not to make generalizations about someone. A friend of mine, while he makes frequent changes in his work, always wants to go to the same restaurant to order the same thing. People who have a Difference pattern in the Context of reading usually have four or five books on the go at any one time. Some people have cottages where they spend their vacation every year; others would not consider going to the same place twice.

When I looked at my own history I discovered that I have moved residences about every eighteen months. I have also discovered that if you do that, banks and other financial institutions will think you are a flake. Guess what pattern they have?

Knowing your own pattern can help you to understand and predict what is happening in your life. When my change bell rang one fall, suddenly I started to notice all the things that were wrong with the place I was living. I was itching to move. I told myself that since I was working on a number of business projects and I needed co-operation from the bank, I would need them to perceive me as a steady, *normal* type. So I had my living room painted, bought some new furniture, moved around the old stuff, and made the whole place *feel different*. After I received the needed financial backing, I cracked and bought a new place.

I have a friend who has a combination of high Options and high Difference patterns in the Contexts of work and study. She started and had not completed three different Master's programs at three universities in different cities. She adopted three children from different backgrounds. After her first undergraduate degree, she went back to school and became a nurse. Every so often she would go back to hospital work because she really liked to take care of people. She would usually stay for a bit, get frustrated by the procedures, and leave. Her change pattern is an average of one to two years, and for some Contexts it is as short as six months.

As a student it was very difficult for her, because if she read a book once, she could not stand the idea of reading it again. She wanted to read something different. She did her Profile with me and decided, "I'm doing this Master's program and I am finishing it." (She also has an Internal pattern.) This was the third attempt, and she managed to build in many different projects towards her Masters degree. For her thesis, she conducted a research project in Asia to complete her degree, while her husband was

"Hamster migration— every seven years."

there on sabbatical. She found a way to *build her need for Difference into her activities.*

Her husband has a Sameness with Exception pattern for several Contexts. He is motivated by evolution and progression, while she prefers to have things changing all the time. How can this work in a marriage? Since none of us is actually living in Reality, who cares what your spouse's patterns may be as long as he *thinks it is getting better* and *she thinks it is totally different?* And so long as he does not bang his shins on the furniture when she moves it around.

For couples with different patterns, I would suggest that you understand your own need for change, as well as your spouse's, and make sure you each feel your needs are being met.

Revolutions and Evolutions: Hiring

There are several things to think about when doing a Job Profile in preparation for hiring. Does the job require a great variety of tasks? How long does each task remain the same? Does the successful fulfillment of the objectives demand creating a revolution (Difference), building upon what is already there (Sameness with Exception), or maintaining the status quo (Sameness)? How much of each?

You can predict that people with a high Difference pattern will create revolutions around them, especially if they also have Proactive and Options patterns. In fact, someone with a combination of Options and Difference can be a compulsive change-artist. I wanted to call on a client with this pattern after not seeing him for two years. I tried the company where he had been working. He had, of course, left and gone somewhere else.

I profiled a man, and told him about his Difference pattern and what that meant for his career. He retorted that he had been a high school teacher and principal for thirty years. I asked him in how many schools had he worked. He had been in *seventeen different schools.* Knowing this pattern will allow you to predict someone's past—a great party trick.

Since the majority of people (65%) in the work Context have a Sameness with Exception pattern, you will be more likely to find those candidates. Many jobs need someone who can build and progress. A fewer number of positions actually require revolutionaries.

People Management

Employees with a Sameness pattern do not respond well to change. They are well suited to tasks that do not change, such as many administrative or production tasks. Managers with this pattern strive to keep standards up and want to provide continuity. This attribute is also appropriate for maintaining a long-term rapport with clients. To motivate Sameness employees, talk about what this task has in common with what they already know.

Sameness with Exception employees will accept change once a year as long as it is not too drastic. They will feel stressed if placed in high-change environments, which explains the stress-related illnesses rampant in the post-recessionary nineties. They are motivated when they can perceive a *progression* in their work. To get them interested in a task, you can tell them how it will make things better, or will build on what they are already doing.

I've Been Moved

To capture the interest of someone with a Difference pattern, you will need to give them lots of different things to work on. Get them to change things (if they are also Proactive) or create changes for them to respond to (if they are Reactive). For some companies this happens frequently anyway. A group of IBM European headquarters managers told me the nickname they have for IBM is "I've Been Moved." Europeans are not used to the American habit of moving people around every few years. (I also heard that the nickname given to the European headquarters of IBM was "La cage aux foils" because no one makes a presentation without overhead foils. *)

Difference people will need to hear how what they are doing is totally different. Remember the line from Monty Python's Flying Circus? "And now for something completely different."

Taking the Pain out of Organizational Change

Once upon a time, large companies had work groups that were called typing pools. Many of the people who worked in typing pools stayed there for a long time, sometimes fifteen, twenty or twenty-five years, typing documents all day long. Then a miracle occurred. Word processors were invented. The agents of change were very excited by all the *different possibilities* these wonderful new machines could offer. They heralded the arrival of the miraculous machines by announcing to the people working in the typing pools: "We have bought some *totally new machines* which are going to *revolutionize* how you do your work." Many people resigned. Countless more panicked and said "I'm too old to learn this. I can't do this. I am a failure." Now, typing pools have completely disappeared from the workplace.

The moral of the story has little to do with the revolutionary machines. If you had been typing for over fifteen years, would you really be interested in revolution? The **language** of change created much unnecessary resistance in the workforce. Forget the word *new*. Forget the word *revolution*. A more appropriate language for populations with Sameness and Procedures patterns would be: "We have bought some machines which are *exactly like* a typewriter. They have the *same* keyboard. They have a *few* extra keys which allow you to go *faster*, work *better*, correct mistakes *easier*,

---

* "Foils" is the British term for overhead transparencies.

but *essentially, they're the same.* And we'll *teach you the procedure* for using them."

From the mid-1980s to the early 1990s, organizations began to notice that large numbers of their workforce balked at frequent changes. Many introduced "Continuous Improvement" programs. They were not called "Dramatic Difference" programs.

The introduction of workstations, personal and networked computers, and statistical process control on the shop floor was (and is) often mishandled in the same way. It is important to prepare the groundwork for major technological and organizational changes. Knowing your workforce and planning your announcements and implementation, by matching the language you use with the people affected, can *dramatically improve* the chances of making the change stick. Resistance is not a necessary outcome of change programs.

I have noticed that those responsible for introducing or implementing change in organizations frequently have a high personal need for change. Often they are mismatched with their environment, and so, *do not speak the same language* as the people they wish to influence.

Why New Coke Didn't Make It

Once again, there is no substitute for good market research. Remember New Coke? Apparently, when they tested the taste of New Coke, the results were conclusive: New Coke tasted better than the old Coke. However, they could not have tested the *name.*

Let's examine, for a moment, the distribution of the patterns in this category. Only a maximum of 30 percent of the population in the work Context is interested in *new,* according to Rodger Bailey's work. But this was the soft drink Context. How many people do you think would want to drink something new in soft drinks, as opposed to what they know, trust, and buy consistently? Apparently, not very many. Coca Cola responded and returned old Coke to the market. They called it Coke Classic, which is Sameness language.

Labatt Blue, a Canadian beer, apparently understood the pattern. They produced a billboard campaign with the slogan: "Tired of the same, old thing? Neither are we."

In 1992 the Saturn automobile was introduced. The commercials announced: "A different kind of company. A different kind of car." My ears perked up immediately. It would be interesting to find out what percentage of the new-car market actually wants something completely different.

When your market has mainly a Sameness pattern, you will need to demonstrate how the product will give them something they know. It must look, sound, and feel like old *reliable.* "You can always count on us" or "We'll always be there," like Roch Voisine's hit song. This can be a creative challenge for new products and services. How about: "Remember when you . . . ? It's back, just the same, and better than ever before."

Sameness with Exception customers want improvements. Show them how your product or service is better than the competition or what they had before, how it will make their lives easier (Toward), with fewer hassles (Away From). They will prefer to buy *upgrades* rather than different software packages.

Difference people want something totally new and different from everyone else: "You'll be the only one in your neighbourhood" (External) or "You can see for yourself how unique this is" (Internal).

If you want to capture everyone, you will need an updated version of *new* and *improved*, since that slogan is now old hat.

Purchasers and Users of Software

Software purchasing and using presents an interesting Context. From my work with some major software companies, my clients and I happened on an interesting conflict of patterns. With regards to the corporate purchasers of software, we have noticed that they seem to have an Options and Difference combination. They want upgrades and new software to look and be totally different, with many more possible applications, even if they do not need them right away. Contrast this with the poor end-user, who suffers through each new installation, having to learn everything all over again. End-users tend to have a Sameness and Procedures combination. (So do I when it comes to software—at this writing, I still haven't upgraded to Windows 95 because I'm afraid I'll have to spend hours and hours learning how to use it.)

For my software clients, we have developed marketing materials and sales processes to reflect both the patterns of the purchasers and the end-users. Part of the process includes educating the purchasers on how to get more enthusiasm from the end-users, and less resistance to new upgrades.

Summary

≋

Decision Factors

Question: What is the relationship between (your work this year and last year)?

Sameness: They like things to stay the same. They will provoke change only every 15 to 25 years.

Sameness with Exception: They prefer situations to evolve over time. They want major change about every 5 to 7 years.

Difference: They want change to be constant and drastic. They will initiate change every 1 to 2 years.

Sameness with Exception and Difference: They like both evolution and revolution. Major change averages every 3 to 4 years.

Distribution: Sameness 5%
Sameness with Exception 65%
Difference 20%
Sameness with Exception and Difference 10%

Influencing Language

Sameness: the same as; as you already know; like before; identical

Sameness with Exception: more; better; less; the same except; evolving; progress; gradual improvement; upgrade

Difference: new; totally different; completely changes; switch; shift; unique; one of a kind; brand new

Sameness with Exception and Difference: Use *both* Sameness with Exception *and* Difference language

𝒰sing the Profiling Worksheet: Motivation Traits

On the following page you will find the Motivation Traits worksheet to help you master both asking the LAB Profile questions and recognizing the patterns of the person you are interviewing. A similar worksheet can be found at the end of the Working Traits section. The full profiling sheet (for both the Motivation and Working Traits) is included near the end of the book.

On the left side of the page are the questions to ask. I have emphasized in **bold** the basic questions, while the Context is in *script*. Remember that for LEVEL (Proactive and Reactive), there are no questions to ask. You simply listen for the patterns while the person is talking.

On the right side of the chart are the patterns and a summary of each of the clues for recognizing the patterns.

When I am interviewing someone I usually start off by putting one check mark each on Proactive and Reactive, since 60 to 65 percent of the population is right in the middle. Subsequently during the interview, if they use mostly one pattern or the other, I add check marks in the appropriate place.

Often I will write down the expressions that indicate a particular pattern, so that I can verify them when I review the results with the person.

Giving Feedback

When sharing the results of the LAB Profile with someone, avoid using jargon such as *Toward* or *Away From*. It will be more meaningful if you simply describe the behaviours of each pattern. For example: "You prefer to solve problems and do troubleshooting rather than working toward goals. What triggers you into action is when there is a problem to be solved or prevented."

I have included a pattern summary in the Appendix to help you use layperson's terminology when speaking to the uninitiated.

The LAB Worksheet: Motivation Traits

Name: _____ Company: _____

Profiler: _____ Position: _____

Date: _____ Context: _____

Questions	Categories	Patterns—Indicators
(no question for Level)	LEVEL	_____ Proactive—*action, do it, short, crisp sentences* _____ Reactive—*try, think about it, could, wait*
• What do you want in your (*work*)?	CRITERIA	
• Why is that (*criteria*) important? (ask up to 3 times)	DIRECTION	_____ Toward—*attain, gain, achieve, get, include* _____ Away From—*avoid, exclude, recognize problems*
• How do you know you have done a good job (*at . . .*) ?	SOURCE	_____ Internal—*knows within self* _____ External—*told by others, facts and figures*
• Why did you choose (*your current work*)?	REASON	_____ Options—*criteria, choice, possibilities, variety* _____ Procedures—*story, how, necessity, didn't choose*
• What is the relationship between (*your work this year and last year*)?	DECISION FACTORS	_____ Sameness—*same, no change* _____ Sameness with Exception—*more, better, comparisons* _____ Difference—*change, new, unique* _____ Sameness with Exception & Difference—*new and comparisons*

© Copyright by The Language and Behaviour Institute and Success Strategies.

Part **3**

Working Traits

 # Working Traits

Questions	Categories Patterns—Indicators
(no questions for Scope and Attention Direction)	**SCOPE** _____ **Specific**—*details, sequences, exactly* _____ **General**—*Overview, big picture, random order*
	ATTENTION DIRECTION _____ **Self**—*short monotone responses* _____ **Other**—*animated, expressive, automatic responses*
• Tell me about a (*work situation*) that gave you trouble.	**STRESS RESPONSE** _____ **Feeling**—*goes in and stays in feelings* _____ **Choice**—*goes in and out of feelings* _____ **Thinking**—*doesn't go into feelings*
• Tell me about a (*work situation*) that was (*criteria*). (wait for answer) • What did you like about it?	**STYLE** _____ **Independent**—*alone, I, sole responsibility* _____ **Proximity**—*in control, others around* _____ **Co-operative**—*we, team, share responsibility*
	ORGANIZATION _____ **Person**—*people, feelings, reactions* _____ **Thing**—*tools, tasks, ideas*
• What is a good way for you to increase your success at (*your work*)? • What is a good way for someone else to increase their success at (*their work*)?	**RULE STRUCTURE** _____ **My/My**—*My rules for me/My rules for you* _____ **My/. (period)**—*My rules for me/ Who cares?* _____ **No/My**—*No rules for me/My rules for you* _____ **My/Your**—*My rules for me/Your rules for you*
• How do you know that someone else (*an equal of yours*) is good at their (*work*)? • How many times do you have to (*see, hear, read, do*) that to be convinced they are good?	**CONVINCER** _____ See # of Examples—*give number* _____ Hear Automatic—*benefit of the doubt* _____ Read Consistent—*not completely convinced* _____ Do Period of Time—*give time period*

ᶜWorking Traits

The next eight categories of the LAB Profile will tell you how people deal with information, what type of tasks and environment they need to be most productive in a given Context, and how they get convinced about something.

These categories will demonstrate how to *maintain* someone's motivation. Each pattern is described in its pure form.

At the end of the Working Traits section, you will find another Summary Profiling Worksheet to help you master asking the Working Traits questions and recognizing the patterns.

⊙he Forest for the Trees: Working Scope

What size chunk of information does the person handle best? The big picture or specific details?

Using the Scope category, you can determine whether someone can handle overviews and grand designs, or whether the details make more sense. There are two patterns in this category:

Specific

Specific people handle small pieces of information well. At the extreme, they cannot perceive or create an overview. They treat information in linear *sequences*, step by step, in all its detail. A Specific person perceives the trees, branches, and twigs, rather than the forest. They may have difficulty prioritizing as a result. If they are interrupted in the middle of a sequence, they tend to either start over at the beginning or resume the telling from the point at which they were interrupted. Specific people work well where details must be attended to, in tasks such as organizing events or handling logistics.

Note: There is a difference between a *sequence*, which Specific people use and a *procedure*, used by Procedures people. While both have a beginning and an end, there may be choice points, branches and several end points in a procedure. A sequence is chronological, linear, narrow and unidirectional. It is possible for a person to *have both* Specific and Options patterns or a Procedures pattern in combination with a General pattern.

Sequence: A — B — C — D etc.

```
                    | --------- C ------- > -------- G ------- H
Procedure:     A ------- B     | ------- E
                    |          |
                    | --------- D
                          | ------- F
```

General

People with a General pattern in a given Context prefer to work on the *overview*, or at the *conceptual level*, though they can concentrate on details for finite periods of time. Because they see the *big picture* all at once, they may present ideas in a random order without stating the link between one thought and another. They concentrate on the forest; having to deal with the trees for long periods of time irritates them.

Distribution _____ **%**

(*in the work Context, from Rodger Bailey*)

Specific	Equally Specific & General	General
15%	25%	60%

Pattern Recognition

While there are no specific questions for this category, you will be able to recognize the patterns within virtually each sentence spoken.

Hint: One simple way you can know for sure is to time your LAB Profile interview. On average, a full interview takes about 20 minutes to complete, not including giving the person your feedback. With a Specific person, the interview will be at least 40 minutes.

Here's how to recognize these patterns in conversation:

Specific
- speak in sequences, step-by-step
- *lots* of modifiers, adverbs, adjectives
- proper nouns for people, places, and things
- if they lose the sequence, they will start over again or continue from where they left off
- only seem to be aware of the step before and after the one they are on; not much perception of the overview

General
- may present things in random order
- overview, summaries
- concepts, abstracts
- simple sentences, few modifiers or details

Examples

Specific:	"Yesterday at 10 A.M. George and I met with Mr. Vivaldi, our big client from Rome, who spoke about renewing our shipping contract for the third year in a row. He now wants the price of the cardboard packaging to be included with the total price next year."
Mainly Specific:	"Yesterday at 10 A.M. George and I met with Mr.Vivaldi, our client from Rome, to discuss renewing our shipping contract. He wants to include the packaging in the total deal."
Equally Specific and General:	"Yesterday, Mr. Vivaldi told George and me that he wants to include the cardboard packaging in the price next year."
Mainly General:	"Next year Mr. Vivaldi wants to renegotiate our contract."
General:	"Rome wants to renegotiate."

Combinations

I am often asked, when someone is answering the Reason question from the Motivation Traits, how one would know if they were Specific or Procedures, if they are telling a story. The Reason question is: "Why did you choose your current work?" To distinguish between a Procedure pattern and a sequence, which is Specific, you will need to pay attention to the amount of detail given.

Here are some examples. The first one is a response from a Procedures person who has a mainly General pattern. "I didn't really choose this kind of work. I was working in another company and they laid off a lot of people. I didn't have a job when this one came up. I applied and got it." Procedures, mainly General.

Here is an example of Procedures with Mainly Specific. "I was working for the Whoofed Cookies Beverage Company as a field engineer from 1973 to 1991. Then the company went into a period of financial difficulties, so in order to stop themselves from going under, they had to let 250 people go. They closed down my department and then I spent eight and a half months unemployed. I had made thirty applications in each of three geographical areas. Then Stephanie Slobdonovich from the Miracle Cure Cleaning Company called me; I had an interview the following day at 10 A.M. and was hired."

Here is what Specific and Options would sound like. "It was exactly the kind of thing I was looking for. I get to work with people. Different kinds of people. I get to work with tall people, short people, fat people, thin people. People with curly hair and people with thin hair and people with no hair on the top of their heads . . . etc." This is not a story; it is all Criteria (therefore Options), and described in what I would call, excruciating detail. (If I have characterized that example as *excruciating*, what does that tell you about my own pattern?)

Here's another general hint:

As you become increasingly familiar with recognizing the patterns in everyday conversation, you will find yourself noticing and hearing many patterns at once, sometimes within a single sentence.

Influencing Language

Generally speaking, it is important to match a person's pattern in exactly the way they talk to you when in conversation.

Specific
• exactly; precisely; specifically; details; use sequences and lots of qualifiers

General
• the big picture; the main idea; essentially; the important thing is; in general; concepts
• leave out the details and multiple qualifiers

When Bad Communication
Happens to Good People

When a person with a General pattern is communicating, negotiating, or problem-solving with a Specific person, you may notice many misunderstandings. The Specific person may be concentrating on each separate example of a problem, for example, and listing what happened in chronological order, while the General person wants to get to the point. There is a huge difference in the size of pieces of information each is treating; one is dealing with each item in great detail, while the other is trying to get at the big picture. Several things will happen:

1. While the General person will be able to follow the specifics for awhile, he will quickly get bored or feel drowned in detail and want to quit, leave or yell, depending on his preferences.
2. The Specific person will insist on giving ever more details of information in an attempt to make things precise for the other person, and will not understand the attempts of the General person to summarize the situation.
3. The General person may speak in such vague terms that she does not give enough information for others to understand what she is actually talking about. She may then lose credibility with the Specific person, who may suspect her of bad intentions.

So what is the cure? There are several options. (Wouldn't you know it?) First, you will need to realize that this situation will take some time to resolve, because of one party's need for detail. This can be an advantage where the specifics of a contractual agreement need to be sorted out properly, and will save time later, as they will not be overlooked. (You would have to have somewhat of a General and a Toward pattern to *overlook* something.)

You could ask a person who has both Specific and General to mediate between the two, essentially *translating* back and forth. If you are mediating, you will need to reassure both parties that their respective approaches are important and relevant, however different they may be.

For the Specific person, you will need to play back their issues and Criteria, and then describe the sequence by which you will proceed, which includes translating items into General terms. For the General person, give them the big picture. "The main thing is making sure you both can understand each other; I'll help by facilitating that process."

Other alternatives include getting the Specific person to make a list of the important issues on one page in order to facilitate the General person's understanding. To help a General person be more clear to a Specific person, ask them sensory-specific questions such as "How would you know when it's right?" or "Can you give me a tangible example?" or "What specifically would have to happen?"

To capitalize on the strengths of each one, have the Specific person check the details of any agreement (especially if they are also Away From, so they can pick out errors and omissions). The General person will be able to determine whether the process is generally on track to achieving an agreement.

The key is making sure that each understand how they themselves and the other person are functioning. They can use these complementary differences to mutual benefit, provided they accept them and adjust the process, as mentioned above, to take into account each person's needs and strengths.

When someone is highly Specific, how can you interact with them to help speed them through to the end of their sequence? One of the things you can do is ask them what happens at the end. This may be perceived as a sort of violation, but at least it is not an interruption.

Why Do All the Songs I Know End in La, La, La?

Here is an analogy to illustrate how someone with a Specific pattern processes information. When people want to remember the words to a song, they usually start singing the song from the beginning, because the words are stored in their brain sequentially. If you interrupt them, they lose their train of thought, and will have to go back to the beginning to pick it up again. Simply talking and responding will not make them go back; it is *being interrupted* that makes them start over. Asking them "then what happened?" may help them to get to the next item. By doing that, you are respecting the sequence and moving them on to the next step. The word "then" presupposes that something happened before, and something happened after. Another suggestion, if they do not have an off-the-scale Specific pattern, is to ask them to fast-forward, almost as if they had recorded their thoughts on tape.

Hiring

Does the job require close attention to specific, sequential details for extended periods of time, or is detailed work of this kind only a small part of the overall responsibilities? Bookkeeping requires someone who can concentrate on specifics for long stretches at a time; deciding financial strategies is much more an overview kind of task. People and project management tend to be Mainly General functions.

Many positions in manufacturing are Specific and sequential in nature, such as assembly-line work. General people would make many mistakes through inattention to detail in this kind of work. Quality control necessitates a Mainly Specific pattern as well as Procedures and Away From.

The essential question to answer when profiling a position is to *what extent is attention to detail necessary?* You would not want a pharmacist to generally get the dosage right when dispensing a prescription.

Difficult Bosses

If a manager has equal preference for Specific and General, she can be very difficult to work for. This kind of manager not only knows *what* needs to be done, but tends to become very specific in telling employees exactly *how* to do it. Because they, as managers, have a handle on both aspects of the work, they often do not delegate, believing that it is easier to just do it themselves, or that they can do a better job themselves. When combined with a Co-operative pattern (please refer to Working Style), they do not leave any territory for their employees to deal with on their own.

One of the advantages of having an equal aptitude for the detail and the big picture is that this person can handle complex tasks and analyses. She can attend to any level or the whole thing.

Sales, Marketing, and Submitting Bids

Prospective purchasers who have a General pattern will want broad descriptions that match their Criteria. As can be expected, Specific people want all the facts, listed in order. Print advertisements for technical products or software often contain a lot of specifics right in the ad. These ads could be accompanied by another one for General purchasers, with a compelling image and a few words.

Many companies, when submitting a bid, do not know whether the purchasing group consists of mainly Specific or General people or both. Why take a chance on either giving too much information or not enough?

Bids *must* contain a lot of detail. The *Executive Overview* will be read by the Generals, with an occasional peek in the Index to find the specific bits they need to complete the picture. The Specifics and people with a mixed pattern will need the full text to make their decision.

Life, the Universe, and Everything

In Douglas Adams' famous science fiction novel, *The Hitchhikers Guide to the Galaxy*, the great question of life, the universe, and everything was asked of the biggest computer ever built. After centuries of computation, and much speculation on the part of Galaxy philosophers, the wonderful computer submitted its answer to the waiting populations. The answer was: 42. Well, what can you expect when you address a General question to a Specific entity?

Pies in the Sky

One of the problems encountered by people who are "pie in the sky" General has to do with the consequences of staying in the conceptual realm. A friend of mine who has a General and Reactive combination had been the head of Human Resources for a large firm in France. He and the company went their separate ways because of some political disagreements.

I asked him, "What are you going to do next?" He responded, "It is important, when one is to work with a company, that the policies and values be the same and what is really important to me is that we establish a humanistic philosophy." I said: "Okay. What are you going to do next to find that kind of company?" He continued: "It is important to understand that the philosophy must be right." I began to lose it: " So what are you going to **do** to find a job?" I shrieked. He needed to break the task of making his next career move into smaller steps and to have a plan of action for meeting his Criteria.

People who are very General may present things in random order (how's that for an oxymoron?), because they are looking at the big picture. They sometimes do not bother specifying the link between items or ideas, since they can see the whole relationship. Often people will not know what they are talking about.

We have discussed the two patterns. Do you get the picture? Or do I need to go into more detail?

Summary

Scope

Question: There is no question for this category.

Specific: Deals with details and sequences. Cannot see the overview.

General: Prefers the overview, big picture. Can handle details for short periods.

Distribution: Specific 15%
Equally Specific and General 25%
General 60%
(from Rodger Bailey, in the Context of work)

Influencing Language

Specific: exactly; precisely; specifically; gives lots of details
General: the big picture; essentially; the point is; in general

hen Hinting Won't Work: Working Attention Direction

≈≈≈

> *Does the person naturally pay attention to the nonverbal behaviour of others, or to their own internal experience?*

The Attention Direction category reveals whether a person can perceive, and respond *automatically* to, the body language and voice tone of other people or not. There are two patterns:

Self

Self people do not show many emotions, although they do have feelings. There is sometimes a time gap between when they receive a stimulus and when they respond to it. They respond based on what *they* consider to be appropriate. These people are convinced only by the *content* of what people say, rather than the accompanying tone, body language, or level of rapport. They have difficulty establishing rapport because they do not notice other people's body language, and therefore they miss many clues. People with this pattern simply do not pick up hints.

They know how well the communication is going, based only on their own feelings. As a result, they tend not to be adept at interpersonal communication. At work, many Self people become technical experts in fields where communication skills are not essential.

Other

Other people have automatic reflex reactions to people's behaviours. They are animated (for their culture) and respond to others with facial expressions, body movements, and shifts in voice tone. They know how the communication is going based on the *responses* they *consciously or unconsciously* observe from the other person. These people are good at creating and maintaining rapport, provided they also have the other appropriate patterns.

Distribution _____ %

(*in the work Context, from Rodger Bailey*)

Self	Other
7%	93%

One in Fourteen People

According to Rodger Bailey's research in the work Context, approximately one in every fourteen people you will meet will have a mainly Self pattern, if these statistics also hold true for the general population. From my experience, I believe that you will find more who are somewhere in the middle between the two patterns.

Pattern Recognition

There is no verbal test for this pattern, as it shows up in body language or the absence thereof. To test for Attention Direction, I usually drop a pencil accidentally on purpose. People with an Other pattern will spontaneously bend down and pick it up, provided they have seen it or heard it drop. Self people will not pick it up. When speaking to someone on the phone, I will sneeze or have a coughing fit in the middle of a sentence. Does the person say their cultural equivalent of Gesundheit or continue on as if nothing had happened?

The following clues will also be apparent throughout the conversation:

Self
- Absence of culturally appropriate behavioural responses such as head nodding, saying "uh-huh," etc.
- reacts only to the content of what you say
- doesn't "pick up the pencil"
- doesn't notice or respond to your voice tone
- little or no facial expression or voice variation

Other
- responds to both content and nonverbal aspects of the communication
- will nod head, move body, say "uh-huh", etc., as a response
- animated (for their culture)

Let's say I were speaking to someone who had a Self pattern and I, with my shoulders drooped, my bottom lip sticking out, and a whiny tone of voice, said: "I'm really happy to be here." She or he would think that I *was* really happy to be here. For this kind of person, unless you actually say: "I am annoyed and irritated" explicitly, they do not pick it up. Hinting will not work, nor will sarcasm as a method of communication.

While only 7 percent of the population at work are Self; probably many more are borderline; that is, they have some of the Self pattern. You can recognize those people when you drop the pencil. They look at the pencil, they look at you, they look at the pencil, and then they may eventually decide to pick it up. It is not spontaneous, not a reflex. A reflex action is something outside of voluntary control. Sometimes you can also recognize these borderline people because, although they may exhibit little nonverbal behaviour themselves (i.e., facial expressions, gestures, and voice variation), they may be able to notice and respond to the nonverbal behaviour of others.

Examples

There are no word examples for this category. Only behaviour observation will allow you to identify "Self" and "Other" patterns.

Here is an example from American television. In a program called M*A*S*H, a character named Radar always knew what the other characters wanted or were feeling before they did. He was picking up signals and clues in a highly intuitive manner, an off-the-scale Other.

For a Self example, we can recall Pat Paulsen, a deadpan comedian who ran for President of the United States more than once in the 1960s. He spoke in a completely toneless manner with a total absence of facial expression or gestures.

When I was leading one of a series of communication and conflict resolution seminars at the CERN (European Centre for Nuclear Research) in Geneva, there was an engineer who had a strong Self pattern. Much to the annoyance of other participants, he kept stopping the discussion to ask for more explicit definitions of terms. He was filtering for the *content* of what was being said. I asked the participants to do an exercise in groups where they were going to practise some confrontation techniques. One person was supposed to observe and give feedback while they each took turns roleplaying. When I went into his group, he was practically in tears because, although he had understood that there was something to be observed, he just could not see or hear anything. I had to do some on-the-spot counselling to help him focus on what *was* possible for him to do.

The definition of a good host or hostess is knowing what your guests want before they become aware of it themselves. For example, when you are in someone's home and cannot find your salad fork, without your having to ask, does one of your hosts notice your dilemma and go get you one? A Self person would not have noticed that you needed one. You would have had to ask for it.

Communication

Some people have asked me if a Self person would feel uncomfortable in social situations. How does a person with a Self pattern usually know if the communication is going well? They will focus on what is being said, and how they themselves feel about it, without noticing the nuances of nonverbal communication, and so may feel quite comfortable. An Other person can evaluate the communication by unconsciously picking up body-language cues and listening to tone of voice. What is more likely is that the Other people, in communication with a Self person, might feel more un-comfortable because of the absence of the nonverbal responses by which they normally get feedback.

When communicating with an Other person, the quality of the rapport that you established is just as important to them as the substance of what you are communicating. Self people are not influenced by the level of rap-port you have with them, so you will need to be absolutely rigorous in the presentation of your arguments or explanations.

Hiring

Self people usually do not succeed in work that requires the ability to create and maintain rapport. They are not suited for customer-service work or dealing with angry customers. Self people do well where technical exper-tise is required.

In the 1980s while I was conducting a series of interpersonal communica-tions courses in a large high tech company, I could often tell a participant was from the Information Services department, usually within the first five minutes of conversation. Many Self people became technical experts in information tech-nology and other technical knowledge-based fields. They tend to do well there, except in situations where knowing how to play office politics is an asset.

Having made that generalization, I must say that I have since noticed many more Other people working in information services than a few years ago, as companies increasingly demand both technical and interpersonal skills. As many of you know first-hand, electronic mail aficionados have even worked out ways to express feelings in text, by including voice tone and emotions in "emoticons" such as :-) (grin), ;-) (wink), :-((sad), :-Q (close but no cigar), and so on. Using the UPPER CASE indicates SHOUT-ING. (My personal favourite is: *%-), which indicates that *I am having a bad hair day and I don't care.*)

Other people, provided they also have the Choice pattern from the Stress Response category, have the ability to empathize with others.

Once a Self, Always a Self?

In theory, the Self pattern can be either *uni-contextual* or *transcontextual*. Transcontextual means that the pattern exists across many Contexts for a person. Both are possible. In my experience to date, I have noticed more Self people who have this pattern across several Contexts than those who are Self in only one Context and not in another. One student told me about her husband, who "never seemed to notice what was going on." She felt she always had to *tell* him.

My advice would be that it is more rigorous to test in different Contexts, rather than just assuming that someone who has a Self pattern will always have that pattern.

Influencing Language

Pay attention to both the level of rapport you have established and make sure that your propositions hold water logically. Remember Mr. Spock?

Self
- keep the communication focused on the content
- match their Criteria and Convincer Channel and Mode

Other
- they are influenced by the depth of rapport

There is no specific Influencing Language for Self people. Pay attention to your content because the relationship is not what they filter for. Be totally rigorous in what you say. Define your terms properly. If they also have an Away From pattern, they will cut your argument to pieces, if it does not completely hold water. There is no point in taking it personally; that is just how they function.

Summary

Attention Direction

Question: There is no question for this category.

Self:	Attends to own experience. Doesn't notice nonverbal behaviour or voice tone.
Other:	Has automatic reflex responses to nonverbal behaviour.
Distribution:	Self 7%
	Other 93%

Influencing Language

Self:	Focus on the content, match their Criteria and Convincer Channel and Mode.
Other:	They are influenced by the depth of rapport.

$\mathcal{F}$reaked Out or Cool as a Cucumber: Working Stress Response

How does a person react to stress in the work Context?

Wouldn't you like to have a way to find out in *five minutes or less*, if someone can handle a high-stress job?

The Stress Response category examines how you respond to the pressures, at work or elsewhere, that are *typical* for the Context you are in. This is not about how someone would respond to major life dramas, since almost everyone would have an emotional response in those situations. People respond to these "normal" pressures in the following three ways:

Feeling

People with a Feeling pattern have emotional responses to the *normal* levels of stress at work. They go into their emotions and *stay there*. High-stress jobs can therefore be difficult for them to handle over the long term. To many other people, they seem to overreact to situations or be hypersensitive. They are well suited for artistic or creative work, where emotion provides the juice. As salespeople, they find it difficult to handle rejection and may not, as a result, prospect for new customers as often as they should.

Choice

Choice people first have an emotional response to the normal stresses at work and then either return to an unemotional state or not as they desire, in a given situation. *They have choice.* Because they feel emotions themselves, they can empathize with others, or choose not to. They tend to perform well as people-managers, as they can combine the personal side of the job and distance themselves when necessary.

Thinking

People with a Thinking pattern do not have emotional responses to the *normal* stressful situations for a given Context. They have trouble empathizing with others, as they themselves do not go into emotional states. They will not panic in most emergencies, but keep a cool head. They are reliable performers in high-stress jobs.

Distribution _____ **%**

(in the work Context, from Rodger Bailey)

Feeling	Choice	Thinking
15%	70%	15%

Pattern Recognition

Question: TELL ME ABOUT A WORK SITUATION THAT CAUSED YOU TROUBLE.

For Contexts other than work, simply substitute the Context for "work situation." That is, tell me about a buying decision that caused you trouble.

When you are asking this question, avoid having the person tell you about *all* the times they had a particular kind of problem. "Whenever a customer is unhappy with our service, I get nervous." Make sure the person picks one specific troublesome (not catastrophic) situation that he remembers. What you are to determine, as they review that situation, is if they go into an emotional state and get stuck there, have an emotional response and come out of it, or have no emotional reaction at all.

Nonverbal Indicators

For the Stress Response category, there are no specific language patterns to listen for. To recognize the pattern, you will need to observe and listen for nonverbal cues, changes in how the person behaves.

Feeling
- they visibly and vocally have an emotional response while describing a difficult situation
- changes in 3 or more of the following are indicators of a change in emotional state:
  body posture, gestures
  facial muscle tension
  eyes drop
  voice will change in timbre, tone, speed and volume

- will stay in their emotional state throughout their recital

Choice
- will go into their emotions initially and return at least once

Thinking
- will not go into their emotions

Warning: It is possible, when you ask this question, that the other person (if they have a Feeling pattern or if they choose to talk about a major catastrophe) may go into a highly negative or painful emotional state. For this reason, make sure that you ask the Stress Response question before the Style and Organization questions: "Tell me about a working experience that was (*your positive Criteria*). What did you like about it?" It is important to ensure that you do not leave someone in a negative state. Reminding them of situations associated with their positive Criteria will help shift them into a more positive frame of mind. If they seem to still be distressed, you may also have them change seats to help them get out of the negative state.

Examples

These patterns can only be recognized by observing and listening to those behaviour changes listed above, not in the language structure.

For a demonstration of the three patterns, please refer to my audio-cassette series *Understanding and Triggering Motivation: The LAB Profile.*[1]

For a good example of the Choice pattern, watch Captain Kathryn Janeway (played by Kate Mulgrew) on the *Star Trek: Voyager* television series.

Hiring

It is very useful to pay attention to this pattern, because certain professions demand certain kinds of responses. For example, the Thinking pattern would be most appropriate for an airline pilot or an air traffic controller. Could you imagine what would happen if a high Feeling airline pilot were to notice another airplane aiming right for her plane? Air traffic controllers whom I trained told me that you usually can tell if the person beside you is having a *close incident*. The heat energy apparently *just pours out*.

If rapport and empathy are important in a job, then Choice is the best pattern to have. Choice people have feelings and can also come out of an emotional state, if appropriate, to look at the situation or take action. When you regularly experience emotions yourself, you can more easily recognize that other people also have feelings. If Harry stays on the analytical, thinking level as a response to Sally's feelings, he probably will not acknowledge the importance of Sally's feelings to her, or even sympathize with them.

---

1. See the Resources section for details

Many people in artistic careers have the Feeling pattern, because art is often an expression of feelings and emotions. I discovered that the principal activity of the staff in many fine dining establishments (especially in Europe) is not customer service, but trying to keep the chef happy. Many chefs are highly emotional people. When they go over the edge about something, all hell breaks loose.

Incompetency Attacks

In sales positions, Feeling people often become demoralized when faced with rejection from prospective customers, because they take it personally. It means that they would often feel stressed in that kind of function, and may even be prone to what a friend of mine calls *Incompetency Attacks*. An Incompetency Attack has nothing to do with one's real level of competence, which may be excellent. It is a strong, emotionally based belief of incompetence, usually felt by someone with a Feeling pattern in that Context.

Career Counselling

When I am counselling someone about career choices, I pay close attention to this pattern, because it gives an indication of how much stress the person can handle.

Passion

There are some other issues to consider. While a high Feeling person may be prone to suffering from stress, they also have a *need* for passion and intensity. When a person has both Feeling and Options patterns in a Context, they are highly passionate about developing alternatives, a very creative combination.

Managing Stress and People

According to Rodger Bailey, most of the population at work has the Choice pattern (70%). This means that when faced with a difficult or troublesome situation they will first have an emotional response. As a manager you can assist by helping these people *disassociate* themselves from their feelings, if appropriate, by helping them change perspectives.

There are a couple of ways to do this. You can distort time by asking them: "Can you imagine what we'll think about this situation two years from now?" You can have them see it from someone else's viewpoint: "I don't think our customers will care much about this." Or you can have them view the whole thing from the outside: "If you were a fly on the wall when this happened, what would you notice?"

For Feeling people you will probably have to practise your conflict resolution and mediation skills. To maintain their motivation, give them tasks that they can get passionate about. As they are working, watch for signs of distress and overload of tension. These people are the most likely to suffer from stress-related illnesses because they feel stressed more often than people with the other patterns. Feeling people may overreact, particularly in tense or conflictual circumstances. It would be useful for them to learn how to dissociate or cool off. (See B'Elanna Torres played by Roxann Biggs-Dawson, the half-human, half-Klingon in *Star Trek: Voyager*, for a clear example of a Feeling pattern.)

When faced with a highly intense reaction from an employee, create rapport by raising your tone to the same level as his while saying something positive or surprising: "I'm so upset about you being upset, that I am ready to tear my hair out!" Saying something like that will get their attention, so that you can then channel their energy onto a more productive path.

Thinking people are highly appreciated where there is need for someone with a cool head. These people spend much time already disassociated from their feelings and can be called on when a rational approach is needed. Do not expect them, however, to create rapport with others who are in an emotional state, because they will have no sympathy. Thinking people, particularly if they have a combination with Internal, can, however, take the heat and be able to stay in the kitchen!

Influencing Language

You can *rouse* people in an extraordinary way by simply *being there* and making *rational sense* of it all.

Feeling
- get them excited about something and focus on the emotion, using words such as:
  intense; exciting; mind boggling; extraordinary, etc.

Choice
- speak in terms that indicate you can go in and out of an emotional state:
  i.e., "You can get excited about this, and then realize that it makes good sense too."

Thinking
- present the *logical* facts:
  the cold reality; hard facts; clear thinking; statistics

Language Range and Culture

The use of highly emotional words is not necessarily an indicator of a Feeling pattern. Some cultures use superlatives as the usual way of speaking, while others avoid them as much as possible.

For example, I suspect that the use of superlatives is another difference between American and English Canadian cultures. You may have noticed that, in comparison to other English-speaking cultures, Americans tend to use vocabulary that hovers at the extremes, from the *COMPLETE DISAS-TER*, on one end, to the *AMAZINGLY WONDERFUL*, on the other. The French and the Québécois also tend to do this.

– complete disaster   **amazingly wonderful +**

English Canadians (and, in my experience, French Canadians from outside Québec) tend to linger closer to the middle, in a range that goes from the *PRETTY BAD* to the *PRETTY GOOD*.

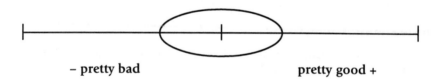

– pretty bad   **pretty good +**

I've heard Americans talk about how difficult it is to get English Canadians excited about something. My advice to Canadians, when listening to Americans describe something, is to apply the Monty Python rule of thumb and divide whatever they say by ten.[2]

By comparison, the English (particularly the upper classes) seem to have an even smaller linguistic range; they go from *NOT GOOD* on the negative side, to *NOT BAD* on the positive side.

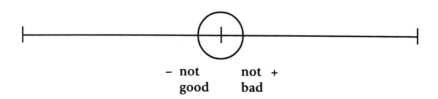

– not   **not +**
good   **bad**

---

2. This "dividing by 10" is from a skit in the British hit comedy television series: **Monty Python's Flying Circus.**

To influence someone using the Stress Response Influencing Language, you will need to choose the kind of language appropriate to the culture.

Summary

Stress Response

Question: Tell me about (*a work situation*) that gave you trouble.

Feeling: Emotional responses to "normal" levels of stress. Stays in feelings.

Choice: Can move in and out of feelings voluntarily. Good at empathy.

Thinking: Do not go into feeling at normal levels of stress. Poor at showing empathy. Keep cool in high-stress work.

Distribution: Feeling 15%
Choice 70%
Other 15%
(from Rodger Bailey, in the work Context)

Influencing Language

Feeling: intense; exciting; mind boggling; wonderful

Choice: empathy; appropriate, makes good sense and feels right

Thinking: clear thinking; logical; rational; cold reality; hard facts; statistics

---

$\mathcal{I}$ Wanna Do It *Myself:* Working Style

> What kind of environment allows the person to be most productive: working alone, with others around, or sharing responsibility?

The Working Style category will allow you to discover (or confirm) how you can be at your best; whether you want to share your work with other people, do it yourself while involving others, or work all on your own.

In this category many people have more than one pattern, a dominant and a secondary Style in a given Context. There are three patterns:

Independent

People who have an Independent pattern in the work Context want to *work alone* and have *sole responsibility.* Their productivity suffers if others are around or if they have to share responsibility. When interrupted, they may lose their train of thought. They prefer to work in an office with the door closed. At the extreme, they may forget to consult with others (especially if they are also Internal). At work, they can go for long periods of time without craving contact with others.

The expression, "A camel is a horse designed by a committee," was probably authored by someone with this pattern. As a manager, an Independent person will do most of the work by himself and probably not establish rapport easily.

Proximity

Proximity people want a *clear territory of responsibility* but need to have *others involved* or around, in proximity. They need well-defined responsibilities; to be productive and stay motivated, and their tasks must involve other people. Their productivity will fall if others share responsibility and authority, or if they have to work totally alone.

Of the three patterns, this one is most suited for people- and project-management positions. They will make sure that everyone knows what they are responsible for. Proximity people do well as the boss, or when they have a boss, as long as territories are well established.

Co-operative

Co-operative people want to work and *share responsibility with others.* They believe in the 2+2=5, the whole is greater than the sum of its parts, Synergy Principle. They have trouble with deadlines and finishing tasks if they have to work on their own. They do not need a territory to be in charge of, and as managers, will want to do everything *with* their employees.

The Californian light bulb joke describes these people. How many Californians does it take to change a light bulb? It takes six: one to change the light bulb, and five to *share the experience.*

Co-operative does not necessarily mean that the person co-operates, in the usual sense of the term, just that she needs to do an activity *with* someone else. When my oldest son Jason was about five years old, he spent an hour building a Lego boat. My youngest son Sammy, then about two and a half, came down from his nap and kicked the boat to pieces. Jason was very upset, but from Sammy's point of view, Jason had *the nerve to do it all by himself.* He did not wait for Sammy to do it *with him.* This was intolerable for Sammy, who usually did not go off by himself and play. He may sometimes be disruptive when he plays, but he needs the company.

Distribution _____ **%**

(in the work Context, from Rodger Bailey)		
Independent	**Proximity**	**Co-operative**
20%	60%	20%

Pattern Recognition

Questions: TELL ME ABOUT A WORK EXPERIENCE THAT WAS (their Criteria)?

- wait for their answer

WHAT DID YOU LIKE ABOUT IT?

For Contexts other than work, you can simply insert the Context into the question: "Tell me about an experience in a relationship that was. . . . "

Make sure the person you are profiling picks a *specific example* of a situation that meets their Criteria. If they have numerous Criteria for the Context you are discussing, simply use one Criterion. Some people may never have had an experience that meets all of their Criteria.

For this category, you will need to listen carefully to what the person talks about. Listen to the answer for the first question and then ask the second question. Does the person talk about doing something *totally alone, in charge with others around,* or *together with others*?

Independent
- says I, I did it, myself, my responsibility
- won't talk about or mention other people
- the activity presupposes that they did it on their own

Proximity
- other people are present but "I did it"
- may or may not mention others, but the *nature* of the activity necessitates the presence of others (i.e. sales or teaching)

Co-operative
- will say: we, us, our job, together, etc.
- includes other people and shares responsibility

Here is how to ask the above questions:

SRC:	Sara, what was one of your Criteria for work?
S:	Challenge.
SRC:	So can you tell me about a work situation that had challenge?
S:	It was a performance issue. There was a question whether a *particular group of people* were performing at the level they were supposed to. *I had to define who was responsible and what to do about it* because the performance wasn't adequate. *I* had to pool that together in different departments and the challenge was to come up with the solution.
SRC:	What did you like about that situation?
S:	I used creativity, it was stimulating, there was a challenge.

In the example that Sara chose to mention, we know that others were involved so it cannot be Independent. Sara says "I" and clearly demonstrates an awareness of who is responsible for what. Her pattern is Proximity.

In the 1970s many of us learned how to say "we" and to "share our dilemmas." This is not necessarily an indicator of a Co-operative pattern. If it really is a Co-operative pattern, the person will talk about the fact that together "we" accomplished something, or that together "we" felt good. If the person indicates that this was his own responsibility, then it is the Proximity pattern.

Examples

Independent:	"I designed the new software and debugged it."
Independent and Proximity:	"I designed the new software and then with my team I got all the bugs out."
Proximity:	"I designed the new software with my team."
Proximity and Co-operative:	"I designed the new software with my team and then together we ironed out the bugs."
Co-operative:	"We designed the new software and debugged it. It was a great team effort."
Independent and Co-operative:	"I designed the new software and then we all sat down and debugged the thing together."

Alternate Question:

How long can you work alone in your office without phoning or going to see someone?

Influencing Language

You can figure this out all by yourself, and use it with other people, so that you will all work well together.

Independent

- do it alone; by yourself; you alone; without interruption; you'll have total responsibility and control; just close your door and reroute your phone

Proximity

- you will be in charge; others will be involved but this is your baby; you will direct; lead; your responsibility is X and theirs is Y

Co-operative

- us; we; together; all of us; team; group; share responsibility; do it together; you won't be alone in this (Away From); let's; we could do that

Team Players? Hiring and People Management

Many management and professional positions advertise for "team players," but what does this really mean? Most management positions require someone who can harness energy, orchestrate activities and create a vision for their team. These activities need a good dose of Proximity with only some Co-operative.

To understand what is needed in a position, you will need to look at the activities and the proportion of time spent in each one. Which ones are *do-it-aloners*? Which activities involve being responsible for the outcome with others involved, and which demand working together at the same time to accomplish the objectives? If the job requires a high degree of proficiency in all three, you are unlikely to find an ideal candidate and may need to redefine the position.

I had a job many years ago where I was the Assistant Human Resources Director in a national youth-development organization for a region that included the provinces of Manitoba, Saskatchewan, and Alberta as well as the North West Territories. My boss had a mainly Co-operative pattern and I have Proximity and Independent patterns at work. She had us decide everything together and I just wanted my *own files*. I needed to have a territory, something that I could be in charge of. She was highly satisfied by our working relationship and I was frustrated.

People who have a mainly Independent pattern at work need space and time to themselves. They excel in those situations that call for someone to keep plugging away by themselves, even when all hell is breaking loose around them. They can concentrate for long periods by blocking out peripheral activities. They do not fare well where constant communication and creating consensus are an integral part of the job.

Since about 60 percent of the population at work has a mainly Proximity pattern, you will notice that most jobs have been designed to give people their own territory as well as necessitating interaction with others. Where the division of tasks has been masterminded by a Co-operative person, there is little mention of individual responsibility, and this confuses and frustrates many employees. I suspect that the "open concept" design of offices was created by Co-operative types. More recently some companies have been experimenting with the "Virtual Office" concept. No one has an office to call her own. You simply reserve a space, depending on the nature of your activity. We'll see if this trend lasts.

Where an Independent person has had a hand in job design, they may have left out defining how people will interface and communicate with each other. This leads to "the left hand doesn't know what the right hand is doing" situation between individuals and departments, common in many organizations.

Pattern Combinations

I am often asked if there are relationships between two or more patterns in the LAB Profile. Is there a relationship between Independent and Internal? These patterns do not necessarily go together. You could want to work all by yourself, not know if your work is good enough, and have to ask, "Maureen, I've just finished this; can you tell me what you think about it?" (Independent and External), or I could publish a report and decide that it was well done, without bothering to get any feedback (Independent and Internal). Most of the patterns can go with any of the other patterns.

Summary

Style

Question: Tell me about a (*work*) experience where you had (*Criteria*). What did you like about it?

Independent: Likes to work alone with sole responsibility.
Proximity: Prefers to have own territory with others around.
Co-operative: Productive when sharing responsibility with others.
Distribution: Independent 20%
Proximity 60%
Co-operative 20%
(from Rodger Bailey, in the work Context)

Influencing Language

Independent: you get to do it by yourself; you alone; total responsibility

Proximity: you'll be in charge; with others around, you'll direct; lead

Co-operative: us; we; all together; share responsibility; let's; do it together

Facts and Feelings: Working Organization

> How do people organize their work? Do they concentrate
> more on thoughts and feelings, or on ideas, systems, tools,
> and tasks?

Working Organization is about how people work, either by getting the job done or focusing on feelings. There are two patterns in this category:

Person

Individuals with a Person pattern pay attention to the feelings and thoughts of either themselves or others. Feelings take on such an importance that *they become the task itself*. They will organize their work so that they can focus on people and their feelings. They are good at establishing rapport.

Thing

Thing people concentrate on products, ideas, tools, tasks, and systems (things). They treat people and ideas as objects, and believe that emotions have no place in the world of work. They want to *get things done*, and have a *task orientation*.

Distribution _____ %

(*in the work Context, from Rodger Bailey*)

Person	Equally Person and Thing	Thing
15%	30%	55%

Pattern Recognition

Since 55 percent of the population have a mainly Thing preference at work, you will hear this pattern more commonly, although specific professions will have their own cultural pattern (i.e., many people in the human services professions have a Person pattern).

The questions are *the same as for the Style category*. In other words, when you ask the questions below, you will receive both the Style and Organization categories of information simultaneously.

Question: TELL ME ABOUT A WORK EXPERIENCE THAT WAS (their Criteria)?

- listen to the answer

WHAT DID YOU LIKE ABOUT IT?

Person
- speak about people, emotions, feelings
- will name people, use personal pronouns
- people are the object of their sentences

Thing
- talk about processes, systems, tools, ideas, tasks, goals, results
- will not mention people often except as impersonal pronouns i.e. "they", or "you"
- people become objects, parts of a process

Examples

Person:	"Mr. Richler was ecstatic with my report. I was quite happy with it too."
Mainly Person:	"Mr. Richler was ecstatic with my report. I was happy too because it meant quite a breakthrough for the whole company."
Equally Person and Thing:	"Mr. Richler was ecstatic with my report. It was quite a breakthrough for the company."
Mainly Thing:	"My report meant quite a breakthrough for the company. My boss liked it too."
Thing:	"My report meant quite a breakthrough for the company."

Other Questions: I recently discovered a test question that will allow you to verify when you are not sure.

"Imagine that you are working very hard to finish a piece of *very important work* that *has* to be done in *thirty minutes.* A colleague whom you *really like and respect* walks in at that moment, appearing quite upset and wants to talk *right now* about a personal crisis. What do you do?"

Either the person will choose to complete the task (Thing), drop everything to comfort the person (Person) or waver between the two, (Equally Person and Thing).

Alternately you could ask the person: "Tell me about a perfect day at work." The person will either tell you about tasks and things, or people and feelings.

Here is another example of someone who is Equally Person and Thing:

SRC: Simon, what is it you liked about helping that person solve a problem?

S: The problem is fixed. And the person is important.

Simon is paying attention both with getting a solution and with the person.

When you ask someone to tell you about a work situation that met their Criteria, and then ask them what they liked about it, they will usually reveal the element that has the most importance for them. The exception is when your interviewee knows the LAB Profile and therefore also knows what you are listening for. "Naive" subjects just give you their pattern.

Influencing Language

Just experiencing how great it is to use just the right words will help you achieve your goals.

Person
- use personal pronouns; people's names; feelings; thoughts; experiencing; this will feel good; for you; for others; the people; our team; our group

Thing
- use impersonal pronouns; things; systems; objects; tasks; objectives; process; get the job done; focus on the task at hand; the goal; the results

Good and Bad People?

Having a Person pattern is not an indication that you are either a "good" or a "bad" person. For example, if someone's profession consists of defrauding others, she would likely be totally focused on the emotions of other people. She will wind and weave emotions while spinning her web. Notice what Robert Redford and Paul Newman were doing in the film *The Sting*. This pattern simply describes *where* you put your attention.

In fine dining establishments, the maître d'hôtel treats all of the patrons basically like objects, placing them in their seats while calling for service. But his job is to make sure that these *objects* are happy. The best example of that kind of Thing pattern, for me, is on commercial airplanes. The flight attendants move down the aisle with the cart between them and you can see they are having a real conversation with each other. They're saying: "And you know what else I heard about him?" Then they plaster on a fake smile and bend down to one of the relatively immobile objects in a seat. "Would you care for a coffee?" You get your coffee and then they can return to their tête-à-tête.

Politicians also refer to people as objects. They talk about *the electorate*. What is the electorate? It is you and I, folks. But to them it is an object, a thing. When the Canadian people rejected the constitutional accords in 1992, many well-known national politicians explained the result by stating that "the electorate was cranky."

Hiring

At work, many jobs are organized to accomplish specific tasks and will need a mainly Thing employee. However, professional recruiters are increasingly looking for people who also care enough about feelings to communicate, establish rapport, and solve conflicts.

Some jobs do require a mainly Person orientation. Customer service and reception are good examples. They also need to have an External pattern, as their customers' feelings must come first. One of the secretaries with whom I worked had a strong Person pattern and was very fond of me. When I would ask her to do something, she frequently would drop everything and attend to me right away. I often had to tell her that it was not urgent and could be done the following week. She would also *not* do someone else's work right away, when she did not like them. In this case, she was also attending to their feelings.

Person salespeople often will have a hard time asking for a close. They are having a lovely time communing with their prospective customers and do not want to end it by focusing on the task at hand. Person managers run meetings that get off topic for long stretches to discuss personal war stories. "That reminds me of the time. . . . " Thing managers will sometimes not recognize feelings and may hurt or embarrass others, and then say, "Feelings have no place at work."

Many people choose counselling or social work as a result of caring deeply about how people feel. Sometimes they forget that the task is to help people become independent and then move on to their next *case*. When they have a high Person pattern, they risk becoming overly preoccupied with the emotions of their clients and suffering from burnout, (especially if they also have Away From and the Feeling Stress Response, which many do). For their own long-term well-being, these professionals need to create boundaries between themselves and their clients, and to focus more on the task at hand (without neglecting their clients' feelings).

In the training field, a survey of corporate trainers was done in the late seventies. It was found at the time that trainers tended not to worry whether they had achieved their objectives as long as everyone felt good. Today, trainers tend to be more task-oriented. Some people will say to me in a training seminar, "This material is very new for me. I don't feel comfortable." Since I tend to be more focused on the task at hand, my inside response usually goes like this: "So, are you being paid to feel comfortable?" However, as a professional, I usually respond by saying, "You know, discomfort is an interesting feeling, because it is a sign that you're stretching. And if you're doing something new that you're not used to, chances are you'll feel uncomfortable. Are you OK with that?" In my mind (with my mainly Thing pattern), making people feel at ease is a **means** to accomplishing the goal of learning.

Blake and Mouton noticed these two patterns when they discussed "Task" and "Maintenance" activities.[3]

Intimate Relationships

This pattern is also important in intimate relationships. Deborah Tannen[4] has noted that, in this Context, men seem to be more concerned with *reporting information* when communicating, while women in relationships tend to communicate in order to establish and maintain *rapport*. She calls this **Report Talk** or **Rapport Talk**. These patterns are similar to Thing and Person. I would suggest that to communicate with a Thing partner (be they man or woman), you could establish rapport by giving or eliciting information. To get a Person partner focused on something, you would want to concentrate on their feelings first, much as I did with the "uncomfortable" example.

Miscommunications between Thing and Person people can happen even over simple things. I was attending a course on Neuro-linguistic Programming in Paris and had lunch with a friend. As I was recounting a funny disaster that had occurred, Suzanne stopped me to ask: "But how did you feel?" "Alright, I guess," I replied, and continued on with the next in the series of mishaps. She did not respond to the funny events, but rather, "But how did they *feel*?" she wanted to know. "I don't know how they felt," I said, starting to become annoyed, "but this is what they did." The two mono-

---

3. Blake, R.R. and Mouton, J.S., **The Managerial Grid** (Houston: Gulf Publishing Co., 1964).
4. Tannen, Deborah, Ph.D., **You Just Don't Understand: Women and Men in Conversation** (New York: Ballantine Books, 1991).

logues continued. "That must have been difficult for you." "Yeah, I suppose, but what happened then was. . . . "

At informal social gatherings, you can usually recognize the Person people. They are the ones who continue talking to you as you are trying to leave. Sometimes they are loathe to break rapport and end your visit.

Sales and Marketing

Person people will buy something for how it will make them feel. Hair colouring and other personal products and services are sold this way. "You're worth it."

To sell to Thing buyers, focus their attention on the product or service and the benefits.

Summary

Organization

Question: Tell me about a (*work*) situation that was (*Criteria*). What did you like about it?

Person:	Concentrate on feelings and thoughts. They become *the task.*
Thing:	Focus on task, systems, ideas, tools, things. Getting the job done is the most important thing.
Distribution:	Person 15% Equally Person and Thing 30% Thing 55% (from Rodger Bailey, in the work Context)

Influencing Language

Person:	use people's names; personal pronouns; feelings; thoughts; feel good; people like
Thing:	things; systems; the thing is; the goal is; process; task; impersonal pronouns

---

$\mathcal{W}$hy Middle Management Got the Squeeze When the Crunch Came: Working Rule Structure

> *What are the rules for behaviour that people apply to themselves and others?*

Rule Structure will give you some information regarding the ability or willingness to manage oneself and others. There are four patterns in this category:

My/My: My Rules For Me / My Rules For You

My/My people have rules for themselves and for others. They are willing to communicate their rules to others. Because they believe that people are similar, they think that what is good for themselves will also suit other people. They will say things such as: "If I were you, I would. . . . " A large majority of people at work have this pattern and probably in other Contexts as well.

My/.: My Rules For Me / I Don't Care

The My/. (period) people have rules for themselves and do not care about others. They do not necessarily harbour malicious intent toward others; it is simply not their problem or concern. These people often get on with what they need to do without thinking about others. Sometimes they are called selfish by others because they simply did not consider anyone else.

I was often awakened in the middle of the night in my sixth floor Paris apartment by people who I believe had this pattern. They would honk loudly at two o'clock in the morning, in a residential district, surrounded by hundreds of people who had, presumably, been sleeping.

No/My: No Rules or Don't Know Rules For Me / My Rules For You

No/My people do not know or do not have guidelines for themselves, but once given the rules, are quite willing to pass them on to others. As a result, they may have difficulty providing direction for themselves or making decisions. Instead, they may get stuck and not know what to do.

My/Your: My Rules For Me / Your Rules For You

People with a My/Your pattern know the rules and policies to follow at work but are reluctant or unable to communicate them to others. They operate from a "different strokes for different folks" perspective. Because they believe everyone is different, they consider it arrogant to tell others what to do. As a result, other people are often unclear as to their expectations.

These are the people who can understand both sides of an argument, as annoying as this may seem to those of us who take strong positions.

Distribution _____ **%**

(in the work Context, from Rodger Bailey)

My/My	My/.	No/My	My/Your
75%	3%	7%	15%

Pattern Recognition

You will need to ask these two questions and notice whether the person answers both or one only, as follows:

Questions:

WHAT IS A GOOD WAY FOR YOU TO INCREASE YOUR SUCCESS (at work)?

- listen for the answer

WHAT IS A GOOD WAY FOR SOMEONE ELSE TO INCREASE THEIR SUCCESS (at work)?

To identify these patterns, you will need to compare the answers to these questions. When someone does not know, they will hesitate a long time and respond with a questioning tone.

My/My:
- Same kind of answer to both questions or answers both questions easily.

My/.:
- Clear response to question one. Indicates lack of interest for question two.

No/My:
- Doesn't know the answer to question one. Has rules for question two.

My/Your:
- Has rules for question one. Doesn't know or wouldn't presume to say for question two.

Examples

My/My:	1. Work harder. Be more organized.
	2. Same way. Work harder. Be more organized.
My/.:	1. Be more organized.
	2. Not my problem.
No/My:	1. Uhm, ah . . . Not sure.
	2. Be organized.
My/Your:	1. Work harder. Be more organized.
	2. Everybody's different.

Influencing Language

If I were you, I would simply pay attention to what the person does because, after all, everyone is different, right?

While there are no specific words for this category, I have created some phrases to give you an idea how to match these thinking patterns in specific Contexts.

My/My:	"You would do that if you were him?"
My/.:	"You're sure about this and it doesn't matter for the others."
No/My:	"Now that you've been informed about what's expected, you can pass that along."
My/Your:	"You know what you should do and you want to leave it up to the others to decide for themselves."

Hiring and People Management

People with the My/My pattern are well suited for people management positions, provided they have the other requisite patterns: Proactive and Reactive, mainly Internal, mainly General, Other, Choice, and so on, (and the knowledge and skill, of course). They clearly state what they expect of their staff, and know and understand the rules by which they guide their own behaviour. If a job or a particular function demands that someone impart expertise, the My/My pattern is best. You would need to be able to tell others what to do.

In situations where a manager has an extreme My/My pattern, and particularly when combined with Internal, he can cause problems for the staff. In an organization for which I had done a large training program, the director decided that all the staff were to go through video-based training. His rationale was that this training had done him a world of good and would therefore accomplish the same thing for the staff. In my opinion, not everyone (at that level) was ready for that kind of experience.

When a manager has the My/Your pattern, she tends to create anxiety around her, because she does not *tell* others what she expects.

When it is important to discover the Criteria, values, goals, and so on, of someone and then work with those, a My/Your pattern is useful. My/Your people make good mediators and negotiators because they can understand each party's views while maintaining their mediator's neutrality. Much of today's standard training in listening and questioning skills for counsellors, coaches, facilitators, trainers, and therapists aims to create a My/Your pattern.

Sales people who have a My/My pattern do well, provided they also have the other desirable patterns for their work (Proactive, some External, mainly Procedures, Choice, Proximity, etc.), because they will ask for the sale. If they have an extremely My/My pattern, they may go overboard about telling others what to do. My/Your sales people may be reluctant to ask for the sale or make suggestions.

So, Why Did Middle Management Get the Squeeze?

The pattern often found in middle management in large, hierarchical organizations is No/My. These people do not typically set the rules for their staff; they find out what the rules are and pass them on.

Since the recessionary period of the early to mid-1990s, organizations have been going through many contortions: downsizing, "re-engineering" their processes, flattening the hierarchy, and in the process, pushing out middle-level managers, among others. Middle managers were perceived as adding little value to many processes, since they seemed to be merely policy and procedure *relay mechanisms.*

This function has been increasingly deemed unnecessary as electronic communication means become more sophisticated, times have been tougher financially, and competition pressures have increased from around the world. The role that middle management plays as people facilitators has been undervalued, in my opinion, as companies were looking to cut heads.

As a result of this process of elimination, a large group of people with a No/My pattern suddenly found themselves looking for work, some for the first time in their lives. What can we predict about these people? It is difficult for them. They haven't got rules for themselves about finding a new career or a new job.

Many support groups have sprung into existence specifically to help this group. They invite speakers to discuss job-finding strategies, raise one's self-confidence, and so on.

Telling Yourself What to Do

I had a career counselling client with the No/My pattern. I asked her, "Do you have trouble sometimes making decisions?" "Oh yes!" she said, "When they concern myself." I asked her to imagine that she was over there in another chair and then had her tell herself what to do. That solved a lot of problems for her. She had no problem telling other people what she expected but she had difficulty deciding what she expected from herself in the work Context.

My/. people do best where they can concentrate on the job to be done and not on others' needs. This kind of work is increasingly difficult to find, as many companies insist that their people communicate and co-ordinate their activities. These people sometimes take the "It's my way or the highway" approach and, if also Proactive and Internal, will bulldoze their way through whatever is going on around them.

I worked with the owner of a small environmental firm who had this combination. He had frightened most of his staff to the extent that they were convinced a pink slip was waiting for them at the end of each day.

Switching Contexts

It is possible to have a My/My pattern at work and My/Your one in a relationship. Since My/Your people do not usually state what they expect from their partner in a marriage, for example, it may be useful for them to switch into My/My from time to time just to let the other person know what they want or do not want. Similarly, people who spend most of their time in a My/My mode in their marriage may want to shift into My/Your to learn how their partner perceives the situation.

I believe that by knowing the different patterns, you can start to choose which one would be the most appropriate at a given time.

Raising Kids

In the Context of raising children, do you also find out from your children what they want, understanding them to be who they are, as well as telling them what you expect? In parenting, it is often appropriate to be in

My/My mode. It is also fitting at other times to use My/Your. One of the goals of parenting is to foster your children's growth and development.

Summary

Rule Structure

Question: What is a good way for you to increase your success (at work)?
What is a good way for someone else to increase their success (at work)?

My/My: My rules for me. My rules for you. Able to tell others what they expect.

My/.:   My rules for me. I don't care about others.

No/My: Don't know rules for me. My rules for you. Typical middle management pattern.

My/Your: My rules for me. Your rules for you. Hesitant to tell others what to do.

Distribution: My/My 75%
My/. 3%
No/My 7%
My/Your 15%
(from Rodger Bailey, in the work Context)

Influencing Language
No specific phrases; just match the thinking processes in specific Contexts.

$\mathcal{D}$ecision Making Processes: Convincer Channel

> What type of information does a person need to gather in order to start the process of being convinced?

The information you will glean from the last two categories in the LAB Profile are especially important for sales people. The Convincer Channel category and the next one, the Convincer Mode, deal with how a person gets convinced about something. Until someone is convinced, they will not take the appropriate actions. At the moment they become truly convinced about something, they are most likely to buy the product or service, or to perform the task at hand.

For each given Context, people generally have a pattern about how they get convinced. There are two phases in this process. First, people will *gather information in a specific sensory channel*, (Convincer Channel), and then they will *treat that information in some way* (Convincer Mode).

Channel Patterns

See	They need to visually "see" a product, service or idea.
Hear	They need an oral presentation or to hear something.
Read	They need to read something.
Do	They have to do something.

Distribution _____ %

(*in the work Context, from Rodger Bailey*)

See	Hear	Read	Do
55%	30%	3%	12%

Pattern Recognition

Question:

HOW DO YOU KNOW THAT SOMEONE ELSE IS GOOD AT THEIR WORK? (or How do you know that a car is worth buying?)

- See—have to see some evidence
- Hear—will listen or hear what someone will say
- Read—read reports, etc.
- Do—have to work with someone to know

Examples

See:	"Just by watching them."
Hear:	"When they explain their decisions you can judge their rationale and thinking process."
Read:	"I read their reports."
Do:	"I have to work with them to get a feel for how they work."

Sometimes people will have more than one answer to this question. For example, they may need to both *see* and *hear* evidence.

Applications

When you wish to convince someone about something, in a sales situation for example, or when assigning a task, you can simply match their Convincer Channel. If you know what kind (Channel) of information they need in that Context, simply give them the information in that form.

Examples

See:	"I would like to *show* you a sample."
Hear:	"*Sounds* alright, doesn't it? Is there anything else you need to *discuss*?"
Read:	"The *figures in the reports* are good."
Do:	"You'll want to *work with it* for a bit to decide."

Influencing Language

You can show a person what you are talking about between the lines, just the same way that they do it. Here is some sensory-based vocabulary for the above patterns:

- See: see, look, show, perspective, image, clear, clarify, light, dark, shiny, colourful, visualize, light up, vague, foggy, horizon, flash, get a look at, picture it, see it in action, view it, etc.

- **Hear:**   hear, talk, listen, wonder, say, question, ask, dialogue, ring, noise, rhythm, in tune, harmonious, musical, tone, discord, symphony, shout, discuss, hear about, tell yourself, etc.
- **Do:**   feel, touch, grasp, gather, in contact with, connect, concrete, pressure, sensitive, solid, closed, open, soft, link, hot, cold, warm, try it out, make sense, work with it, grapple with it, try it on, test it out, etc.

Summary

Convincer Channel

Question: **How do you know that someone else is good at their work?**

See:	Needs to see evidence.
Hear:	Needs an oral presentation or to hear something.
Read:	Needs to read something.
Do:	Needs to do something with the evidence.
Distribution:	See 55%
	Hear 30%
	Read 3%
	Do 12%
	(from Rodger Bailey, in the work Context)

Influencing Language
Match the sensory channel (see, hear, read, do) with your language.

C linching the Deal: Convincer Mode

> *What does a person do with the information previously gathered in order to trigger a conviction?*

After a person has gathered the information in a specific sensory Channel, they will need to treat it in some way in order to become *convinced* about it. This treatment is called the Convincer Mode.

There are four patterns:

Number of Examples

Number of Examples people need to have the data a certain number of times to be convinced, or to learn something.

Automatic

People with an Automatic pattern take a small amount of information and decide immediately based on what they imagine the rest to be. They jump to conclusions and, once decided, do not easily change their minds. They will often give the benefit of the doubt.

Consistent

Believe it or not, Consistent people are never completely convinced. Every day is a new day and they need to re-evaluate every time. I call this pattern the *Scarlett O'Hara* pattern, because "Tomorrow is another day."

Period of Time

Period of Time people need to gather information for a certain duration before their conviction is triggered.

Distribution _____ %
(in the work Context, from Rodger Bailey)

Number of Examples	Automatic	Consistent	Period of Time
52%	8%	15%	25%

Pattern Recognition

Question: HOW MANY TIMES DO THEY HAVE TO DEMONSTRATE THIS (see, hear, read, do) BEFORE YOU ARE CONVINCED?

Number of examples
- will state a specific number of times

Automatic
- one example or assume people are good
- give the benefit of the doubt

Consistent
- never really convinced
- judge each time

Period of Time
- will talk about a duration or period of time they need

The question, as designed, asks for a specific number of times. People will either be able to answer that question or it will, at first, flummox them. Then you will know, by the process of elimination, that the pattern is *not* Number of Examples.

Examples

Number of Examples:	"Two or three times."
Automatic:	"I can tell right away."
Consistent:	"You have to judge each piece of work."
Period of time:	"Over a couple of months."

Here are some sample dialogues, to show you how to test to make sure.

SRC:	Gillian, how do you know that an equal of yours is good at their job?
G:	I just need to see and hear them once.
SRC:	Once?
G:	Yeah, I can tell right away.

There's a hint here. Sometimes you will get the answer to both the Channel and Mode questions when you ask the first one. Gillian needs to see and hear, and has an Automatic Convincer Mode.

SRC:	Jim, how do you know someone else is good at their job?
J:	I'll see what they've accomplished and hear good things about them.
SRC:	How many times do you have to see and hear that to be convinced that person has done a good job?
J:	Two or three times.
SRC:	(Let's test to be sure.) So if you saw and heard that twice, would you be totally convinced that they're good?
J:	Maybe.
SRC:	If you saw and heard that three times, would you be totally convinced?
J:	Yes (nodding his head).

Jim needs to see and hear; Number of Examples: 3

SRC:	Natasha, how do you know someone else is good at their job?
N:	I would want to work with them for a while.
SRC:	How many times do you have to work with them?
N:	Uh, I don't know. How long?

Natasha's Channel is Do; she also revealed her Period of Time pattern while answering to the first question, confirming it in her second answer. Now we need to find out how long she needs to get convinced:

SRC:	How long would you have to work with someone to be convinced that they are good at their job?
N:	Oh, a couple of weeks.
SRC:	So if you worked with someone for a couple of weeks, you would be convinced?
N:	Yes.

SRC:	Adam, how do you know that a colleague of your is good at their job?
A:	I read their monthly reports.
SRC:	How many times would you have to read someone's monthly reports to be convinced that she or he is good?
A:	Well every report is different. You could do a good

job on one and not on the next. You have to read each one.

Adam needs to read (Channel) and has a Consistent pattern for his Convincer Mode. He is never completely convinced once and for all; he judges each time.

Applications

Most of the population (52%) has a Number of Examples pattern (in the Context of Work), which means that they need to have the data a certain number of times to be convinced. Advertising often works on the theory that if you repeat a message six times within a given time period, most people will get the message and act upon it. Many personal development tape programs also recommend that you listen six times. The six repetitions will reach most people, because the majority need three or fewer to be convinced.

Consistent people take nothing for granted. Combined with Away From, this pattern is ideal in tasks that involve checking for mistakes or in any kind of quality control. You would not want Joe to think that, since he "knows" Charleen performs well, he does not really need to check.

Learning

Let's take education as a Context for a moment. A child is learning addition or subtraction at school and needs to repeat the sums twelve times to be convinced that she has learned it. The chances are that during school hours she will never get the number of examples she needs to convince herself that she can add or subtract. Lessons are usually designed with a certain number of repetitions of skill sets. If a teacher can detect how a student having difficulty gets convinced that she knows how to add, then exercises can be adapted to provide the necessary repetition.

This information can also be useful for parents to help their children with school work. "How would you know that someone can read well?" "When they can get all the words right away." (Channel: Do) "How many times would they have to get all the words right away for you to be *sure* that they can read well?" "Ummm, lots of times." "Lots? If someone could read all the words right away three times would you be sure?" "Hmm, I'm not sure." "Well, let's say they read all the words five times right away; would you be sure then?" "Yeah, of course." Then, as a parent, you can make sure that, at each stage of reading, the child counts the number of times up to five that they got the words. Once the child gets the *proof* they need, they will believe that they can do it and will read with more confidence.

You will sometimes need to discuss the proof with the child. If getting *all* the words or *always* getting the right answer is unrealistic, then maybe you could help them use a more attainable proof.

If a child has Consistent pattern (never completely convinced) in the Context of learning, you will notice that she will need to get convinced that she knows something *each* time she does that activity. You might want to point out that this time is like *each other time*, inasmuch as the child was able to do it, once again.

Tough Customers

Automatic people take a small amount of information and decide immediately based on what they extrapolate. In other words, they hallucinate the rest, then they decide. They are the sort of people who jump to conclusions or make snap decisions. If you are trying to convince an Automatic person of something and they say no in the first breath, do not bother going back to try to reconvince them. They only rarely change their minds.

As customers, Consistent people are the most difficult to deal with. You will need to re-establish your credibility each time you serve them. They may love your service one day and hate it the next and love it again the following day. They appear skeptical and just will not get convinced. Use the same Influencing Language as for an Internal person, paying attention to match their Convincer Channel. "I suggest you try it out before you decide" (Do, Consistent), or "Look it over and tell me what you think" (See, Consistent). This group is the most likely to return items that they have bought, or to change their minds on something they have agreed to in a negotiation.

Period of Time people need to have information over a set duration before they get convinced. Your customer may tell you that she needs to discuss (Hear) your product for a couple months. You can either wait for that period or phone her a few weeks later and say that you have been so busy, it feels like a couple of months have gone by.

Influencing Language

Each time you are with people, you can give them the benefit of the doubt that they will consistently take the time they need to make up their minds.

(Remember to also match the Convincer Channel)

Number of Examples:	(Use the number)
Automatic:	You can assume; benefit of the doubt; decide fast; right now
Consistent:	try it; each time you use it; every time; consistent performance; don't take my word
Period of Time:	(match the period of time)

Summary

Convincer Mode

Question: How many times do they have to demonstrate (see, hear, read, do) this for you to be convinced (that they are good at their work)?

Number of
Examples: They need to have the data a given number of times to be convinced.

Automatic: They take a small amount of information and get convinced immediately. They hardly ever change their minds.

Consistent: They are never completely convinced. Every day is a new day and they need to get reconvinced.

Period of
Time: They need to gather the information for a certain duration before their conviction is triggered.

Distribution: Number of Examples 52%
Automatic 8%
Consistent 15%
Period of Time 25%
(from Rodger Bailey, in the work Context)

Influencing Language

Number of
Examples: use their number

Automatic: assume; benefit of the doubt

Consistent: try it; each time you use it; daily; every time; use Internal Influencing Language

Period of
Time: match the period of time

$\widehat{\mathcal{O}}$he LAB Profile Worksheet: Working Traits

On the following page is the second half of the worksheet to assist you in profiling someone's Working Traits. I have again included the indicators for each pattern to help you practise recognizing the patterns.

You can find a complete profiling sheet for both the Motivation Traits and the Working Traits in the Summaries section at the back of the book.

LAB Profile Worksheet: Working Traits

Name: _____ Company: _____

Profiler: _____ Position: _____

Date: _____ Context: _____

Questions	Categories Patterns—Indicators
(no questions for Scope and Attention Direction)	**SCOPE** _____ **Specific**—*details, sequences, exactly* _____ **General**—*Overview, big picture, random order*
	ATTENTION DIRECTION _____ **Self**—*short monotone responses* _____ **Other**—*animated, expressive, automatic responses*
• Tell me about a (*work situation*) that gave you trouble.	**STRESS RESPONSE** _____ **Feeling**—*goes in and stays in feelings* _____ **Choice**—*goes in and out of feelings* _____ **Thinking**—*doesn't go into feelings*
• Tell me about a (*work situation*) that was (*criteria*). (wait for answer) • What did you like about it?	**STYLE** _____ **Independent**—*alone, I, sole responsibility* _____ **Proximity**—*in control, others around* _____ **Co-operative**—*we, team, share responsibility*
	ORGANIZATION _____ **Person**—*people, feelings, reactions* _____ **Thing**—*tools, tasks, ideas*
• What is a good way for you to increase your success at (*your work*)? • What is a good way for someone else to increase their success at (*their work*)?	**RULE STRUCTURE** _____ **My/My**—*My rules for me/My rules for you* _____ **My/. (period)**—*My rules for me/ Who cares?* _____ **No/My**—*No rules for me/My rules for you* _____ **My/Your**—*My rules for me/Your rules for you*
• How do you know that someone else (*an equal of yours*) is good at their (*work*)? • How many times do you have to (*see, hear, read, do*) that to be convinced they are good?	**CONVINCER** _____ **See** __ **# of Examples**—*give number* _____ **Hear** __ **Automatic**—*benefit of the doubt* _____ **Read** __ **Consistent**—*not completely convinced* _____ **Do** __ **Period of Time**—*give time period*

© Copyright by The Language and Behaviour Institute and Success Strategies

Part 4

Applications

$\mathcal{A}$pplications

In this section, I have included examples of different applications of the LAB Profile. You will find lots of hints and subtleties on the uses of the questions, and on using the Influencing Language.

The following topics will be covered:

- Career Counselling and Personal Profiles
- Corporate Culture Diagnosis and Change Measurement
- Hiring Employees Who Perform
- Building a High Performance Team
- Negotiating
- Analyzing Your Target Market
- Political Campaigns
- Education and Learning
- Default Profiles

Career Counselling and Personal Profiles

When people come to me for career counselling, we usually start by doing a LAB Profile. Also, managers have asked me to profile their employees to determine their strengths and weaknesses, either for the job they are presently doing, possible promotion, or transfer.

It is important to remember to establish clearly the Context with the person being profiled. Since most of the people interviewed do not know much about the LAB Profile, I usually include, in their report, the LAB Profile Summary, found near the end of this book.

Here are two examples of reports for career counselling:

LAB PROFILE REPORT
Bill X

Context: Work

Motivation Traits

The following patterns describe those things that will trigger Bill's motivation.

Mainly Reactive with some Proactive

Bill is more likely to think and consider than to jump into action. He is mostly motivated by situations where he gets to understand, analyze, and think. He may wait for others to initiate and feel more comfortable responding.

Criteria

The following words and phrases are his hot buttons about work. He will be motivated when he thinks of or hears them:

> personal and professional satisfaction, sense of purpose, sense of passion, sense of excitement, sense of accomplishment, part of something larger, provides a purpose for my life, sense that I am empowering people and organization

Mainly Away From

His motivation is usually triggered to move away from bad situations. He is primarily energized when there is a problem to be solved, a situation to be avoided, gotten rid of, or not have happen. He is a natural trouble shooter. He will need to refocus on his goals at regular intervals to avoid being sidetracked.

Mainly External

In situations where he has to decide for himself, he can and will, but he doesn't have a particular need to be the one who decides. His motivation is triggered when he gets feedback, either from other people or from results. In the absence of such feedback he will become demotivated. He may accept information as instructions.

Mainly Options

Bill is usually motivated to develop new options, alternatives, possibilities. He often has difficulty *following* procedures, but is usually good at *developing* procedures. When asked to simply follow a procedure, he may try to fix the procedure. Breaking the rules is irresistible to Bill.

Sameness with Exception and Difference

He likes his work situation to change often. When he is sure that he knows his job, he is happy doing that job for a couple of years. For some aspects of his work life he likes to do a job for five to seven years; for other aspects he likes one to two years. His task clock seems to average at about three years.

Working Traits

The following patterns describe the work environment that Bill needs, the kind of tasks that suit him, his response to stress, and how he gets convinced about something.

Mainly General

Bill usually makes sense of his work as an overview and prefers to work on the big picture, but he can work with detailed sequences for extended periods if necessary.

Other

He accepts the emotional content of his communications with others. He has automatic reflex responses to the behaviour of people, which facilitates interpersonal communication. He makes sense of communication with others based on the nonverbal part of the communication.

Proximity with some Independent

Bill usually likes to work with others around and involved. To be most productive, he needs to have his own clear territory of responsibility. For some aspects of his work he wants to be totally alone, without interruption.

Thing with some Person

At work, Bill concentrates on the task at hand. While he recognizes the importance of feelings, given the choice, he will focus on the job to be done.

Stress Response—Choice with some Feeling

Bill initially reacts to job pressures emotionally, and may stay in emotional feelings longer than necessary. He is usually able to adapt to stressful situations and will respond based on his own belief of appropriateness. He is best suited to tasks where empathizing with others is an asset.

Rule Structure—My/My

Bill expects others to work the way he works. He has no difficulty telling others at work what he expects. He is well suited to people-management tasks because of this trait.

Convincer Channels—Seeing, Hearing, and Feeling

He is primarily convinced about projects or ideas by seeing the evidence or observing the product or process. He is also convinced by hearing or discussing it. To be fully convinced, he also needs to "get a sense" of something, a feeling.

Convincer Mode—Number of Examples

Bill is convinced by three to four examples. This is the number of times he needs to see, hear, and feel something to be convinced. Fewer than this number leaves him unconvinced.

Ideal Work Situation

The following points describe Bill's ideal work:

- time to reflect, analyze, and understand, with some time for initiating
- problem-solving and troubleshooting
- feedback in terms of results or by significant others
- possibility to create options, design new procedures; less apt to follow procedures himself
- evolution and revolution; wide variety of tasks and major change about every three years
- prefers to work on overviews, rather than detail

- with own territory of responsibility, others around; some time totally alone
- concentrate on ideas, tasks, systems, and some feelings
- avoid high-stress work

Suggestions

Bill needs to refocus on his goals at regular intervals. This will help him to assess his present activities as to whether they bring him closer to his goals and reflect his deeply held values.

Since Bill has an aptitude to create alternatives and to reflect at an overview level, he will need to team up with someone who is more Proactive and more Procedures and detail-oriented to complete and finish the ideas he will develop. To succeed at an endeavour, he will need to divide what he has to do into steps, and follow them.

High-stress work with looming deadlines, for example, will not be healthy for him over the long term.

The checklist and suggestions at the end of the report can be used by the client when evaluating choices.

Depending on the profile of the client, you can either suggest options or give them a procedure for finding work, starting a new career, and so on.

Here is another sample report for a client who was considering moving her part-time business to full-time:

LAB PROFILE REPORT
Claudia Y

Context: Work, present and future

Motivation Traits

The following patterns describe those things that will trigger and maintain Claudia's motivation.

Equally Proactive and Reactive

Claudia initiates or waits for others to initiate. She does either with equal ease. She can be energized, while at the same time she can think and not act. Understanding is just as important as action. She is just as likely to consider as to act. She needs her work to provide the opportunity to do both.

To successfully set up and run her own business, Claudia will need to actively engage her Proactive part, particularly to generate new business.

Criteria

The following have a high level of importance for Claudia in her work. They are her *hot buttons*:

always have things to learn, work with words and language, contact with the outside world, team work, well paid.

The experiences represented by these words are what Claudia is looking for in her work.

Toward

Claudia is motivated to move "toward" her goals. She is motivated by goals. She wants to attain, achieve, get, and is so goal-oriented that she may not recognize real or potential problems. She would benefit by having someone with a facility for recognizing problems help her when she is planning.

Mainly Internal with some External

Usually Claudia decides for herself and is motivated when she gets to decide. To a lesser extent she needs feedback from others to check how well she is doing, but generally Claudia knows within herself. She usually takes that information from others and evaluates it by her own standards. In her ideal work situation, she would have the opportunity to judge her work for herself, using feedback from others as input.

Mainly Options with some Procedures

Claudia is usually motivated to develop new options and find other ways of doing things. She is very creative. She may have difficulty completing procedures, because her main motivation is to develop alternatives. If Claudia runs her own business, it will be important for her to make sure that procedures are completed and that her ideas are taken to their logical conclusion before starting on a new project.

Sameness with Exception

She likes her work situation to progress and evolve. Claudia likes to do the same work for about five to seven years. She can accept changes once a year, provided they are not too drastic. This is an excellent pattern for building a business, as Claudia will stick with the setup and development phases, provided she is doing activities she enjoys.

Working Traits

The following patterns describe the work environment Claudia needs, the kind of tasks that suit her, her response to stress, and how she gets convinced about something.

Mainly General and some Specific

Claudia prefers to think about her work in an overview. She can work with specific details for extended periods. As a manager or co-ordinator of other people's work, she must remember to let other people focus on the how while she manages the general overview. She can see the big picture at work but deal with details when she has to.

Other

Claudia is sensitive to the nonverbal behaviour of others, such as voice tone, facial expression, body posture, and so on. She has automatic reflex responses to the behaviour of people. She makes sense of the communications with others based on the nonverbal part of the communication.

Stress Response—Feeling with some Choice

Claudia initially reacts to job pressures emotionally and tends to stay in emotional feelings longer than necessary. She is usually able to adapt to stressful situations and will respond based on her own belief of appropriateness. She is best suited to tasks where empathizing with others is an asset.

Proximity

Claudia likes to work with other people around. She likes to be the boss or to have a boss, as long as her territory of responsibility and authority is clear. Her productivity will suffer if she has to work totally alone or if she has to share the responsibility with others.

Mainly Person with some Thing

While at work, Claudia focuses mainly on people's needs. This means she will be responsive to clients' and her boss' feelings. She can also be task-focused. At times she may drop the task to take care of someone's personal feelings. At these times, she may need to remember the goals and decide on priorities, which she has the ability to do.

Rule Structure—My rules for me / My rules for you

She expects others to work the way that she works. She understands the rules and unwritten policies of the workplace and she has no difficulty telling others what those rules are, an essential quality for management.

Convincer Channel—See and Hear

Claudia needs to hear and see evidence when getting convinced about something. To a lesser extent she needs to do something with the product or person to input the necessary data to start the process of being convinced.

Convincer Mode—Period of Time

Claudia needs to hear, see, and do something consistently with the evidence for a period of six months before she is convinced. Less than this amount of time will leave her unconvinced.

Ideal Work Situation

In summary, Claudia needs the following elements in her work:

- opportunity to take the initiative and to reflect
- work toward goals (she needs to have elaborated specific goals or she will be demotivated)
- work that she can judge for herself with input from others
- opportunity to develop systems, procedures, and ideas
- progression and personal growth in five to seven year cycles
- concentrate on the big picture with a bit of detail work
- have the responsibility and authority with others involved
- rapport and empathy with others

Things for Claudia to Consider when Deciding on Developing Her Business:

- be proactive about prospecting for clients
- have someone help during the planning stage who can easily perceive potential and actual problems. Explain their role clearly to them
- make sure that the procedures needed to make the business a success will be taken care of
- evaluate the business ideas and make sure that each plan is completed
- plan for incorporating growth and development in the work she does

---

THE KEYS TO PERSONAL PROFILES

1. Decide on the Context and the purpose of the profile.
2. Adapt the questions to the Context.
3. Describe the patterns using layperson's language for the patterns, when giving feedback to the person.
4. Make sure to include the ramifications of any relevant combinations; For example, with Away From combined with Person, you can predict that your client will drop whatever he or she is doing to take care of others' needs.
5. Test your diagnosis by asking the alternate questions when you are not sure.

Corporate Culture Diagnosis and Change Measurement

There is a very simple, unscientific way to figure out the culture of an organization in LAB Profile terms: Ask the people who work there. In my experience, I have been surprised by the high degree of consensus among employees and managers about the profile of their company. While groups with whom I have conducted team building operations usually begin on agreeing about nothing, except that they have problems, they will instinctively know whether the organization has mainly Options or Procedures, Internal or External, Toward or Away From, Difference or Sameness with Exception, and so on.

At the IBM International Education Centre in La Hulpe, Belgium, the managers of management development from each country did a Present State—Desired State analysis of the LAB Profile of the corporation. They affirmed that the company had an Internal pattern, trying to shift to External, from Procedures to adding Options, and from Sameness with Exception to adding some Difference. This analysis enabled them to understand exactly what kind of attitudes their programs should be encouraging. We then worked on some of the strategies they were using and could use to those ends. (But that is another book.)

To accomplish the analysis, I simply described the attributes of each pattern and asked the participants where they thought IBM was. The process took about three hours and was achieved by consensus.

You can also use the LAB Profile to measure the effectiveness of organizational change operations.

Do a *before* corporate-culture diagnosis with a random group of people from the organization. Implement the desired changes with the appropriate strategies, paying attention to match your language to the Decision Factors patterns (Sameness, Difference, etc.) that are prevalent in the organization. About six months to a year after you have put the major changes in place, pick a different random group of employees. Have them describe the present culture using the LAB descriptions. The *effective* changes should show up by changes in the LAB patterns.

You can also design internal corporate communications after you have diagnosed the culture in LAB Profile terms. I will soon be publishing another book on this topic.

161

Hiring Employees Who Perform

An engineering and manufacturing company had advertised for a production manager. They received *300 applicants* and, out of that group, found
only one good candidate. I was asked to profile the position and the senior
management team to whom the successful candidate would report. I wrote
their next ad with the appropriate Influencing Language, designed to attract
the right people and turn off the ones who wouldn't fit. They received *100
applications* and *eight good candidates.*

Job Profiles

To profile a position, you will need certain information about the job
itself, the environment, and the culture that the successful candidate will be
working in.

For the position itself, you will need to understand what the specific
tasks are and the *responsibilities* that the person will hold.

The following elements will help you determine the profile of a job.

Does the job demand that the person:

- just go and do it / think about it / think and do (Proactive-Reactive)?
- manage priorities, attain goals / identify and solve problems (To-
  ward-Away From)?
- decide by oneself, hold standards / adapt to feedback (Internal-Ex-
  ternal)?
- follow procedures / design them (Procedures-Options)?
- revolution, frequent change / evolution / maintain standards (Dif-
  ference-Sameness with Exception-Sameness)?
- big picture / detail (General-Specific)?
- rapport with others (Other, Choice)?
- high / medium / low stress (Stress Response: Feelings-Choice-Think-
  ing)?
- work alone / in charge of own territory with others around / together
  as a group (Independent-Proximity-Co-operative)?
- focus on feelings / tasks to be accomplished (Person-Thing)?
- communicate rules and own expectations / transmit received rules /

just get it done / understand both sides (My/My - No/My - My.- My/ Your)?
- check for errors, quality control (Consistent and Away From)?

Here is the job description for the Production Manager mentioned above. This company designs and builds equipment for the manufacture of different kinds of plastic film:

PRODUCTION MANAGER
JOB DESCRIPTION

Manufacturing Production Management:
Manage plant workforce through supervisors.
Balance plant production levels with sales requirements.
Determine manpower and material requirements.
Carry out studies on unit (trade category) loading, capacity analysis, and performance.
Monitor production reports and investigate causes of errors in production, shipping and data entry.
Release work orders to departments in accordance with master schedule.
Devise detailed production plans and schedule machine setups for trials and shipping.
Develop standard costing systems.

Ensure that shipments are properly done:
- completeness of order
- correctly crated/packaged/protected for shipment so that damage will not occur during shipment
- necessary assembly / electrical installation drawings are included
- shipping costs
- quality control

Interface with Engineering to establish priorities for jobs to be released.

Materials and Inventory Management:
Responsible for all WIP and stock.
Order and time deliveries from suppliers to co-ordinate with production requirements.
Maintain optimal inventory levels.
Co-ordinate and direct all activities relating to physical inventory audits.
Oversee bills of materials, determine production standards and part number.
Implement automated materials / inventory control system when feasible.
Co-ordinate / oversee purchasing department.
Negotiate prices / terms with major suppliers.

Select / establish new suppliers
Bring new ways / methods to make the purchasing function more effective and ensure that it changes to reflect the current environment.

Government Compliance:
Overall responsibility for compliance with applicable government regulations with the plant. This would include:

* OHSA—Safety compliance and due diligence
* Workers' Compensation
* hazardous waste removal
* WHMIS compliance
* evaluations
* discrimination

Facilities Maintenance:
Prepare annual budgets for supplies, spare parts, and accessories. Establish procedure for equipment selection, operation, maintenance, and replacement.

Using the above job description, and having profiled the senior management team to whom the Production Manager would report, I came up with an ideal LAB Profile for this position. I have included it here to show how I write job profiles.

PRODUCTION MANAGER-JOB ANALYSIS

The following characteristics are to be preferred, based on the job description and the relationship with the directors.

Motivation Traits

Mainly Proactive with some Reactive

The job requires a high level of energy and the ability to initiate; to a lesser extent the person must be able to analyze and reflect.

Mainly Away From with a little bit of Toward

The successful Production Manager needs to be constantly troubleshooting, inspecting for errors, and making corrections. The directors will need to be goal-focused, with an eye on managing priorities.

Internal

The Production Manager will have to set standards and evaluate against these standards. To fully assume the workload, he/she will need to know internally when things are good or bad, and not have to rely on the constant feedback of the directors. To work well with the directors, they must agree on a set of standards and how they will be evaluated, and then let the Production Manager get on with it.

Mainly Procedures with some Options

The Production Manager will need to be motivated by following procedures most of the time. He/she must be the sort of person who is compelled to complete and finish what he/she has started. To a lesser extent he/she will have to develop new procedures.

Sameness with Exceptions and Difference

The Production Manager will need to manage improvements and progression over time *and* be able to introduce new procedures and systems. He/she must also be able to handle a wide variety of tasks simultaneously.

Working Traits

Mainly General with a good dose of Specific

To work effectively the Production Manager needs to always have a handle on the overview. This would allow him/her to delegate when appropriate. However, several of his/her tasks necessitate that he/she handle specific details for extended periods. Normally a person who is equally General and Specific has a difficult time delegating, which could lead to frustration on the part of his/her staff, and burnout over the long term for the person him/herself.

For this reason, a person who is mainly General is preferable.

Other

The person must be responsive to tone of voice and body language to supervise and communicate with staff and negotiate with suppliers.

Stress Response—Choice

The Production Manager will need to be able to empathize with others and be able to control his/her internal state, to handle the work load without burning out when things go wrong.

Mainly Proximity with some Independent

Most of the tasks require someone who needs and understands the need for having a territory of responsibility while working with others around. For some of the tasks, he/she will need to work/think while completely alone.

Mainly Thing and Some Person

The person must remain focused on the task at hand and be responsive to feelings. Given ambitious production deadlines, the task must take priority over feelings.

Rule Structure—My/My

He/she has to be able to give clear directions.

Convincer—Consistent

Ideally, a person who is "never completely convinced" is the best choice for a position that demands quality control and inspection. This means that he/she will constantly check and not assume that things are okay because they were last week.

MOST IMPORTANT PATTERNS

Upon analysis of the job description, and taking into consideration the Profile of the three directors, the following patterns are the most important for the new Production Manager:

Mainly Away From
Internal
Mainly Procedures

I used the following comparison chart to compare each of the short-listed candidates from the first advertisement (that the company wrote), relative to the 'ideal' for the job.

──── COMPARISON CHART ────

PROFILE PATTERNS	PRODUCTION MANAGER	BOB	JOHN	MIKHAIL
Proactive-Reactive	Mainly Proactive	Equally Proactive & Reactive	Mainly Proactive	Mainly Proactive
Toward-Away From	Mainly Away From	Mainly Toward	Away From	Mainly Toward
Internal-External	Internal	Mainly External	Internal	Mainly Internal
Options-Procedures	Mainly Procedures	Mainly Procedures	Equally Options & Procedures	Mainly Options
Sameness & Difference	Sameness w/ Exceptions & some Difference	Sameness & Difference	Sameness w/ Exceptions	Difference & some Sameness w/ Exceptions
Specific-General	Mainly General & some Specific	Mainly General	Mainly General	Mainly General
Other	Other	Other	Other	Self & Other
Independent-Proximity-Co-operative	Mainly Proximity, some Independent	Co-op with some proximity	Proximity	Mainly Proximity with some Co-operative
Person-Thing	Mainly Thing & some Person	Equally person & Thing	Mainly Person & some Thing	Mainly Thing
Stress Response	Choice	Choice	Choice	Choice
Rule Structure	My/My	My/Your	My/Your with some My/My	My/My
Convincer	Ideally, Consistent	Consistent	Period of Time	Large Number of Examples, possibly Consistent

RECOMMENDATIONS

In my opinion, regarding the attributes of each candidate (not the skills or knowledge base), John is the most suitable, followed by Bob. I believe that John is the best because of his ability to perceive, predict, prevent, and solve problems and because of his proficiency at making decisions. He is the most likely to relieve the directors of many responsibilities.

Bob is more goal-oriented and may tend to overlook problems. Because he is more External, he is more likely to need feedback on a continuing basis to help him decide.

Attracting *Only* the Right People: Career Advertisements

To demonstrate how to write an advertisement, here are the two ads used for the Production Manager position.

The ad placed by the company before I was asked to profile the position:

PRODUCTION MANAGER

Private fast-growing engineering company manufacturing high-tech quality machinery for worldwide export has immediate opening for decision maker to manage production division.

Production to double within the next year necessitates efficient co-ordination of rapidly expanding department.

Right candidate must have minimum 10 years related experience. Emphasis on organization, planning, and purchasing. Candidates must have excellent people-management and leadership skills.

Here is the ad I wrote after doing the profiles:

PRODUCTION MANAGER

Immediate opening for a proactive Plant Manager who will grow with this engineering company, which manufactures high-tech quality machinery for worldwide export.

The right candidate will manage the production division, solving technical, people, and government-compliance issues by following procedures and developing new ones when necessary. You will set standards and assure they are consistently met, even under the pressure of ambitious delivery targets. You are highly experienced and skilled in project and people management and purchasing, and can prove it.

The first step is to call now for all the information you need.

I suggested that the candidates call, because only Proactive people will actually pick up the phone. Can you identify the specific Influencing Language used in the second ad?

$\mathcal{B}$uilding a High-Performance Team

As a people manager, it is incumbent upon you to assess accurately the strengths of your people. Beyond being aware of their knowledge and skill levels, when you also know their LAB Profile, you are better placed to redesign or adapt individual task assignments (where you are able to do this).

One way is to list all the activities that must be done in your department, and verify that each one is indeed necessary and useful. (Many companies are now doing such task analyses with consultants to determine just what tasks are needed, given increased customer expectations.) Using the elements from the Job Profile section, you can list the ideal LAB Profile patterns beside each activity, along with the knowledge and skill requirements.

Once you have profiled and given feedback to each of your staff members, you can adjust task assignments based on what needs to be done and the profile of your staff. I suggest that you do this in a consultative manner, taking into account preferences where feasible.

Let's look at the team as a whole. What are the elements in LAB Profile terms that characterize your team? What are the strengths and weaknesses when you consider the tasks that need to be accomplished? How can you maximize these strengths? How can you attenuate, or take advantage, of the weaknesses when pursuing team goals and objectives?

This is an area where there is no one miracle recipe. Your team will first need to decide its vision, mission, and goals (within the larger context of the organization, of course). There are many books on the numerous available methods for doing this. The next step is to assess your resources (including your people) and evaluate where you are now in terms of performance. Any intervention you decide upon will then come as a result of comparing (1) your desired state and your resources with (2) your present state.

I would like to give you an example where I used the LAB Profile to help a team improve its performance. I assisted the department of pharmaceutical services at a leading-edge university hospital. After they had clarified, in both general and specific terms, where they were going, I profiled the entire team and the tasks to be accomplished.

Here is a comparison chart of what I found when comparing three Contexts—the *overall* work of the pharmacists, work in the *dispensary*, and the *clinical* work they do on the wards—with the group profile.

PHARMACIST LAB PROFILE

OVERALL JOB	DISPENSARY WORK	CLINICAL WORK	PHARMACISTS n=17
Proactive & Reactive	Mainly Reactive	Proactive & Reactive	Proactive & Reactive
Mainly Away From, some Toward	Away From	Away From	Mainly Away From
Mainly Internal	Internal	Internal & External	evenly distributed between Internal & External
Procedures to Options (2 to 1)	Mostly Procedures	Options & Procedures	Mainly Options
Sameness w/ except & some Difference	Sameness with Exception	Sameness w/ Exception	Mainly Sameness w/ Except, some with double pattern
Mainly Specific & some General	Mainly Specific	Mainly Specific	Mainly General
Other	Other	Other	Other
Proximity	Proximity	Proximity	Mainly Proximity
Thing with some Person	Thing	Person & Thing	evenly distributed Person, Thing & both
Choice	Choice or Thinking	Choice	Mainly Choice
My/My	My/My	Mainly My/My & some My/Your	My/My

While it is obvious that there are strengths where the group profile matches the job to be done, and possible weaknesses where the patterns do not match, there are also other performance factors to consider. This particular group holds frequent departmental meetings to discuss how to work with patients, how to introduce and manage new technological developments and how to move the department towards its goals in improvement of quality.

Given that the group has a mainly Away From pattern, with about half highly Internal and mainly Options, I was able to predict what their meetings were like. A problem would be raised, and solutions suggested;then long-winded disagreements would ensue on what was wrong with the analysis and suggested solutions. Many members of the team were frustrated by the length, frequency, and lack of productiveness of these meetings.

We discussed ways to create more effective meetings by taking advantage of the strengths in the team. For example, they would need to discuss and agree on Criteria and standards to be met (Internal). "What do we want instead of the current situation?" They also specified what tangible evidence would demonstrate that standards had been met by asking: "How would we know we had achieved what we wanted?" Then they could explore options for how to get there. The Away From people would have free rein to examine the suggested solutions for problems and fix them. Lastly, the Procedures people on this team could ensure that the resulting tasks would be completed.

Interestingly enough for this group, given that the profile of their job had a good dose of following Procedures, most of the group fell on the Options side of that continuum. This may be an example that illustrates how one needs to take into account the culture of the organization. This hospital is a teaching and research hospital, known for its innovations in health care. Perhaps the institution itself attracts Options people to work there because of its reputation. I questioned the pharmacists about how they view their job. Do they see their day-to-day work as basically following procedures? Many of them said that each patient is different, with a problem that needs to be solved, as they search for *new options* with their multi-disciplinary team of doctors, nurses, and so on. I would like to be able to profile Pharmacists in other institutions to see if this group is actually different.

They recently hired a more Procedures manager to balance the team. She has contributed greatly by establishing more protocols and ensuring that they are followed. I continue to help them with hiring new staff.

While it is difficult to make generalizations about how to create a high-performance team, I believe that the starting points are a thorough knowledge of your team members and the jobs to be done. You will need to reflect upon the individual attributes of your team members in comparison to the mission, tasks and specific goals. (Am I My/My or what?)

Using the LAB Profile to do employee and group profiles, and comparing the profiles to the tasks that need to be done, will enable you to identify areas that need improvement and areas where your team can go from good to great. You will need to have some Options thinking about this, because no one step-by-step process will fit all cases.

Negotiating and Bargaining

While the LAB Profile itself is not a protocol for negotiating, it can be used effectively for understanding the needs and communication style of all parties. It will allow you to present your proposals in ways that your partners in negotiation can best accept.

At the risk of making a gross generalization, certain groups or sectors have identifiable cultures that can be understood in LAB Profile terms. For example, a combination found frequently in union bargaining units is the following: Reactive, Away From, Internal, Procedures, Sameness, and Consistent. People with this combination will react to management initiatives by noticing what is wrong (from their perspective) with any proposal, decide based on their own standards and Criteria, insist on following the same procedures to the letter, and protest loudly when conditions and demands change.

They tend to ask for identical treatment of workers (Sameness) and therefore will fight the introduction of systems such as merit pay (Difference). *Fairness* is a word one hears often in this Context. It is a Sameness word. *Fair* usually means the same treatment for everyone.

As a result, to negotiate effectively with a partner having the above combination, I would recommend that you give your rationale in terms of the problems for the workers that would be prevented or solved. As they probably have an Internal pattern, you could ask them to *consider* information on the disastrous alternatives. Forget about suggesting options. "The *right way*, to avoid treating anyone *unfairly*, would be to . . . "

Remember that if you are negotiating with people who have a Consistent pattern, you will need to re-establish rapport and credibility at each contact, whether in person, on the phone, or in writing. I put the Consistent pattern in perspective for a newly hired general manager. He was taking his company through a turnaround, starting in a situation with historically bad labour-management relations. "In order to convince your workforce that you want to make the company and the workers thrive," I told him, "you will have to prove your good faith many times. You will only need to screw up *once*, in their eyes, to destroy all the goodwill you have been creating" (Consistent).

For union negotiators, I would suggest that your proposals be put in Toward and Internal terms, listing the concrete benefits for them to consider. Management tends to understand and agree more readily to forward-moving, goal-oriented proposals. Management cultures also may have an Options pattern and not want to be tied down to following a given procedure, such as a collective agreement.

Preparation Is the Key

To get ready for a negotiation, spend some time analyzing your counterparts in LAB Profile terms. In cases where you have yet to meet, and cannot pre-establish contact by phone, look at any written communication you have received from them for phrases that resemble the Influencing Language patterns.

Alternatively, you could plan to ask some of the LAB questions in your first meeting, such as "Why is that important?" or "How will you know when this negotiation is successful?"

When I am negotiating, I usually assume that the person I am negotiating with has an Internal pattern in that Context, unless there is proof to the contrary. This assumption allows me to avoid being perceived as disrespectful, and creates a climate where both our views will be honoured.

Sometimes you will find that a person has an Internal preference in the Context of the negotiation but an External pattern to her or his perceived constituency. In this case you will need to use both sets of Influencing Language, while being careful to place each in the correct Context. "Only you can judge if your constituents will approve this," or "Having studied this to the depth you have, when you decide on the right answer, your people will show their appreciation for all the work you've done," or "What do *you* think about the impact this will have?"

The key to using the LAB Profile in negotiating situations is to take the necessary preparation time to figure out your counterparts' (and your clients', if you are representing them) main patterns. Your diagnosis will guide you in how to present or discuss issues with them.

*H*itting the Target: Analyzing Your Market

Rodger Bailey, the developer of the LAB Profile, and I did some consulting for a major software company. They wanted to have a profile of their print advertisements (both media and flyers) to find out who they were reaching, and to test consistency within the advertisements. Specifically, we looked at two elements: the overall visual aspect (that which would first attract a person to look at the ad), and what was contained in the content (mainly text) of the ad.

We examined the ads and found that nine of the fourteen categories were represented. Here is a summary of our findings.

- **Level** (Proactive—Reactive): The ads matched the normal pattern for the general population at work.
- **Direction** (Toward— Away From): The ads were skewed in the Toward direction.
- **Source** (Internal—External): The ads focused mainly on attracting an Internal audience, although this pattern was not as clear as some of the others.
- **Reason** (Options—Procedures): The ads represented both Options and Procedures.
- **Decision Factors** (Sameness, Sameness with Exception, Both, Difference): While the ads generally showed a normal distribution (mainly Sameness with Exception),[1] the visual aspects of the ads were much more Difference than the body text. This means that people with a high Difference pattern would be attracted to the ad and then *not* find what they were looking for in the content.
- **Scope** (General—Specific): While a normal distribution is skewed towards General, the ads contained much more Specific data. Our client and ourselves felt that this overrepresentation of Specific matched the corporate buyer of software fairly closely.

---

1. Based on Rodger Bailey's findings

- **Style** (Independent—Proximity—Co-operative): The ads reflected heavy clusters around Proximity and Independent. We suggested that it would be useful to determine if our client's marketplace is actually shaped that way.
- **Organization** (Person—Thing): The ads contained a strong Thing orientation, which was probably appropriate for the Context.
- **Convincer Channel** (See, Hear, Read, Do): For the flyers, the visual aspects used mainly Do, while the text was mainly See and Read. Once again, what attracted the reader was not to be found in the content.

As a result of this analysis and an analysis of the desired audience, our client was able to determine whether their ads and flyers were reaching their target for the two products we profiled. By using data collected from their 800 information telephone line, they could test whether people with certain patterns were or were not responding to the ads.

We also demonstrated a startling fact for our client. I put the ads into two piles stating that one group had been written by one person and that the other group was written by someone else. This was verified by the account executive of their advertising company. We had clearly demonstrated that the writing was more influenced by the writer's profile than by the ability to reach a certain audience.

We would have liked to do more work with them to help specify the ideal Influencing Language for each of the products, based on re-interpreting market research already done into LAB profile terms. Unfortunately for us, our client, needing high Options and Difference at work, had left the marketing-director position and had moved on within the company. He now works for a competitor, in a different city. Plus ça change. . . .

Market Research

Surveying your marketplace can be done simply and inexpensively using the LAB Profile. You can do it by phoning your sample group. You will need to adapt your questions for the appropriate Context: toothpaste, using rail service, buying a car, and so on. You may well find, after profiling, that only a few of the categories are relevant for your product or service. You can then design your advertising or sales processes around the Influencing Language for the people most likely to buy.

Alternatively, if your product meets the needs of groups you are not presently reaching, you can switch some of your language and images.

You can also use the LAB Profile to re-interpret research that you have already completed. For one of the products in the software example, the *innovators* and *early adopters* segments of the market match the Difference pattern in the LAB. *Mid and late adopters* together, have generally the same distribution and behaviours as Sameness with Exception people.

The advantage of translating your research into LAB terms is to determine exactly what *Influencing Language* will be the most effective in your marketing campaign and sales literature.

Sales, Sales, and More Sales

You can produce extraordinary sales results by using the LAB Profile. You will first need to adapt the LAB questions for your particular product or service. I suggest that you go through the list of questions and add in your particular Context, as follows:

"What do you want in a house?" or "What is important to you when you purchase software?" (Criteria)

"Why is reliability (their Criterion) important for you right now?" (Toward—Away From)

"How would you know if you did a good job at buying a car?" (Internal—External)

"Why did you choose your last life-insurance broker?" (Options—Procedures)

"What is the relationship between the place you live in now and your last one?" (Sameness—Difference, etc.)

"How do you know that a stereo is worth buying?" (Convincer Channel)

"How many times would you have to (see, hear, do, read) that to be convinced it's for you?" (Convincer Mode)

As you adapt the questions you will notice that certain of the patterns are more relevant to your product or service than others. In my experience, I find that paying attention to the Motivation Traits and the Convincer Channel and Mode are sufficient in most sales situations. Also, your product or service may naturally attract people with particular patterns in that Context. For example, rust paint is usually sold to avoid or fix rust problems.

When you are in the process of finding out what your prospective customer needs, you can weave the adapted questions into your normal conversational procedure. You will then know how to present your product or service, by matching their Criteria and using the appropriate Influencing Language.

By following this simple process you can shorten your sales cycle dramatically and increase customer satisfaction at the same time.

Who Can Sell and Who Can't?

Those of you attracted to multilevel marketing (MLM) businesses and other sales careers *solely* because of "unlimited income possibilities" (Options) need to realize that your chances for success are, in fact, limited. Those of you who would do almost anything rather than pick up the phone and speak to someone you don't know (Reactive), need either to overcome this obstacle or consider going into retail sales. Most of the time customers do not come to you delivered on a silver platter. This is your career, and it is in your own best interest to find one with tasks that suit you.

Most sales activities consist of *following a procedure*. For you to succeed in sales over the long term, you will need to be able to follow a procedure over and over again. This means having a mainly Procedures pattern in the Context of your work. For outside sales and generating new business you will also need to be in a very Proactive mode, to go out and prospect for new business.

Sales is a wonderful career for those of us who like to go out and take people through the process of finding what they really need and want. When you systematically use the tools in *Words That Change Minds* to help you satisfy your customer's desires, you will find that the results astonish you.

$\mathcal{P}$olitical Campaigns

Political campaigns provide the most dynamic example of the LAB Profile in action. The 1993 Canadian federal election is a case in point: The winning Liberal party used language that precisely matched the mood and aspirations of the voting public.

The polls indicated that voters were very cynical about politicians, their campaign promises, and likely behaviour once elected. In LAB Profile terms we can interpret this as an Away From and Internal combination. The theme of the governing Conservatives was "We are *different,*" relying on the pre-election popularity of their *new* leader, Kim Campbell. Wrong pattern. With the prevailing mood of cynicism, no one believed them. (Remember George Bush's famous pronouncement: "Read my lips. No new taxes.")

The Liberals produced their Red Book, with their commitments for governing after the election. Instead of telling people what to do (which would only work for people who are External), they told the public "we understand you are *fed up* with campaign rhetoric" (Away From). They presented their program from the Red Book and asked voters to *decide for themselves* (Internal). They also proposed that since they had put it all in writing, the electorate could *judge their performance* (Internal) once in power by verifying whether they had kept their commitments.

But the Liberal party went further than matching voter cynicism. They redirected the electorate by creating hope, with their positive visions for the future of the country. Contrast this with Kim Campbell's flat declaration that there would be no upswing in employment until the year 2000. Which party would you rather vote for?

The Conservative party not only lost its large majority but returned only two Members of Parliament to the House of Commons. (This makes the Conservatives the only party in the history of Canada to have achieved gender parity.)

The Notwithstanding Clause

Notwithstanding the impact of the language used, I am sure that the general unpopularity of the Conservative party, and particularly that of former Prime Minister Mulroney were important factors in the outcome of the election.

In the 1995 Ontario provincial election, the Liberal Party used the same strategy as their federal colleagues, producing a red book of promises. But the mood (and hence the LAB Profile) of voters had shifted. The Conservative party won a majority with their "Common Sense Revolution" slogan. Sameness AND Difference: the good ol' days as a revolutionary concept.

If political parties want to improve their chances of successfully communicating their message to the voting public, they might consider adapting some of the LAB Profile questions for their pre-campaign polls. These questions can also be used to judge the mood of the media, important potential allies in any campaign. The power of the LAB Profile lies in its ability to *measure the mood* of the public and *indicate the language* to which people will be the *most receptive*.

$\mathcal{E}$ducation and Learning

It is not my intention to criticize public-school education in this section, but rather to provide some food for thought.

Why are educational programs designed the way they are? It is usually because the authors believe they have discovered the *best way* to learn a subject. Often they are right about large percentages of the groups they hope to reach, but what about the smaller percentage of students for whom this is not true?

My comments are about these *other* students, for whom a given model does not work, and who therefore are more likely to drop out of school. In the work I have done with educators on the topic of reducing the number of dropouts in secondary school, we discussed strategies for keeping kids interested *throughout the school cycle*.

My advice to individual teachers in primary or secondary school would be to first identify the pupils who are not turned on by class activities. Secondly, profile them to discover what will trigger and maintain their motivation. Once the individual's motivation patterns are known, you can then adapt activities to suit their needs, using the resources and methods available, and inventing some when necessary. Lastly, you will notice a marked improvement in the participation and performance of these previously hard-to-reach students.

For example, Options students may have difficulty following the prescribed procedure, and as a result may become frustrated or disruptive in the classroom. These students are more likely to stay motivated and focused if they are given more choice and the possibility to develop their own process. Procedures students may have difficulty knowing how to start an open task. They would appreciate having a procedure to follow to get started. In each case you would need to make sure to use the Influencing Language that matches the student's pattern. "Think of all the possible ways to do this!" (Options); "Here are the first steps to get started" (Procedures).

You can also design or use activities to encourage flexibility in the LAB categories—following and completing procedures as well as developing options.

For Internal students to stay motivated they will need to make their own decisions. You can get them to evaluate their own work. When making

185

suggestions to this group, you might want to use phrases such as: "You might want to consider," or "Can I make a suggestion for you to think about?" External students will need lots of feedback to know how well they are doing. To encourage the development of both Internal and External patterns, you can provide a balance in activities—self-evaluation (Internal) and adapting to feedback received (External). You will be able to see and hear who responds best to which patterns merely by observing the students' reactions to the tasks.

Much of someone's ability to use what they have learned is dependent on the *level of confidence* they have about having mastered it. When someone's Convincer patterns have been satisfied, they are more likely to use the material or do the activity more confidently.

If a child needs six or 7seven repetitions of a skill to be convinced he knows it, it is unlikely that he will get enough repetition in the course of a school day. My suggestion to teachers, when they notice a child feels unsure of what they have learned, is to ask the Convincer Channel and Mode questions. "How do you know when someone else is good at addition?" "How many times do you have to see them do it right (or hear that they got the right answer, or do the work with them, etc.) for you to be *convinced* that they are good at addition?" Then you can assign homework based on the number of repetitions or period of time needed. If the student has a Consistent Convincer Mode, (never completely convinced), you will find that she *knows* she can do it one day and perhaps is unsure the next. Remind her of the previous times when she knew she could do it. She is still the *same* person.

Adult Learners

Learning is a Context in and of itself. The act of *learning* something is about taking in new material and acquiring it for oneself, while *using* what one has learned requires a different set of behaviours.

As you can probably deduce, this process is a sequence of Contexts: Learn something new in External; evaluate it in Internal; use it and determine the results in Internal and External.

For someone to learn something *new*, she will need to be in an External mode. If someone is attempting to take in something new while remaining in Internal mode, the new material will find itself banging up against previously held standards and Criteria within the person. As a result, the ability to actually acquire the new material is limited. In many adult education courses, the learners are asked to put aside for awhile what they already know about a topic, to facilitate taking in a new way of thinking about it. They are invited to reinstate their critical thinking caps once they have mastered the material. However, I personally hate being told to leave my knowledge and experience at the door when I take a course, especially since it took me so long to acquire it.

You might wish to consider a more elegant way to help your students shift into an External mode for the *learning* part of the activities. Simply establish your credibility, so that your students become External *to you*. This credibility is particularly important for adult learners, as any corporate trainer will tell you.

In educational Contexts the LAB Profile is useful in two ways. First, it can be used to diagnose and plan for students who are not doing well with the programs in vogue. Second, it can help teachers understand what patterns they are *unconsciously* encouraging or discouraging as a matter of course.

Default Profiles

Defaults are the standardized settings on your computer. They are what your computer *assumes*, unless you give it instructions to the contrary. It occurred to me recently that you can also use the LAB Profile patterns to make assumptions about people and situations that you may not have been able to research in advance. What patterns can you assume to be operating *unless* you get proof to the contrary?

For example, when I begin a presentation to a group of people whom I do not yet know, I find it useful to assume that the members of the group will probably have the following patterns:

- **Internal** to me: They are each wondering: "Who the hell is this woman and what makes her think she has something of value to offer to me?"
- **Away From** with regard to what I am presenting: They will notice faux pas, any inappropriate remarks, or examples that are not relevant to them.
- **Consistent:** They will like me when I say or do something they agree with and dislike me should I step out of line, with regard to their expectations.

Although these kinds of assumptions may seem negative at first glance, in fact they help me prepare. If I assume that a group has an Internal pattern (at least at the beginning) then I do two things right at the start of my presentation: I take steps to establish my credibility and I use Internal Influencing Language. "I will be presenting some information for you to consider in your work. I invite you to compare it to your own experience and decide what you think."

For the Away From pattern I suggest: "You know your working environment better than I do. We will have the opportunity to adapt these ideas to your milieu. I'm sure you'll notice which parts are appropriate and which *aren't*." To deal with the Consistent pattern, I constantly monitor the individuals in the group to notice signs of disagreement, confusion, and concern. I will invite someone with a concerned face to tell me what they are thinking, so that I can respond to it.

Once you know the behaviours associated with each pattern, you can predict the Default Profile for many situations. You can identify which patterns are *safe* to assume unless you get evidence to the contrary. I use the word "safe" intentionally: If you had unconsciously assumed the opposite pattern would a disaster result?

For example, you might assume (outside of your awareness) that a group to whom you were to present had an External pattern to you, just because they hired you. When you began your presentation, you might forget to establish credibility, presupposing that they believed everything you say. Under these circumstances, it is quite likely that you will be attacked on a substantive issue by a member of the group.

I often tell the students in my presentation skills workshops: "Only God can demand blind faith. Everyone else has to prove their case." Proving your case means both establishing your credibility and providing information to support your points. This will address the Internal and Away From patterns in your audience.

In sales situations, you can develop Default Profiles for your prospects and customers. Let's say you are a computer consultant. It may be safe to assume that many customers have an External pattern to you. They come to you for expertise and might run away if you asked them what they thought the best solution was.

The marketing group for a large pharmaceutical company presents their new marketing strategies quarterly to the sales representatives. We did Default Profiles for both the sales reps and the end customers: physicians. The marketing group felt that the sales reps had the following Profile when they were in the field, working their territories:

Mainly Proactive; Toward (focused on the sale); External (to physicians); Procedures and Sameness with Exception.

They also thought that the sales reps had a different profile when dealing with Head Office and the Marketing Group:

Mainly Proactive; Away From (picking holes in marketing strategies); Internal (we know the field better than those guys at Head Office); Procedures and Sameness with Exception (don't keep totally changing what we are supposed to do).

As a result of this analysis, the marketing group listed Influencing Language to use and to avoid in their presentations. They also redesigned their strategies to take into account the two different Profiles of the sales reps (for two different Contexts) and the customers' (physicians') Profile.

If you are a therapist or counsellor, you can assume that your clients have an Away From motivation when they come to you for help. You might consider using Away From Influencing Language in your promotional materials and when working with them. "You've decided that you are fed up enough with this problem to want to get rid of it, once and for all."

Default Profiles are an example of a Generalization. They are useful if you make sure to pay attention and adapt to the exceptions.

What Else?

Words That Change Minds is the fruit of my experience using and playing with the LAB Profile in many different Contexts. It can help you just do things, as well as help you to stop and think about them. You will achieve many of your goals, while at the same time preventing and solving communication problems.

As you use these tools, you will notice what a difference it makes for the others you live and work with. The possibilities are endless for communicating in just the right way. You can make a big difference, improve what is already good, and maintain relationships that are important to you.

Whether you use the material in this book in great detail or just focus on the big picture, you will understand what is said to you and notice behaviours in new ways. This material can raise many passions and provide for rational thought. When you are working alone, with others around, or together in group harmony, you can feel great about what you accomplish.

If I were you, I would take these tools for myself and use them to guide me and help me understand how others are different. You will see, hear, and feel the improvements that working with the LAB Profile will instantly provide, over and over again, consistently, for as long as you want.

While I have discussed quite a few applications and ideas, I am sure that there are *many other ways* to use this tool. So I put the question to you:

"Now that you know how to understand, predict, and influence people's behaviour by finding out what will trigger and maintain their motivation, what else would you like to do with it?"

I look forward to hearing from you.

Shelle Rose Charvet
success strategies
1264 Lemonville Road
Burlington, Ontario
Canada L7r 3X5
phone 1 (905) 639-6468
fax 1 (905) 639-4220
Email: info@successstrategies.com
Website: www.successstrategies.com

Appendices

Summaries and Useful Bits

In this section you will find:

- LAB Profile pattern summaries and distribution figures that you can include in reports you give people
- An Influencing Language summary to help you plan what to say or write
- Research Abstracts
- Resources
- LAB Profile Worksheets to use when profiling people

I hope you have as much fun as I have using
Words That Change Minds.

ℒAB Profile Pattern Summary

Motivation Traits

How a person triggers their interest and, conversely, what will demotivate them. Each pattern is described below in its extreme form.

LEVEL: Does the person take the initiative or wait for others?

Proactive: Acts with little or no consideration. Motivated by doing.
Reactive: Motivated to wait, analyze, consider and react.

CRITERIA: These words are a person's labels for goodness, rightness, and appropriateness in a given context. They incite a positive physical and emotional reaction.

DIRECTION: Is a person's motivational energy centered on goals or problems to be dealt with or avoided?

Toward: These people are motivated to achieve or attain goals. They have trouble recognizing problems. They are good at managing priorities.
Away From: They focus on what may be and is going wrong. They are motivated to solve problems and have trouble keeping focused on goals.

SOURCE: Does the person stay motivated by judgments from external sources or by using their own internal standards?

Internal: They decide based on their own internal standards.
External: They need outside feedback to know how well they are doing.

REASON: Does the person continually look for alternatives or prefer to follow established procedures?

Options: They are compelled to develop and create

procedures and systems. They have difficulty following set procedures.
Procedures: They prefer to follow set ways. They get
stumped when they have no procedure to follow.

DECISION
FACTORS: How does a person react to change, and what
frequency of change do they need?

Sameness: They want their world to stay the same.
They will provoke change only every 15 to 25 years.
Sameness with Exception: They prefer situations to
evolve slowly over time. They want major change
every 5 to 7 years.
Difference: They want change to be constant and
drastic. Major change every 1 to 2 years.
Difference and Sameness with Exception: They like
evolution and revolution. Major change averages
every 3 years.

Working Traits

How people treat information; the type of tasks; the environment they
need to be most productive; how they go about making decisions.

SCOPE: How large a picture is the person able to work with?

Specific: Details and sequences. They cannot see the
overview.
General: Overview, big picture. Can handle details ·
for short periods.

ATTENTION
DIRECTION: Does the person pay attention to the nonverbal
behaviour of others or attend to their own internal
experience?

Self: Attends to own experience. Doesn't notice
others' behaviour or voice tone.
Other: Has automatic reflex responses to nonverbal
behaviour.

STRESS
RESPONSE: How does a person react to the normal stresses of the
work environment?

Feeling: Emotional responses to normal levels of
stress. Stays in feelings. Not suited for high-stress
work.

Choice: Can move in and out of feelings voluntarily. Good at empathy.
Thinking: Does not go into feelings at normal levels of stress. Poor at establishing rapport or showing empathy.

STYLE: What kind of human environment allows the person to work best?

Independent: Alone with sole responsibility.
Proximity: In control of own territory with others around.
Co-operative: Together with others in a team, sharing responsibility.

ORGANIZATION:

Does the person concentrate more on thoughts and feelings or on tasks, ideas, systems, or tools?

Person: Centered on feelings and thoughts. They become the *task*.
Thing: Centered on tasks, systems, ideas, tools. Getting the job done is the most important thing.

RULE STRUCTURE: Does a person have rules for themselves and others?

My/My: My rules for me. My rules for you. Able to tell others what they expect.
My/.: My rules for me. I don't care about you.
No/My: Don't know rules for me. My rules for you. Typical middle management pattern.
My/Your: My rules for me. Your rules for you. Hesitant to tell others what to do.

CONVINCER CHANNEL: What type of information does a person need to start the process of getting convinced about something?

See: See evidence.
Hear: Oral presentation or hear something.
Read: Read a report.
Do: Do something.

CONVINCER MODE: What has to happen to the information or evidence previously gathered to make a person become "convinced" of something?

Number of Examples: They need to have the data a certain number of times to be convinced.

Automatic: They take a small amount of information and get convinced immediately based on what they extrapolate. They hardly ever change their minds.
Consistent: They are never completely convinced. Every day is a new day and they need to get reconvinced.
Period of time: They need to gather information for a certain duration before their conviction is triggered.

PATTERN DISTRIBUTION

From Rodger Bailey's research, in the Context of work, the Language and Behaviour Patterns have the following distribution:

LEVEL	Equally Proactive &		
Proactive	Reactive	Reactive	
15%–20%	60%–65%	15%–20%	

DIRECTION	Equally Toward &		
Toward	Away From	Away From	
40%	20%	40%	

SOURCE	Equally Internal &		
Internal	External	External	
40%	20%	40%	

REASON	Equally Options &		
Options	Procedures	Procedures	
40%	20%	40%	

DECISION FACTORS			Sameness with
	Sameness with		Exception &
Sameness	Exception	Difference	Difference
5%	65%	20%	10%

SCOPE	Equally Specific &		
Specific	General	General	
15%	25%	60%	

ATTENTION			
Self	Other		
7%	93%		

STRESS RESPONSE			
Feeling	Choice	Thinking	
15%	70%	15%	

STYLE			
Independent	Proximity	Co-operative	
20%	60%	20%	

ORGANIZATION	Equally		
Person	Person & Thing	Thing	
15%	30%	55%	

RULE STRUCTURE			
My/My	My/.	No/My	My/Your
75%	3%	7%	15%

CONVINCER CHANNEL			
See	Hear	Read	Do
55%	30%	3%	12%

CONVINCER MODE			
Number of Examples	Automatic	Consistent	Period of Time
52%	8%	15%	25%

$\mathcal{I}$nfluencing Language Summary

Motivation Traits

LEVEL

Proactive: do it; go for it; jump in; now; get it done; don't wait

Reactive: understand; think about; wait; analyze; consider; might; could; would; the important thing is to . . .

DIRECTION

Toward: attain; obtain; have; get; include; achieve

Away From: avoid; steer clear of; not have; get rid of; exclude; away from

SOURCE

External: so-and-so thinks; the impact will be; the feedback you'll get; the approval you'll get; others will notice; give references; results

Internal: only you can decide; you know it's up to you; what do you think; you might want to consider

REASON

Options: break the rules just for them; opportunity; choice; expanding; options; alternatives; possibilities

Procedures: speak in procedures: first; then; after which; the right way; tried and true; tell them about the procedures they will get to use

DECISION FACTORS

Sameness: same as; in common; as you always do; like before; unchanged; as you know

Sameness with
Exception: more; better; less; same except; evolving; progress; gradual improvement

Difference: new; totally different; completely changed; switch; shift; unique; revolutionary; brand new; one of a kind

Sameness with
Exception and
Difference: (both sameness with exception and difference
                   vocabulary will work)

Working Traits

SCOPE

Specific: exactly; precisely; specifically (and give lots of details
                   in sequence)
General: the big picture; essentially; the important thing is; in
                   general; concepts

ATTENTION DIRECTION

Self: (keep communication focused on the content)
Other: (influenced by the depth of rapport)

STRESS RESPONSE

Feeling: happy; intense; exciting; mind boggling; wonderful
Choice: empathy; appropriate; makes good sense and feels
                   right
Thinking: clear thinking; logical; rational; cold reality; hard
                   facts; statistics

STYLE

Independent: do it alone; by yourself; you alone; without interrup-
                   tion; total responsibility and control
Proximity: you'll be in charge with others involved; you'll direct;
                   lead; your responsibility is X; theirs is Y
Co-operative: us; we; together, all of us; team; group; share respon-
                   sibility; do it together; let's

ORGANIZATION

Person: (use personal pronouns and people's names);
                   feelings; thoughts; feel good; people
Thing: (impersonal pronouns) things; systems; process; task;
                   job; goal; organization; company; accomplishments

RULE STRUCTURE

                   no particular words or phrases—you can match these
                   patterns as you talk

CONVINCER CHANNEL

See:	(must see data to get convinced)
Hear:	(must hear data to get convinced)
Read:	(must read data to get convinced)
Do:	(must do it, or work with someone to get convinced)

CONVINCER MODE

Number of Examples:	(use their number)
Automatic:	assume; benefit of the doubt
Consistent:	try it; each time you use it; daily; every time; consistent
Period of Time:	(match period of time)

ℛesearch Abstracts

LAB Profile Inter-Judge Reliability

Inter-judge reliability of the LAB Profile was verified in two separate studies using the Statistic Kappa[1] (Cohen, 1986). In the first one, conducted in 1993, the data analyzed were obtained from recorded interviews with thirty-four subjects. During the second study in 1995, eighty-four people were interviewed in the Context of career decision making.

For each of these studies, analysis showed a statistically significant reliability coefficient for eleven of the thirteen categories covered by the LAB Profile. In both 1993 and 1995 the Stress Response category did not obtain a significant result, possibly because the judges worked from audio recordings of the interviews, and therefore could not take into account the noverbal communication of the subjects. For the 1993 study, the Scope category was also not significantly reliable. In 1995, the Level category did not give a significant result.

For each of the above-mentioned categories, there are no specific questions in the LAB Profile to elicit the patterns. In such cases, inter-judge reliability depends on the level of training and experience of the judges.

In summary, in both of the studies, ten of the LAB Profile categories obtained a statistically significant reliability coefficient: Direction, Source, Reason, Decision Factors, Attention Direction, Style, Organization, Rule Structure, Convincer Channel, and Convincer Mode.

These two studies demonstrate that it is possible to obtain inter-judge reliability for the LAB Profile categories that use specific questions to elicit the patterns, and that one can train judges who will get the same results from data obtained from the LAB Profile answers.

Étienne Godin, Université de Moncton

Cohen, J. (1960). "A coefficient of agreement for nominal scales." *Educational and Psychological Measurement*, 20(1), 37-46.

Godin, É. (1997). *Inter-Judge Reliability of the LAB Profile*. manuscript, Université de Moncton, Moncton, N.B., Canada

---

1. The Statistic Kappa was introduced to measure nominal scale agreement between a fixed pair of raters (p. 378, *Psychological Bulletin*, 1971, Vol. 76, No. 5).

The LAB Profile and Career Indecision

An exploratory study was done with sixty-one students aged between 17 and 24. The purpose of the study was to determine whether the LAB Profile would show differences between students who were able to make career decisions that they were comfortable with (n=41), and students who were indecisive and uncomfortable with their indecisiveness (n=20) with regard to career decisions. The students completed the Professional Decision Profile (Jones, 1986) and went through LAB Profile interviews.

The ordinal data from the LAB Profile interviews underwent an inter-judge reliability test (Godin and Sirois, 1995). Reliability was statistically significant for nine of the eleven categories used in this study.

The frequency distributions of the two groups were different on the following eight LAB Profile categories: Level, Direction, Reason, Decision Factors, Scope, Stress Response, Rule Structure, and Convincer Mode. From an analysis using McCullagh's regression model for ordinal data, these results were significant with a 95 percent confidence interval. However, in the Level and Stress Response categories, there was insufficient inter-judge reliability to have complete confidence in these results. There were no significant differences in the following three categories: Source, Style, and Organization.

While the results do not indicate that any of the categories fit one or the other group exclusively, they do show tendencies for each group. For example, while there was a high percentage of subjects in both groups having the Away From pattern, the percentage was slightly higher for the group who were indecisive and uncomfortable with their indecisiveness. Similarly, there was a slightly greater tendency to have the Sameness pattern, as well as a slightly smaller tendency to have the Difference pattern in the indecisive and uncomfortable group than with the decisive and comfortable group. However, these patterns were found within both groups. Also, all the people who had a Toward pattern were in the group who were able to make career decisions that they were comfortable with.

These findings, among others, have prompted the researchers to suggest that further studies on the LAB Profile and career indecision also include other elements. Apart from profiling the subjects, researchers should probably also include in their data whether the subjects have found in their environment the resources that meet their needs, as identified from the LAB Profile. For example, if individuals need to follow a procedure, were they able to find a suitable one from their environment? If so, how much more likely is it that they will be in the decisive and comfortable group?

Another aspect that might also be researched would be whether one can help the indecisive and uncomfortable people become more decisive by a judicious use of the appropriate Influencing Language.

Micheline Sirois, Université de Moncton

Godin, É. and Sirois, M. (1995). *Inter-Judge Reliability in 83 LAB Profile Interviews.* Unedited document, Université de Moncton, Moncton, N.B., Canada.

Jones, L.K. (1986). *The Career Decision Profile.* North Carolina: Lawrence K. Jones (instrument).

McCullagh, P. (1980) *Regression Models for Ordinal Data.* J.R. Statist. Soc.B. 42(2), 109-142.

Sirois, M. (1997). *Comparative Study of the LAB Profile Patterns in Groups of Decided and Undecided Individuals With Regards to Career Decision-Making.* Unpublished Master's Thesis, Unversité de Moncton, Moncton, N.B., Canada.

I appreciate all the work that Micheline and Étienne contributed toward legitimizing the LAB Profile and also wish to thank Dr. Lorraine Bourque, who directed this NLP research and gave them much encouragement. Thanks also to Dr. Réal Allard, who co-directed Micheline's thesis and provided many insightful questions and comments.

We spent many hours discussing the theoretical aspects relating to career decision and the LAB Profile, as well as the implications of the findings and the nature of the tools used to measure decisiveness and indecisiveness. We developed hypotheses on possible combination patterns that might make a person less or more decisive in the Context studied. After much debate and statistical analyses, we all felt that, while one could measure decisiveness (using Jones' test), perhaps decisiveness is actually a function of having one's needs met, whatever those needs may be.

But this remains to be proven. Anyone interested?

esources

Consulting and Training in English and French:

Shelle Rose Charvet
Success Strategies/stratégies de réussite
1264 Lemonville R oad, Burlington, Ontario, Canada L7R 3X5
Phone: 1(9 05) 639-6468 / F ax: 1(9 05) 639-422 0
Email: info@successstrategies .com
Web Site: http://www .successstrategies .com

Audio Programs:

Rose Charv et, Shelle; **Understanding and Triggering Motivation.** The LAB Profile, audio cassette series , available in English or French from Success Strategies .

Rose Charv et, Shelle; **Health and Metaprograms,** audio cassette series , available in English from Success Strategies .

NEW Internet-based LAB Profiling Tool for groups and individuals:

http://www .jobEQ.com — y ou can try out a sample test for y ourself.

The NLP Personal Profile and Guidebook, Arthur , Jay and Greg Engel. Available from:

LifeStar
2244 S. Oliv e Street, Denv er, Colorado, 80 224-25 18 USA
Phone: 1(3 03) 753-9355 / F ax: 1(3 03) 753-9675
Email: lifestar@rmii.com

A written profile with similar content to the LAB Profile which can be administered to individuals and groups .

LAB PROFILE Consultant/Trainer Certification Program:
For locations and dates , please contact:

Success Strategies/Stratégies de réussite
1264 Lemonville R oad, Burlington, Ontario, Canada L7R 3X5
Phone: 1(9 05) 639-6468 / F ax: 1(9 05) 639-422 0
Email: info@successstrategies .com
Web Site: http://www .successstrategies .com

LAB Profile Worksheet

Name: _____	Company: _____
Profiler: _____	Position: _____
Date: _____	Context: _____

Motivation Traits

(no question for Level)	**LEVEL** _____ _____	**Proactive**—*action, do it, short, crisp sentences* **Reactive**—*try, think about it, could, wait*
• What do you want in your (*work*)?	**CRITERIA**	
• Why is that (*criteria*) important? (ask up to 3 times)	**DIRECTION** _____ _____	**Toward**—*attain, gain, achieve, get, include* **Away From**—*avoid, exclude, recognize problems*
• How do you know you have done a good job (at . . .) ?	**SOURCE** _____ _____	**Internal**—*knows within self* **External**—*told by others, facts and figures*
• Why did you choose (*your* current work)?	**REASON** _____ _____	**Options**—*criteria, choice, possibilities, variety* **Procedures**—*story, how, necessity, didn't choose*
• What is the relationship between (*your work this year and last year*)?	**DECISION FACTORS** _____ _____ _____ _____	**Sameness**—*same, no change* **Sameness with Exception**— *more, better, comparisons* **Difference**—*change, new, unique* **Sameness with Exception & Difference**—*new and comparisons*

Working Traits

(no questions for Scope and Attention Direction)	**SCOPE** _____ _____	**Specific**—*details, sequences, exactly* **General**—*Overview, big picture, random order*
	ATTENTION DIRECTION _____ _____	**Self**—*short monotone responses* **Other**—*animated, expressive, automatic responses*
• Tell me about a (*work situation*) that gave you trouble.	**STRESS RESPONSE** _____ _____ _____	**Feeling**—*goes in and stays in feelings* **Choice**—*goes in and out of feelings* **Thinking**—*doesn't go in feelings*
• Tell me about a (*work situation*) that was (*criteria*). (wait for answer) • What did you like about it?	**STYLE** _____ _____ _____	**Independent**—*alone, I, sole responsibility* **Proximity**—*in control, others around* **Co-operative**—*we, team, share responsibility*
	ORGANIZATION _____ _____	**Person**—*people, feelings, reactions* **Thing**—*tools, tasks, ideas*
• What is a good way for you to increase your success at (*your work*)? • What is a good way for someone else to increase their success at (*their work*)?	**RULE STRUCTURE** _____ _____ _____ _____	**My/My**—*My rules for me/My rules for you* **My/. (period)**—*My rules for me/Who cares?* **No/My**—*No rules for me/My rules for you* **My/Your**—*My rules for me/Your rules for you*
• How do you know that someone else (*an equal of yours*) is good at their (*work*)? • How many times do you have to (*see, hear, read, do*) that to be convinced they are good?	**CONVINCER** _____ See _____ Hear _____ Read _____ Do	____ # of Examples—*give number* ____ Automatic—*benefit of the doubt* ____ Consistent—*not completely convinced* ____ Period of Time—*give time period*

© The Language and Behaviour Institute and Success Strategies ☎ TEL 1(905) 639-6468 FAX 1(905) 639-4220

LAB Profile Worksheet

Name: _____ Company: _____

Profiler: _____ Position: _____

Date: _____ Context: _____

Motivation Traits

(no question for Level)	**LEVEL**
	_____ Proactive
	_____ Reactive
• What do you want in your (*work*)?	**CRITERIA**
• Why is that (*criteria*) important? (ask up to 3 times)	**DIRECTION** _____ Toward _____ Away From
• How do you know you have done a good job (*at . . .*) ?	**SOURCE** _____ Internal _____ External
• Why did you choose (*your current work*)?	**REASON** _____ Options _____ Procedures
• What is the relationship between (*your work this year and last year*)?	**DECISION FACTORS** _____ Sameness _____ Sameness with Exception _____ Difference _____ Sameness with Exception & Difference

Working Traits

(no questions for Scope and Attention Direction)	**SCOPE** _____ Specific _____ General
	ATTENTION DIRECTION _____ Self _____ Other
• Tell me about a (*work situation*) that gave you trouble.	**STRESS RESPONSE** _____ Feeling _____ Choice _____ Thinking
• Tell me about a (*work situation*) that was (*criteria*). (wait for answer) • What did you like about it?	**STYLE** _____ Independent _____ Proximity _____ Co-operative
	ORGANIZATION _____ Person _____ Thing
• What is a good way for you to increase your success at (*your work*)? • What is a good way for someone else to increase their success at (*their work*)?	**RULE STRUCTURE** _____ My/My _____ My/. (period) _____ No/My _____ My/Your
• How do you know that someone else (*an equal of yours*) is good at their (*work*)? • How many times do you have to (*see, hear, read, do*) that to be convinced they are good?	**CONVINCER** _____ See _____ # of Examples _____ Hear _____ Automatic _____ Read _____ Consistent _____ Do _____ Period of Time

© The Language and Behaviour Institute and Success Strategies ☎ TEL 1(905) 639-6468 FAX 1(905) 639-4220

Index

'This fabulous little book manages to be both practical and humorous. An enormously useful resource for anyone diagnosed with breast cancer, or supporting someone with breast cancer.'

Dr Ian Goodwin MBChB, FRANZCP
Specialist Psychiatrist

'I liked the chapter on how to manage worry after a diagnosis of breast cancer. It is pithy, concise, and well focused. It is a very helpful chapter, for all of those involved.'

Dr Rob Shieff MBChB, FRANZCP
Psychiatrist and Cognitive Behaviour Therapist

'Brilliant! I wish this book was published when I went for my biopsy. It's such an easy read.'

Chrissie T.

'Gwendoline's humour helps to guide you through the sense of shock on receiving news of breast cancer. Her story shows how manageable the process can be, with the expertise of wonderful doctors and nurses and those who love and support you, back to life and living with breast cancer.'

Marilyn W (Diagnosed with breast cancer 2009)

'Very good information and guidance for a support person ... Your humour is the best medicine.'

Rexy W (Marilyn's Support Team Leader)

Breast Support

If you or someone you love has breast cancer,
you need this book!

GWENDOLINE SMITH
M.Soc.Sc. (hons), Dip.Clin.Psych.

First published 2011

Exisle Publishing Limited,
P.O. Box 60-490, Titirangi, Auckland 0642, New Zealand.
'Moonrising', Narone Creek Road, Wollombi, NSW 2325, Australia.
www.exislepublishing.com

Copyright © Gwendoline Smith 2011
Gwendoline Smith asserts the moral right to be identified as the author of this work.

All rights reserved. Except for short extracts for the purpose of review, no part of this book
may be reproduced, stored in a retrieval system or transmitted in any form or by any means,
whether electronic, mechanical, photocopying, recording or otherwise, without prior written
permission from the publisher.

National Library of New Zealand Cataloguing-in-Publication Data

Smith, Gwendoline.

Breast support : if you or someone you love has breast cancer,

you need this book! / Gwendoline Smith.

Includes bibliographical references and index.

ISBN 978-1-921497-91-9

1. Breast—Cancer—Patients—New Zealand—Biography.

l. Smith, Gwendoline—Health. II. Title.

362.196994490092—dc 22

For further information on this book:
www.breastsupport.com.au
www.breastsupport.co.nz

10 9 8 7 6 5 4 3 2 1

Text and cover design by Christabella Designs
Printed in Singapore by KHL Printing Co Pte Ltd

This book uses paper sourced under ISO 14001 guidelines from well-managed forests and
other controlled sources.

To my wonderful mother Bette,

to my marvellous surgeon Wayne Jones,

and to a beautiful soul Rena, who died of cancer

during the writing of this book.

PERTH & KINROSS COUNCIL	
05710077	
Bertrams	13/02/2013
362.1 HEA	£12.95
AKB	

CONTENTS

Acknowledgements

I have so many people to thank. I love all of you equally, and I thank all of you equally because you are all part of the reason I can be here today to write this book.

So, in no particular order:

My darling Murray Grindlay, who accepted and loved me without breasts and ignored my scars.

My wonderful dog Gerry, who loves me anyway.

A main muse and a wonderful photographer, Damien Nikora and his beautiful wife and family. You introduced me, in the form of art, to everything I have been through and I love you for that, Damien. I thank you for the healing that mother Bette and I went through. Special!

Lindsay, my wonderful friend and office manager, who made sure I was able to re-establish my life, and her darling husband Al, who has his own battle with cancer.

Dr Rob Shieff and Dr Ian Goodwin, who have also given me another chance at restarting my life.

My amazing GP, Dr Jeffrey Fetherston.

All the wonderful medical professionals I came in contact with.

Dr Chris Walsh and her partner Sue for their contribution to the section of the book regarding lesbian relationships, and for their wonderful battle for Herceptin funding.

All my dear friends and supporters, without whom I can't imagine what life would have been like.

My family, my inspirational mother Bette and her sisters with their own breast cancer experiences.

All the other women who, as members of the Breast Cancer Club, shared with me and inspired me with their hope and enthusiasm.

My darling Jennifer, one of the first people close to me to go through all this, who introduced me to the BCC.

My dear friend Lisa Couldrey for her illustrations, and David Shields for his photography.

My dear friend Ross Kinnaird, who illustrated my thoughts in the cartoons about psychiatric disorder and oncology.

Georgia Shattky, who patiently put together endless rewrites and tolerated my panics during the establishment of the drafts.

I would also like to acknowledge my colleagues at Exisle Publishing, who have enabled this book to become a reality.

Illustrations

The author and publishers gratefully acknowledge the assistance of the following people and organisations for the photographs and illustrations in this book:

Damien Nikora: pp. 114, 163, 168, 170, 175, 176, and special thanks for his assistance with photographic reproduction.

Lisa Couldrey: pp. 18, 102, 141

Ross Kinnaird: p. 111

Verna Langslow: p. 162

Annabel Mackenzie: pp. 134, 136

Kathryn Quirk: p. 161

Mark Roman: pp. 16, 22, 147, 153

David Shields: p. 113

Siemens Healthcare: pp. 28, 96, 155

Foreword

Unfortunately breast cancer is a common disease. Within our social circles we all know a female family member or friend who has had this disease. It is a problem that touches us all. But when it happens none of us is prepared for the complexity of information and the rollercoaster of emotions that ensue. What does often surprise us is the outpouring of love and support from those people around us. It sometimes comes from surprising places, from people who have previously been acquaintances rather than friends, but who help with their extraordinary strength. They are true supporters.

Being diagnosed with breast cancer is a life-changing event. It is no laughing matter; however, approaching this problem, like so many other difficulties in life, with a sense of humour can ease the burden. This book does just that. It is a story of one woman's journey through the lows and highs of investigations, diagnosis and decision making, peppered with practical and humorous anecdotes.

Gwendoline uses the analogy of travelling down the Breast Cancer Highway, a variant of the well-known cancer journey, in her discussion. This is very apt because the concepts of moving quickly, the fear of being out of control, the need for lane or direction changes, negotiating on-ramps and off-ramps, and staying safe are quite relevant to the situation. This is in some ways a travelogue of experiences, and in others a map and checklist of what and who to take along.

We live in an age where there is an overload of information. Advice and treatment choices are available at our fingertips. The difficulty is navigating through the internet pages and sorting the relevant and factual from the weird and fantastic. Gwendoline, with her psychology training and intensely personal perspective, has done the research, gathered the resources and presented them in a very practical way. This will be enormously helpful to other women and their support teams as they embark on their own cancer journey.

Wayne Jones BHB, MBChB, FRACS
General, Breast & Endocrine Surgeon

INTRODUCTION

A most reluctant membership

Well, I must admit I never thought I would be writing this book, just as I suspect you never thought you'd be buying one like it. But you are, and I'm so sorry that you've had bad news.

I am, of course, making the assumption that you, or someone you love, has just been diagnosed with breast cancer.

When I first got the news I recalled a comment my dear friend Jennifer (still well and truly alive, 11 years on) had made when she was first diagnosed: 'Breast cancer — it's the club you never wanted to be a member of.'

Which reminds me of the good old Groucho Marx resignation joke: 'I don't want to belong to any club that will accept me as a member.' Except with this club you don't get to decline or resign. There are no age barriers to membership, no dress codes, no class discrimination, just the diagnosis. With horror and great reluctance, I became a member (so to speak) early in 2009.

This book is a recollection of my experiences and a synopsis of my learning. It's designed to be a helpful, informative and at times entertaining guide to assist you, and your loved ones, through this previously inconceivable reality.

It's not my intention to bore you with statistics, but take a quick glance now at these. For a club with such a reluctant membership, the worldwide figures as I write are quite a phenomenon.

Here's a pictorial snapshot of global membership figures:

Breast cancer incidence and mortality worldwide 2008

Estimated number (thousands)

Territories	Cases	Deaths
World	1384	458
More developed regions	692	189
Less developed regions	691	269
WHO Africa region (AFRO)	68	37
WHO Americas region (PAHO)	320	82
WHO East Mediterranean region (EMRO)	61	31
WHO Europe region (EURO)	450	139
WHO South-East Asia region (SEARO)	203	93
WHO Western Pacific region (WPRO)	279	73
IARC membership (21 countries)	729	210
United States of America	182	40
China	169	44
India	115	53
European Union (EU-27)	332	89

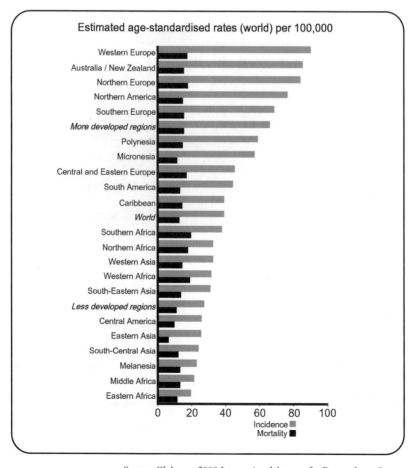

Source: Globocan 2008 International Agency for Research on Cancer

Worldwide risk statistics for breast cancer: breast cancer is the fifth most common cause of death worldwide.

1. The United States has an incidence of one in eight (13 per cent).
2. In the United Kingdom the lifetime risk is one in nine.
3. In Australia breast cancer is the most common form of invasive cancer and one in 11 women will be diagnosed before the age of 75, an increase of 18 per cent from 1995 to 2005. More recent figures (2010) now reveal the incidence in Australia to be one in seven.
4. In Canada one in nine women is expected to develop breast cancer during her lifetime. Since the mid 1990s, however, both the incidence and the mortality rate have been on the decline.
5. Where I live in New Zealand, one in nine women will develop breast cancer.
6. The highest incidence occurs in Northern and Western Europe, North America, Australia and New Zealand, and in the south of South America, notably Uruguay and Argentina.
7. Breast cancer does occur in men, though rarely. That being the case, I would like to add that while not minimising the existence of breast cancer in men, this book is written about female breast cancer (no offence intended, gentlemen).
8. It is by far the most prevalent of the cancers. In a group of people who have been diagnosed with any type of cancer in the past five years, 18 per cent would have pink ribbons.
9. The incidence has increased from one in 20 in 1960 to one in eight in 2008.

Source: *Breast Cancer Research*. 2004: 6(6): 229–39

It is important to draw attention to the fact that the higher incidence in more affluent regions is due in part to the presence of more sophisticated screening services that detect the early, invasive cancers. Some of these would otherwise have been diagnosed later, or not at all.

I think you'd agree these are sobering facts. An awful lot of mothers, wives and sisters, daughters, girlfriends, aunties, grandmothers, cousins, nieces, friends, nuns, colleagues …

A tabloid depiction could look like this:

Breast cancer is now the most common cancer in both developed countries and developing regions, with an estimated 1.38 million new cases diagnosed in 2008. As you can see, mortality rates are much lower in developed regions, which have more sophisticated and accessible treatment and earlier diagnosis.

In Western countries, 89 per cent of women diagnosed are alive five years after their diagnosis. My focus in *Breast Support* is on these women. You could choose to focus on the 11 per cent who don't make it, and it is important to acknowledge the plight of those women. But how will focusing on the 11 per cent help you now?

If you don't know *how* to adjust your focus, or manage your worry, refer to Chapter 17, 'How to get off the worry roundabout'.

I'm not a medical expert in the fields of breast surgery or oncology (the study of cancer). However, I have written *Breast Support* to provide you and your loved ones with reference material that will give you easy access to a cross-section of evidence-based information from top experts in these fields.

And just in case you were wondering, *Breast Support* is not the kind of book that trades on pleas for sympathy, cries of bitterness and victimhood as some form of personal catharsis. I've never been big on spoiling a perfectly good book with endless pages of psychological purging. I will, however, disclose honest descriptions of my pain, fear and, at times, profound loneliness. Because I know that will be helpful.

Sometimes I'll change hats (as changing bras isn't an option right now) and speak to you from my expertise as a psychologist.

But most of all I want you to be inspired and hopeful.

My purpose is to guide you towards that point by sharing with you my experiences of human kindness, hopefulness and laughter.

For where there's humour, there's hope.

The 'why' of the book

The 'why' question is one I take great pains to avoid when it comes to most aspects of my life. I've found that attempts to answer it can open the way to a labyrinth of great complexity and, even worse, to a minefield of adamant, unwavering opinions. All steadfastly supported by unshakeable beliefs.

We need to remember, however, *that beliefs are not facts.*

But in this instance, the 'why' of the book is really quite simple: *I was diagnosed with breast cancer. Fact.*

The purpose of the book

This is slightly more complicated, but still only requires a twofold response.
(i) To provide you with as much factual information and direction as I can to ease the ride.
(ii) To provide your loved ones, your very own breast support team, with as much information and direction as I can, to help them help you. And, I hope, to make the ride just a little bit easier for everyone.

The origin of our word 'disease' lies in the 14th century French word *des-aise*: *des* is from the Latin prefix *dis*, meaning 'without', 'away' or 'having a reversing force'. And *ease* of course refers to freedom from pain or tension, from anxiety or care.

So the role of the support team is to help create an environment where pressures are eased, whether they're physical, financial, psychological and/or emotional.

Essentially, their job description is to render life less difficult. That may seem like a complex task, but it's really quite simple. It's about trying to relieve and where possible reduce the burden, to lighten the pressure.

I love the concept of easing the way for people at difficult times in their life, and for me that's a good enough reason for writing this book.

The 'how' of the book

I deliberated over this question for many, many hours   for weeks in fact, and the weeks became months — until finally it became apparent that I was no longer deliberating, I was in fact procrastinating. Like any skilled procrastinator, I always had an excellent reason.

It was okay… as long as I was on the phone talking about *Breast Support*, or emailing people about *Breast Support*. Or, as an absolute last resort, cleaning my keyboard, tidying and cleaning the filing trays that would be housing anything to do with *Breast Support*.

Yes, you've got the picture! I got stuck. You might well ask, '*Why* did you get stuck on the *how*?'

To which I would reply: 'Because *how* the book is put together, and how it's used, had to be designed to assist with and contribute to the process of easing.' It was important that the book was accessible and user-friendly. And not too technical or scientific. A book that all those involved could find their way around; a book that would help them to identify where, when and how to help. And for those of us most directly concerned, the 'diagnosed', a guide to:

- What you need to do when, where and with whom, and what to expect.
- What you need to do to be prepared, and what to pack.
- Some idea of what they're wearing for breast surgery these days (vital information for any girl, as far as I'm concerned). I'd require the same information if I was going somewhere exotic or, for that matter, meeting the prospective step-children.
- *Who* can do *what*, *when*, *where* and *how*.

I hope you don't mind the use of the verb 'diagnosed' as a noun. It's just that I refuse to use words like 'victim', 'the identified patient'; even the term 'survivor' grates with me sometimes. Factually, the point of difference is that we have been diagnosed with breast cancer, hence 'the diagnosed'.

Breast Support is a handbook, a reference source, a directory. You can dip in and out of the book, depending on where you are in the process. In fact, considering the stress levels involved, it is far more useful to approach the relevant chapter just prior to requiring the information.

By all means flick through to see what's ahead, but don't expect to recall all the relevant information. Your concentration span will be distracted by the number of new people, the amount of new information and a myriad of new tasks, but remember: keep it simple, and keep it easy.

There will be guidance and instruction for your supporters as they move in parallel beside you. This book should function like a map, for both the travellers and the navigators. It's designed to ease the way as you find yourself travelling, at great speed, along the Breast Cancer Highway (see map on next page).

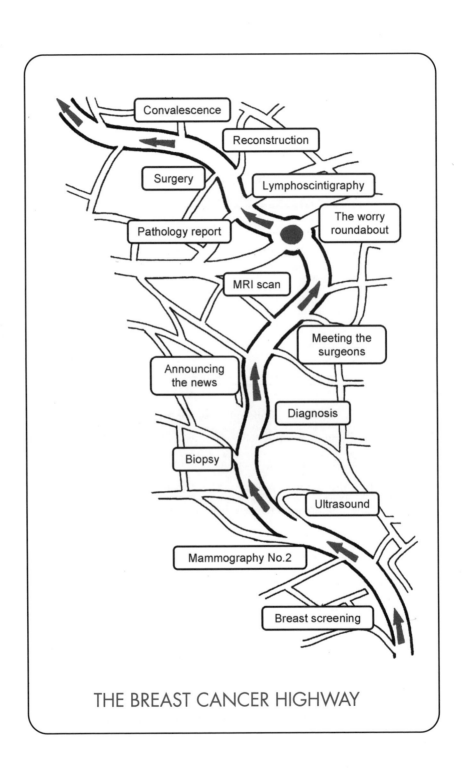

THE BREAST CANCER HIGHWAY

1

How it all happened

Well, I was just minding my own business really. I had enrolled in some unpretentious low-maintenance yoga classes. Very suitable, as well as comfortable for women of a certain age. I was particularly keen on the fact that I didn't have to stand on my head. I never wanted to stand on my head, even during infancy, when it was more easily achievable. I certainly had no intentions of starting now, despite the revered blood-flow benefits.

All the women's magazines, along with a bit of more serious research, had me convinced that stretching and breathing, breathing a bit more and getting in touch with the spiritual side of myself would be a very self-nurturing activity.

Muscle (AKA flab) toning was a big thing for me at the time, having long since acknowledged the growing phenomenon of the 'royal wave', as we girls of a certain age call it (for the benefit of you boys who don't know, or are polite enough not to mention it, it's that flesh just under the upper arm that tends to move of its own accord, with no muscle tone or resistance to gravity.)

One sunny lunchtime, having stretched and breathed for an hour, I happened as I was leaving to notice an exceptionally large van with 'Free Breast Screening' written boldly on the starboard side. Well, I thought, free for women of a certain age (50-plus, if you must know). I guess there has to be some benefit attached to increasing maturity.

In I went for that familiar process of squeezing and squishing and flattening, and then being asked if you could just tolerate another tonne of pressure per breast quarter. Gasping for air, you manage to choke out, 'No, no problem, that's fine.'

I've often, in my more cynical moments, wondered — usually during a mammogram — how much pressure would be applied during a penisogram. But I don't dwell on it, because I know you boys get dealt to during prostate examinations, so I guess we can officially call that a touché.

I'd been having mammograms annually since my late thirties after my mother (as well as the occasional maternal aunt) had been diagnosed with breast cancer. Better safe than sorry, I thought and, besides, it was never going to happen to me.

Screening

To screen or not to screen, that is the question.

And the answer is quite simply, Yes.

I've never really been one for self-examination. Having lumpy breasts made it all a bit confusing. I remember the morning I felt a lump: my life flashed before my eyes and I came out of the shower in tears. It turned out to be a pimple, aggravated by the wire insert in my new bra. Clearly the reaction of a woman with no breast tissue familiarity whatsoever. Particularly given that the pimple in question could be seen by the naked eye and was a thumbnail distance from the nearest breast.

I was more familiar with genetic predisposition than with lumpy textured breast tissue (which sounded to me like an unsuccessful attempt at making hollandaise sauce).

When you speak to breast cancer professionals, 40 seems to be the magic age at which they recommend we start regular screening. However, mammograms may be selectively used in younger women.

Early detection saves lives

Whoever came up with that line had it absolutely right. Certainly, mammogram screening isn't perfect. Along the way, you will undoubtedly speak to other women and read stories in women's magazines of lumps undetected during screening.

Nonetheless, mammograms are recognised as the gold standard for breast cancer screening and early detection, helping detect 85 to 90 per cent of all breast cancers, even before you can feel a lump.

So maybe it was a little spark of spiritual goodwill on the part of the universe that put the van outside my yoga class (cheers, Marilyn), beckoning me in with the word 'free'. Or perhaps it was my Scottish heritage making that one of the more seductive adjectives in the English language.

Whatever the reason, mammography saves lives, and it is as a result of the wonderful advances in this technology that I am alive to tell this story.

The phone call

It had been a couple or three weeks since I'd had the mammogram, and no news is good news — that's how it usually goes. Besides, I was somewhat distracted by being in the middle of a severe depressive episode (the 'dark side' of manic depression, otherwise known as bipolar disorder).

I won't go into why this had happened. It's only important as a way of introducing you to my state of mind at the time of the phone call. Anyway, there I was in bed and depressed. I very reluctantly picked up the phone next to my bed, where I'd spent the best part of a month. Hearing that I had to go in for further mammography films was neither here nor there in the scheme of things. In fact, when the caller asked me when I would like to come in, she sounded somewhat mystified when I said, 'What do you have at the end of next week?'

'You can come much sooner than that.'

'No, the end of next week will be fine.'

I was unable to conceive of getting out of bed and driving to the clinic, so the delay was considered and intentional on my part — it certainly wasn't a reflection on the service. My psychic pain at the time had deadened me to any fear, or even concern. Quite unlike the adrenalin surge when I discovered the aforementioned pimple. Besides, only other people got cancer, and so what if they needed a few more pictures?

Fortunately, by the time the appointment came around my medication was working and off I went. Got a car park right outside — all was well with my world, no need to panic.

I didn't know it, but I was about to undertake ...

2

The triple assessment

Part 1: Mammogram number two (just double-checking)

So, first things first: the checklist. You will find checklists throughout *Breast Support*. Remember to refer to these before each appointment as they will provide you with all the information you'll need for that particular day.

1. No SPECIAL precautions.
2. Remember not to apply lotions, deodorants, powders, or creams to your chest before the procedure. They can interfere with the imaging.
3. You will be asked to undress from the waist up, so wear jeans, track pants or a skirt if you're racing between meetings. Essentially, just be prepared to be naked from the waist up, so make it easy and wear a two-piece outfit. You'll be more comfortable all round.
4. If you have exceptionally sensitive skin you may experience a slight irritation or aching after the mammogram. Take some soothing gel or cream and/or an over-the-counter pain-relief medication.

Support team

1. This is not a day when it's vital that you're there, but if you can co-ordinate a time it's always nice to have company. Be prepared to take about two hours out of the day as the clinic may be busy or running behind time. If you and yours do have time to spare, there's nothing like a beverage on the way home and a bit of a debrief. Nothing may come of this second mammogram, but a little bit of anxiety is only natural when faced with even the possibility of the 'C' word.

2. If children are at home, it may be more helpful to offer to sit with them for a few hours.

Expect a bit more squeezing from the mammography machine, a slight fear of bosom implosion — although only fleetingly.

I looked up pressure ratings just in case any of you were interested, and found the whole topic far too confusing to bother with for the purposes of *Breast Support*. Sure it's uncomfortable, but it has to be done, and as for that god-awful squeezing… apparently the heftier the squeeze the better. Certainly, there's nothing else to worry about. Lots

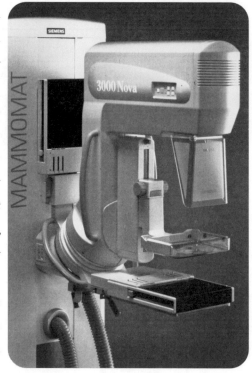

of us girls have to go back for a second photo shoot; technology isn't always reliable — perhaps the caravan had been on a lean.

Once that was done, I found there was a bit of running around, doors opening and closing, other women sitting in robes with their clothes in little plastic baskets, waiting their turn. With cups of tea and gingerbread on offer, the day could have been worse. I could have still been in bed depressed. Things were really looking up, to my way of thinking.

Part 2: The ultrasound (aka sonography)

A few moments later, I was gently and politely ushered off into another little suite for an ultrasound. The health professionals are so sensitive and caring in this system — they're a resource to value and be proud of. So there I was, poised on my back, positioned for an ultrasound on my left breast. The nurse had explained that there was just a little area of concern, just making doubly sure. That's lovely of them, I thought — taking the time to just make sure, how kind. Still, nothing to fear … I don't have cancer, this is just part of a thorough routine.

We'll talk science and the practicalities a little later in this chapter. Just briefly though, I'd like to tell you a bit about what it feels like. So, from a purely subjective point of view, it goes something like this.

Once again, be prepared to be naked from the waist up. You'll lie slightly towards one side, comforted by a few pillows, to ensure the best access and exposure of the area that has created this additional concern. Then out of a tube comes enough lubricant (as cold as KY Jelly but without the excitement to follow) to cover the identified spot or spots, for the purposes of a little, hand-held transducer (wand-like object) to be rolled and massaged over the area of the breast in question. Focusing on the area that needs to be imaged, the gel helps the magic transducer glide and make good contact with your skin. Once the gel warms to a few degrees above freezing point (well, that's what it feels like), it's all over, and with no pain whatsoever.

The ultrasound imaging can be witnessed on a screen, but at a quick glance it seems like looking for a breadcrumb in a large bowl of blancmange. Not riveting viewing, and when the ultrasound operator attempts to get you involved by explaining the process, it is about as interesting as going swimming in an even larger bucket of blancmange. But watching is a matter of choice for the individual. I tend to daydream, usually about the last time I reached for a tube of KY Jelly; rather different circumstances, but that goes without saying ...

On a more serious note:

1. As part of the initial assessment and detection portfolios of many areas of medicine (e.g. obstetrics, cardiology, abdominal structures, the detection of blood clots), ultrasound is recognised as an excellent tool. Not limited to diagnosis, ultrasound can also be used in screening for disease and to aid in the treatment of diseases or conditions.

2. Ultrasound carries no known risks. It is also safe for pregnant women.

3. Preparation for ultrasound for breast screening purposes is minimal. You'll most likely still be dressed in your 'Be prepared to be naked from the waist up' outfit. You will be given a gown that's open at the front and with not a sequin in sight.

4. The room will be dimly lit for no other reason than to enable the operator to see the images of your breast more clearly.

5. The ultrasound is generally performed by a specialist technician, as it was in my case. All those working in a breast clinic are not only specialists in their craft, but also have a specialist interest in breast cancer.

6. Ultimately a radiologist will examine and interpret your images.

7. Ducts, lobes, cysts, abscesses, fibroadenomas and breast masses can be seen on ultrasound. In other words, a lot of stuff important for your assessment and subsequent diagnosis — as well as abnormalities that would never be discovered via self-examination.

8. The ultrasound can also clarify whether or not the abnormalities detected by the mammogram are cancerous or benign.

9. If you get sent for an ultrasound by your doctor, this does not mean that he or she suspects you have breast cancer; it just means that a clearer picture of your breast is needed.

Support team

You could offer to go along to the ultrasound appointment, or to look after the children for a couple of hours, if that is applicable.

Anyway, it didn't end there and, to err even further to the side of caution, it was decided that a biopsy was called for.

Part 3: The biopsy

Now this started to change the landscape. Local anaesthetics were being discussed and rather large needles were being prepared. Again I chose not to look, as slipping into the 'comfort of denial' has always provided me with a certain kind of preventative pain relief.

Local anaesthetics are a wonder drug these days, working instantaneously. In they go with a syringe-type contraption, at which time you're warned of a thunking sound, which is samples of your flesh being removed to be popped into test jars for further analysis. This was a stage I was *so* not interested in seeing. But, once again, it's your choice whether you wish to observe the procedure; you're always invited to take either option. Considerable effort is put into making sure you are as comfortable as possible, and that at all times you are informed *how* the procedure will take place, what to expect with regard to discomfort or pain levels, and explanations of *what* is being done and *why*.

The main reasons *why* are:

1. To find out the true nature of a breast mass that is causing concern as a result of the mammogram.

2. So that, using a 'hollow-core needle', larger samples of the breast mass as well as nearby healthy tissue can be taken (when they use the word 'larger', they're still talking tiny, but those of you with a needle phobia just don't look.)

3. The tissue samples then go to a pathologist for examination. The pathology report goes to your doctor and your surgeon. A negative result means that no cancer was found — sometimes what shows up can be things like calcifications or just harmless little lumps. A positive result means that there is a malignancy, and further tests will be needed to secure the diagnosis.

How the biopsy is done depends on the size and/or location of the breast mass being sampled. I'm pretty sure I had an ultrasound-guided needle biopsy, as there were no lumps to be felt and, as the lump was deep, the ultrasound provided a way of 'seeing' where to take the sample.

The alternatives are a freehand biopsy, a stereotactic needle biopsy, or a vacuum-assisted biopsy. The health professionals will explain the type they are using, and make you as comfortable as possible, so try not to worry. Having a biopsy isn't pleasant, but it's necessary and it doesn't take long.

What to expect: You will be awake, with your breast numbed. The lump will be located by touch or imaging. Three to six samples will be taken. You will feel some pressure, but don't hesitate to mention significant pain. A few bruises will be the only aftermath. You can return to work, or go home straight away.

Then it was over: a final bit of gentle pressure to stop the bleeding and a few dressings, waterproof of course — which was fine in my books, meaning that even in the shower I still wouldn't have to face looking at any possible indicators of breast cancer.

The women were great. They offered another cup of tea (which I declined), a few panadeine (which I accepted with polite haste, being exceptionally pain-sensitive). On the way out, another appointment was made to discuss the biopsy findings, but again nothing to worry about: lots of girls have err-on-the-side-of-caution biopsies.

Off I drove, and again thought nothing of it. Didn't mention it to anyone, because what would be the point in creating worry in those around me for a check-up — no more frightening than going to the dentist.

The weather had changed slightly so I was no longer in plunging necklines, which would have exposed the rather patchy, unfashionable dressings. In reality, though, the royal wave had put an end to the plunging necklines with pencil straps quite some time before.

I must admit to the week dragging a little and my sleep becoming somewhat disturbed prior to the next appointment. But not to worry. My depression was lifting, and I was able to spend time with friends and engage in conversation, and my first experience of laughter returned during this time. I was so relieved to be in so much less emotional pain that the biopsy and its potential outcome tended to fade into the background.

It's more than likely that you may experience restlessness or sleep disturbance. The medical term for this is *anticipatory anxiety*. This form of

If you find you're not sleeping much at all, or waking up worrying in the early hours of the morning and not getting back to sleep, you should consult your doctor.

anxiety is created by worry. The brain starts to predict all the possible negative outcomes. Unsurprisingly, with the C word on the immediate horizon, these predictions are likely to be alarming.

There are very helpful, non-addictive medications that will assist with the worrying and guarantee you a good night's sleep. Some of you may prefer to try herbal sleep supplements; if these work for you, that's good news — if not, get a script from your doctor.

If you are prone to worry then you will also be worrying during waking hours. For management techniques refer to Chapter 17, 'How to get off the worry roundabout'.

3

Cancer diagnosed

The day of the biopsy results

It was a busy day at the screening clinic. Lots of women were there with their support people. These came in the form of friends, daughters, husbands, translators. They filled the waiting room in combinations of pairs, some obvious and some not so apparent. The men all seemed to be clutching the daily newspaper like a security blanket.

I, of course, was unaccompanied by a support person. Why would I need one? A bruised breast was really no more uncomfortable than period cramps, and I'd certainly never needed a support person to go to the pharmacy. So why would I need one just for a bit of a chat about a few tiny flesh samples?

There was plenty to read: informative brochures about breast screening, breast cancer and the accompanying contact numbers for breast cancer support groups. Clearly, nothing of relevance for me — this visit was going to be the last stop in an inconvenient run of medical appointments.

It wasn't too long before I was called. The lovely nurse, who the week before been so busy dishing out gingerbread between going in and out of numerous doors, escorted me into the room to meet the consulting surgeon. He stood to greet me, and there for the first time was a clue. Introductions were made, hands were shaken, gently but assertively. There were smiles, but no real laughter.

There was a feeling of sadness in the room, but not of pity. Then the lovely nurse sat close to me on my left, with the surgeon facing me across the desk. As I felt her presence become nurturing, I could hear my heart start to thump. As I looked down at the desk, the consultant delicately slid an outlined picture of breasts, viewed from various angles, across the desk in my direction. Then he began to draw on the template as he described the detected type and patterns of my cancer.

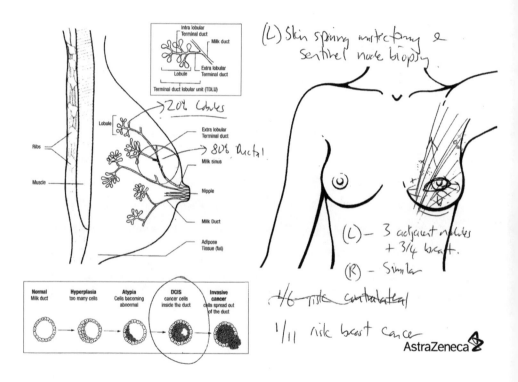

So that was what I looked like. Yours will be unique to you, and a lot of concentration and effort will go into explaining, slowly and carefully, what the findings of the biopsy are, what the recommended treatment procedures are, and what options will be open to you.

I would at this junction also like to point out that it would appear from this drawing that *breasts do come in pairs*. Stating the obvious? Apparently not. This particular piece of general knowledge seems to have escaped certain of our insurance companies. Anyway, we'll get to that.

Then it comes: 'The news isn't good, Gwendoline.'

And that's about all I heard, really. Oh, apart from a few other words that seemed to resonate at a deafening pitch in my mind: *cancer, breast, mastectomy.* They shattered my denial like a shard of glass falling from a great height. It continued to fall until it impaled my soul. Then I began to weep. The tears ran down my cheeks in what seemed like a never-ending flow of water from my inner being.

I leapt from everyday reality into the surreal. I stared across the room as the lovely nurse slipped the tissue box closer to my right hand, something I had done many times as a therapist. Tissues, the acknowledgment of our need to cry, to wipe away the tears and make room on our faces for more.

With the tears still streaming down my face, I tried to concentrate on the outline drawings of breasts with all the little circles of milk ducts. Then came the final instalment, the part where the devilish little cancer cells start taking over and wanting more room, primarily in the rest of your system. Out they go, breaking free from the duct walls, heading off looking for lymph nodes and anywhere else they can call home.

The professionalism of the surgeon and the nurse, still there on my left comforting me, was impeccable. Such compassion, and the precious theme of human kindness, was something I continued to experience throughout. The only thing missing at this time was my ability to hear, interpret, integrate or remember any of what was being explained to me. The words *cancer* and *mastectomy* continued exploding in my head, echoing and thundering like a violent storm on a tin roof.

As I pointed out a little earlier, I didn't take a support person with me after all, I wasn't about to get diagnosed with cancer. *Mistake number one.* Of course it was a lesson quickly learned, and I never made it again. You can't know the outcome of those early appointments, so take a supporter. Better to be safe than sorry, as I was on that day.

A friend of mine, also a member of the Breast Cancer Club, eloquently explains why, and I quote:

> Thank God I had taken a friend with me on the second recall day. I sat, stoically, not hearing what they were telling me, except that whatever it was it eventually overwhelmed me and I broke down in tears. My friend was there to ask the questions.
>
> *Mindfood Magazine,* May 2000

So take it from me, and the millions of women worldwide who have been diagnosed with breast cancer:

Do NOT go to any follow-up appointments on your own.

No, you're not some weak, pathetic creature. It's just that you'll turn into a weeping deaf mute, unable to comprehend this terrifying reality that has changed your life in a New York minute.

I was offered a cup of tea and time to calm down before leaving, but I had an overwhelming desire to leave. Not that I had anywhere in particular to go, but I needed to escape from that environment. That strange, alien place, full of kindness but containing nothing familiar, only constant surreal reminders of what I had just been told.

So I graciously declined the offered cup of tea and having grabbed a new handful of tissues, pamphlets, reading materials and contact numbers, I put on my sunglasses to hide my tears, refreshed my lipstick and walked back out into the world. A world that was changed forever.

My first thoughts were, how am I going to live, how am I going to support myself, how will I work? I screamed inside: *No! Not now!* How could this be? Where was the fairness? Where was the justice?

If there's a God, why is there cancer?

Before we continue with the actual events, and the likely path of events for you, I want to digress for a time to discuss concepts to do with God, faith and universal justice. And to address questions like, what happens to your faith when cancer is diagnosed?

I couldn't help but notice that once the C word is on the horizon, there seem to be a lot of references to the spiritual, religious and cultural aspects of life — and often from the most unlikely friends and family members. They want to know why — if there's a loving God — does cancer exist, and why do nice people get cancer.

These questions and observations may also play a part in your own grieving, and in your struggle to come to terms with this devastating news.

I have to be honest and admit to thinking, Oh God no, please no! I can't take this, I can't take any more pain. I have no shame in declaring my leanings towards pantheism, but I feel certain this particular plea would be described as good old-fashioned 'foxhole religion'.

Despite my somewhat dry and even cynical sense of humour at times, I do pride myself on my acceptance of other views on life and the universal human right to religious belief and faith in the existence of a higher being.

While saying that, I'm adamant that adult human beings need to evaluate and rank the importance of their beliefs in relation to their potential to cause harm, both to themselves and others.

I, for instance, am confident in describing myself as a 'nice person', and still I was diagnosed with breast cancer. If you or someone you love and cherish has just discovered they have breast cancer, you may feel angry with God or your higher power. You may question your faith and look to the heavens in dismay, but take a moment to absorb these words from one of the greatest thinkers of our time:

> I cannot conceive of a God who rewards and punishes the objects of his creation, whose purposes are modeled after our own ... A God, in short, who is but a reflection of human frailty.
>
> Albert Einstein (pantheist)
> Obituary, *New York Times*, 19 April 1955

Even to entertain the belief that you have been 'chosen', or that you are being punished, is mistaken, and this type of belief won't help you recover. The belief that somehow you are in the firing line for universal retribution is irrational and of absolutely no value to your health.

Although that's not to say that it doesn't feel like that at times. Register this:

Just because you believe or feel something doesn't make it fact.

While we are on the subject, let me just provide you with a brief introduction to a newish field of study in both science and medicine: psychoneuroimmunology (PNI). A very big word, but essentially what it refers to is the theory of mind/body connectivity. This is something that I, both as a scientist and a lay person, have a great deal of time for.

To give you some idea of the depth and breadth of the research: PNI has evolved from the interaction of psychology, neurobiology, immunology, theology, yoga, shamanism and the space programme. Finally achieving scientific respectability, various body–mind techniques perfected for optimal performance in astronauts and athletes are at last entering the health arena and making a significant contribution.

If you wish to read more about this fascinating field of science, http://www.caitresearchgroup.com/collaborators/Barrett-spirit-science-PNI.pdf will inform you about a lot of credible and respected research. However, at a time like this you may prefer to take my word for it.

Essentially, whether it's through prayer, meditation, yoga, athletics or scrabble, the reduction of worry and anxiety can only ever be a good thing. So, rather than feeling angry that the universe doesn't 'give a shit' — just accept that it doesn't. In the words of Christopher Hitchins, author and journalist (diagnosed with cancer in 2010): 'To the dumb question, Why me? the cosmos barely bothers to return the reply: Why not?' (*Vanity Fair*, September 2010).

Looking back, my favourite quote was:

> The great lesson is that the sacred is the ordinary, that it is to be found in one's daily life, in one's neighbours, friends and family, in one's backyard.
>
> Abraham Maslow (Founder of Humanistic Psychology)

And that is exactly where I placed my faith: in my wonderful surgeon, the myriad of health professionals who held my hand (and, at times, my breasts), and my friends and family. I made it through as a result of their dedication, their confidence and optimism, their compassion and acts of human kindness.

Faith co-exists with cancer, as we do. As a result of our technology we are increasingly able to live with cancer; we don't have to die from it.

4

How to make the announcement

When, how and who to tell

An announcement is defined as: 'To make known publicly; proclaim; to declare the arrival of; the act of announcing' (*Collins English Dictionary*). All of which suggests something quite glorious really, like a birth or an unexpected visit from a friend.

Unfortunately, this announcement will impact just as powerfully on all of those around you who love you and care for you, but will hardly result in the same euphoric enthusiasm. They too, will experience that sense of initial disbelief. Then they'll feel frightened, for you but also for themselves. After hearing my news, some of my girlfriends rushed to the phone to make appointments for mammograms, realising that in our busy lives there's always a tendency to put health last (well, at least until the end-of-season sales are over).

Close encounters with potentially terminal illness induce in all of us a sense of our own mortality. That is, unless you're like a woman I knew years ago whose most memorable malapropism went like this: 'Terminal illness? Like when you get sick at the airport?'

What can you say? Only that ignorance, sometimes, is bliss.

But back to where I was: that's right, I'd just had the news. Adjusting my sunglasses in the hope of hiding the tear streaks, I headed towards my car. My first brush with the real world came when I was startled out of the thoughts thundering through my mind by my cellphone ringing. It was a girlfriend, Sue, checking the validity of the rumour that I'd been called back to the breast clinic for a biopsy.

Oh, that's right — I forgot to mention that late one summer evening a pleasant breeze had caught the collar of my shirt, exposing a rather obvious little tapestry of bloodstained dressings. This irregularity was spotted by Brett (another dear friend of mine), and living as we do in a village, he'd clearly instigated a chain of communication among my nearest and dearest.

Unable to contain myself, I pulled over to the side of the road; I can remember the exact spot. I cried out in pain: 'Susie, I have breast cancer!' There it was. I'd said it out loud. It was real.

Having made that first announcement via my phone, I quickly excused myself and kept on driving. I had to find someone. I needed to be held; I needed to touch another human being, to feel something, anything, that would somehow ground me. I needed someone to hold me while I gasped for air, while I attempted to bring some sense of comforting familiarity to this nightmare.

From the moment I connected with Dene (another loving friend), the gates opened. Not only the floodgates of my tears, but also the gates to the network that was going to take care of me in the months to come: my supporters. Phone calls were made and phone calls started to come through. Statements of empathic disbelief as well as condolences abounded, along with offers of help and the beginnings of networking with other members of the Breast Cancer Club — women who were still very much alive and keen to share their knowledge, typically delivered with great humour.

One at a time, girlfriends and boyfriends arrived to provide me with company and solace. I recall being on my deck with Sylvia and Toni as they sat patiently while I rang my mother, and my nearest and dearest. Having had breast cancer herself, my wonderful mother Bette immediately reminded me that she was living proof, at a very sprightly 80, that it's a survivable illness, and even more so if caught early.

Advice on making the announcement:

1. There will be those that you do want to tell the news to yourself: your family and your closest friends. But you will find that telling the story, from the mammogram recall to where we are now, draining and emotionally exhausting. There will be overlaps where groups of friends connect, so allow the announcement of the news to evolve.

2. Hand over the telling of the news to your support team. Have it conveyed that you do want people to know, but you're still too shell-shocked to make contact, and that you'll talk to them soon. On the other hand, if you and your family are private people, you can still monitor to whom the news is conveyed. This way the people you love get to know, but without putting too much pressure on you. This a time where the removal of avoidable strain will become a priority.

When breast cancer is diagnosed it affects all of those around you and, most of all, your darling companion.

Men worry too ... and often don't know what to do

I was officially between husbands when I was diagnosed, so this wasn't a consideration for me at the time. (You will be pleased to know that like any good product, I wasn't left on the shelf for long, breasts or no breasts, and am now very happily living in sin with my new boyfriend.)

However, breast cancer being — as I mentioned earlier — primarily a female disease, men can feel somewhat powerless. Men like to fix things, and this diagnosis isn't something they can fix, no matter how many power tools they have.

This is an announcement that threatens the life of their mate (and still, hopefully, their sexy best friend) and the mother of their children. Research shows us that men don't tend to have the ease of emotional expression that women have, particularly when it comes to vulnerability. This is an experience that destabilises men, who are often more comfortable with the expression of anger, an emotion that serves to shift anxiety (via the production of such biochemicals as noradrenaline) and maintain their illusion of control.

But getting angry doesn't help. Besides, who or what do you get angry with?

I have always wanted *Breast Support* to be like the *Lonely Planet Guide* to getting through from diagnosis to what lies beyond, while still managing life and staying sane. Like a road map of the Breast Cancer Highway, showing you where to stop and why, what to wear and what to pack for the trip. A resource that you can dip in and out of as you approach the next day, the next series of appointments. So I have endeavoured to keep the text easy to read and accessible. At a time like this, with all your attention focused on how to treat the disease, there isn't a lot of time or energy for in-depth reading. So, husbands/partners/fathers/sons/brothers, you all have an important part to play.

I am not a believer in reinventing the wheel, so when I come across a resource that's well-researched and provides more specialised and in-depth material, I prefer to point you in that direction; then, of course, you get to choose if you follow through.

On that note, I would like to introduce you to a wonderful book I came across, entitled *Breast Cancer Husband*, by Marc Silver (Rodale, 2004).

This book includes topics such as talking with your children about the diagnosis, the nuances of the diagnosis, intimacy issues. Topics that men need to better understand to be helpful and supportive partners in the battle against breast cancer.

Dr Mikael Sekeres, oncologist

With all credit due to Marc Silver, I would like to provide a synopsis of some of his most helpful tips:

- At a loss for what to do as a supporter? Ask your wife/partner for a to-do list.
- At www.menagainstbreastcancer.org you'll find volumes of tips aimed at husbands/partners.
- To relieve support fatigue, take time out for yourself, go for a run or a walk, or even just watch a bit of sport on TV.
- If your loved one craves company but isn't up to long visits, volunteer to police the number of visits and the time of each visit.
- If she begins to tell you how upset and worried she is, don't say, 'Cheer up, it's not that bad,' or, 'Can we talk about this later?' Try, 'Is there anything I can do to make you feel better, or do you just want to talk?'
- Empathise, don't criticise.
- If you're looking for uninterrupted time to talk, go for a drive or a leisurely walk.
- No matter how stressed you may be feeling, try not to say things you will later regret, such as, 'I've had this feeling for a while that I'm not sure if I'm still in love with you.'
- Involve her parents and yours. They can and will want to be a significant part of the support effort. Grandparents are often especially fabulous at taking care of the children. Being with their grandparents can also normalise things for children.
- Involve the extended family. It doesn't matter who does what, it's just important that someone is doing what's required.
- Try to be at as many doctor's appointments as you can. You will provide a necessary set of ears, and a memory. Construct a list of questions the night before an appointment. Call ahead and find out what she requires for her appointments, i.e. mammogram films, medical records.

- Learn about the treatment options so you can be an informed set of ears when she goes through her decision-making process.
- Be careful, but do try to introduce a bit of humour. Like, 'Mmmm, I get to help choose a new set of breasts, even though I'll miss the boobs I fell in love with.'
- Even try talking to any other men you know that have been through a breast cancer diagnosis. I know that's a somewhat alien concept, but try it — you'll find it works. That's why women talk and network so much; it's not all gossip and talking about the men in our lives.
- In particular, keep talking to each other. She will tell you what's helpful.

5

Lesbian love and breast cancer

Not all partnerships or marriages are between men and women. Lesbian love is unique within the context of breast cancer, in that both members of the relationship have breasts.

I felt incredibly inspired when I began preparing this chapter. I began to further develop my understanding of the politics of breast cancer and funding. I was already familiar with the workings of 'pharmaeconomics' (the economics of pharmaceutical funding), but only through my work as a founder of a destigmatisation programme for mental health in New Zealand.

As so often happens in life, when I used my network to connect with lesbian women who would be prepared to be interviewed, I was doubly blessed. I interviewed two fantastic women who were not only a significant force in the political battle for the funding of Herceptin (the drug for HER2 positive breast cancer) in little old New Zealand, but who were also both diagnosed with breast cancer in the course of that fight. You will meet them later in this chapter.

In my hunt for the best possible information I could provide you with about breast cancer, I came across Dr Susan Love, an adjunct professor of surgery at UCLA and the medical director of the Susan Love MD Breast Cancer Foundation. She was appointed to the National Cancer Advisory Board by President Clinton.

Often referred to as one of the 'founding mothers' of the movement to eradicate breast cancer, her book *Dr. Susan Love's Breast Book* was described by the *New York Times* as 'the bible of breast cancer'. A point of difference that comes through strongly in her research is not only her determination to continue to develop treatment, but also her belief that the goal is the eradication of breast cancer.

I could go on, as there is so much fantastic research coming out of her efforts, including her dedication to researching smaller communities, such as lesbian and transgender, as well as the small group of men who get breast cancer (about 2000 in the US). Love says, 'By looking at sub-groups, we might be able to discover hints about the causes of breast cancer that get washed out when looking at the broader population. The transgender community also provides a group that have been exposed to many different types of hormones.'

Whatever site you go to affiliated with Dr Love, her work, dedication and passion emerge as phenomenal. As an out lesbian, she has pioneered a lot of research into breast cancer and lesbian women. She has also undertaken research into any possible significant differences in causality, social impact and subjective experiences of the health system for lesbian women.

Dr Love's advice is to be out to your doctors; if a doctor has a problem with your sexuality, you want to know and get yourself another doctor. It's bad for your health to be worrying about what people think of you when you're dealing with something as serious as cancer.

A handful of studies have specifically addressed lesbian cancer risks and experiences, but the findings have been inconsistent and research group sizes have been too small. What I found disturbing during my research into any idiosyncratic differences between heterosexual and lesbian women with breast cancer was that, even when cost is not an issue, previous or feared negative responses from healthcare providers frequently keep too many lesbians from seeking routine screenings.

The following visual exercise introduced me to another point of difference for lesbian women.

If you are heterosexual, imagine, for a moment, that you enter a waiting room where all the forms are designed for lesbians and all the magazines are lesbian-related. Then imagine that the doctor assumes your partner is female and you have to correct them and point out that he's male. More than likely, you'd feel uncomfortable and unwelcome.

Liz Margolies (Ex. Dir. National LGBT Cancer Network
www.cancer-network.org)

I loathe prejudice. I can't bear the fact that my girlfriends get exposed to this additional 'shit' — as if dealing with breast cancer isn't more than enough. In my ideal world, we are all just earthlings, living with difference, inhabiting … www.planetgoogle.com

I love decent human beings, and some of the nicest women in my life are lesbians. And there's another group of women that I love who are not lesbians. Then there's that other group of women I belong to and love, the Breast Cancer Club. Then there's a whole lot more women I love who don't have breast cancer. I rest my case. We are all women and, unlike certain human beings, cancer does not discriminate.

Now, as promised, I would like to introduce you to two of the women who were among the Herceptin Fund Fighting Heroines, and 'fighting heroines' does not overstate their dedication to the cause of having the treatment drug Herceptin funded for 12 months in New Zealand for HER2-positive early breast cancer. For more information, email: BCAC@breastcancer.org.nz

Dr Chris Walsh and her darling Sue agreed, much to my delight, to be interviewed for *Breast Support*.

What follows is a transcript of Dr Chris Walsh's own story as she related it in the course of our interview.

I am 52 years old and was brought up in a small town in the Bay of Plenty.

My mother, perhaps it was her Catholic background, told her children never to tell a lie. My father was big in the union movement and taught us to speak out if we thought something was not right and stand up to people who we thought were doing something wrong. This has got me in a lot of trouble over the years, but with experience and more wisdom I have learnt to pick my battles. This campaign for Herceptin funding is one such battle.

Being diagnosed with HER2-positive breast cancer in March 2006 is another battle. Unfortunately I had little choice in this one. I had no idea what being HER2-positive meant even though I have a nursing background. Since my diagnosis, life has changed dramatically. I now have curly hair from chemotherapy but, more seriously, have learnt a lot about breast cancer.

I believe that the issues around funding for Herceptin have been clouded and largely driven by fiscal concerns rather than humanitarian ones, sound research and good health outcomes.

I believe that all women with breast cancer in New Zealand should have the standard of care that those in 23 other OECD countries have.

What has helped me so far to continue with this battle has been the loving support of my partner, family and friends. They continue to support me even though they worry about the stress all this causes. They also know that I will continue to speak out. I am so fortunate to have them behind me in this battle.

Chris Walsh

Sue, as the loving partner, was there every step of the way, involved with everything that occurs when such an enormous battle is taking place. A huge concern for Sue was the impact of the battle on Chris's health. Then, as if that wasn't enough to contend with, Sue was also diagnosed with breast cancer on 15 February 2008 — Chris's birthday! I did ask Sue if she had considered alternative gifts, perhaps an apron with matching oven mitts? (Just a thought.)

I asked them both if they thought the experience was a very different one for lesbian women in their relationships than it was for heterosexual women in partnerships with men.

Both said they believe that the degree of emotional support would be different. That a female partner would have more of an understanding of how it would feel. That communication would be easier, as men often tend to struggle with emotional language. However, as I was putting these questions to them, Chris and Sue pointed out that asking about difference presupposes a comparison across the differing gender configurations of relationships.

At one stage during our time together I found myself thinking, what would be the chances of this? All the women in this room have dealt with breast cancer, reconstruction and, as Chris pointed out (in post-modern terms), 'breast deconstruction'.

The three of us discussed how individual the choices are on how to go ahead, particularly with reconstruction. That as a woman your breasts are so much a part of how you feel about yourself, your image of yourself as a woman, regardless of what your sexual preference might be. That discussing your thoughts with your partner is important, but the final decision is yours alone. I couldn't agree more.

The biology of breast cancer

The biology of breast cancer should never be overlooked. We can learn about this via genomic medicine, which essentially is built on the exploration of our DNA.

The human genome can be likened to a big control panel, and the genetic information stored in our chromosomes is unique to each of us. Through this branch of science we will eventually learn much more about our individual predisposition to disease, as well as the treatment types we respond to best.

To summarise current knowledge:

- There is little evidence (in 2010) linking stress to breast cancer causality. Genetic links are more likely to predispose to cancer.
- We get cancer because we are women: this is the most significant factor.
- The literature says that alcohol consumption, being overweight, smoking and insufficient exercise make you more likely to get cancer, just as you are more likely to suffer from high blood pressure, have a heart attack, and so on.
- Chris agrees with me that the strongest evidence lies in the biology; the triggers are yet to be revealed.

My personal view

Reviewing so much literature to help me write this chapter has reinforced for me once again that the main reason we get breast cancer is because we are *all* women, whatever our sexuality.

Although studies that include minority groups — like the transgender community — may provide invaluable information, particularly with regard to the influence of hormones, my own clinical standpoint is that the answer to breast and other cancers (along with other terminal disease) lies with the human genome (DNA).

I did find it distressing to discover that what was most troubling for lesbian women in some communities and countries was the inability to be open about their sexuality. That such additional stress should be imposed on them strikes me as criminal in the 21st century. I guess that, metaphorically speaking, I'm a bit like this illness — I don't discriminate either.

We are all sisters in our biological womanhood, and whether we like it or not there is no discrimination when it comes to membership of the Breast Cancer Club.

6

How, when and what to tell the children

When I was much younger than I am now, I chose not to have children. I had observed that bringing up children must be one of the hardest job descriptions ever. It also appears to be a 24-hour-a-day vocation, with enormous responsibility. Particularly if you want to come up with a really good end product: balanced adult human beings. I decided to satisfy any lingering maternal instincts through my career.

I can't imagine what it must be like to have to tell your children that you have a potentially life-threatening illness. Hence I've spent time interviewing parents, and of course researching endlessly.

How you tell your children will depend a great deal on their age. It's something you'll want to discuss with your husband/partner. You may find it helpful to ask other women how they approached this very sensitive question. I do suggest, however, that you wait until you know more from your specialist. This is a very treatable cancer; it's important that jumping to conclusions is avoided, and that an intangible sense of fear isn't communicated to the children (of whatever age) without further evidence and prognostic information. Children have very active imaginations.

I would like to share with you the conversation I had with my girlfriend Jennifer about telling her daughter Chani when she was diagnosed. Jennifer brought her thoughts as a mother, wife and psychologist to this discussion.

I told Paul first, naturally, and he was gutted, and in so much pain. We had to get through our own feelings before we could safely work out the plan for telling Chani, who I recall was about eight at the time. So we processed our own pain, fear and distress first.

I think one of the major advantages of being trained as a psychologist was my ability to detach, to bracket the emotional impact, and also to interpret research. So I immediately embarked on a massive review of the literature, and made decisions around treatment. I also looked at the literature around disclosure to children. Based on what I read, we made a decision to explain to Chani that I had a serious illness, that I would have to have an operation and that I would try my absolute hardest to get better.

We explained that we were all feeling frightened, and that was okay. Children are finely tuned and perceptive; they're also egocentric — they can easily misinterpret the intense feelings, the glances, the whispers behind closed doors — and they may believe that they are responsible.

As a psychologist I say there is no right way of telling a child (not every child should be told — the decision must be made on an individual basis), and the amount of information should be kept simple and minimal. It's important to talk calmly about the daily routine, what arrangements will be made to care for them, who else will be helping out. In other words, do everything you can to keep the family routines going; this creates a sense of normalcy and security during a very stressful time.

I was really fortunate that I have always cultivated the notion of 'many mothers', so I knew that even if I didn't make it through to guide my child into adulthood, there were many beautiful strong women in our lives who loved her and whom she loved, who would be great 'other mothers' — this helped me to stay calm.

I adore this concept of many mothers, and I was also a part of that network. It seems to me that each friend of the family, each close relative, brings something unique to the life experience of children. Cancer is very much a part of contemporary life, and losing your mother to breast cancer is also a part of life. I remember how frightened I felt when my mother Bette was diagnosed with breast cancer. As an adult living a long way from my parents, I couldn't be there to help that much, but then another two 'mothers', her sisters Margaret and Grace, were there to take charge.

Not having children of my own, I would never claim to be an expert on how to explain such news. The more I read, the more it became apparent that there were different approaches based on the culture of the family. There are, however, a number of pointers that most of the research revealed and the parents I spoke to agreed upon.

Tips for talking to your young children (three to nine years)

Support team, as grandparents, friends and family members, this is important information for you too. Continuity of the message is also essential to enable children to adapt to the changes they can observe around them.

1. Experts agree that it's not a good idea to shield children from the fact that their mother has breast cancer, despite your desire to protect them; they're kids, you'll be thinking — they shouldn't have to be worrying.
2. Younger children don't need detailed information, but they do need honesty and reassurance.
3. Honesty builds a sense of trust, helping them to face this situation, and their ability to be resilient throughout the difficult times in their lives.
4. Plan out the conversation in advance. Involve the other older siblings, as they can provide different insights.
5. Don't avoid using the word cancer. Try to provide them with simple explanations about cells, and what the doctor may have to do to make sure the cancer is all gone.

6. Due to their childlike sense of being centre of the world, ensure they understand that they haven't done anything to cause the cancer. And ensure they understand that it's not contagious, like a cold or chickenpox.

7. Explain to them as best you can (these factors will change with further prognostic information), how you will be affected by the treatment, e.g. feeling sad, or tired, having to go to hospital. And that you may lose your hair. Clearly this is a step-by-step decision-making process.

8. Explain to them that relatives and/or trusted family friends will be there to help, as there will be certain things you are unable to do, like collecting them from school, playing outdoor games, picking them up for a hug. However, you can still have time with them, reading, looking at books, watching a video.

9. It may be tempting out of both love and fear to want to indulge them and give them extra treats. In the big scheme of things this isn't that harmful, but it may increase their anxiety around change, and induce a feeling that something bad is happening.

10. Other trusted adults who spend time with the children, e.g. teachers, school counsellors and sports coaches, need to know what is happening. Decent human beings like to be able to help at times such as this. Don't shut people out. Other adults can help by alerting you to any dramatic behavioural changes the kids may exhibit, which could indicate they're struggling.

11. Invite the children to ask questions and, depending on their ages, think about taking them to a doctor's appointment. Try to remain optimistic, but without making promises.

Further tips for fathers

You still have your own feelings to manage. These will probably fluctuate widely, and will include fear and powerlessness in the context of the male urge to fix and protect the family. Along with that, you're trying to present as happy for the children even as you're dealing with your own feelings of terror.

I've revisited Marc Silver's book *Breast Cancer Husband* (pages 75-89) in search of a few tips specifically for 'flustered fathers':

- Don't leave it to the children's mother to do everything. This is a time when mother and father must take equal responsibility.
- Be truthful; don't make promises to your children in an attempt to make them feel better. This will mean that if there is further bad news they will experience even more distress.
- Guide them towards asking you for things when Mum gets home from hospital or appointments.
- If your hours at work are long, this is the time to ask for help.
- Keep things as normal as possible. Where you can, try to keep the kids at home even when their mother is in hospital.
- Check in with them regularly to get a handle on what they are thinking and feeling.
- Ask the kids to help when and where they can.
- Try in spite of everything to make time to have fun with them.

Talking to older children, teenagers and young adults

Although a lot of similar considerations apply, there are of course differences when it comes to older age groups. Teenagers and young adults in particular have access to a lot more information via friends and the media about the serious nature of the disease.

Here are some points to keep in mind:

- Be truthful about the diagnosis, the types of treatment you are considering and why.
- Schedule discussion times; they may not always have anything to ask, but keep the lines of communication open.
- You may need to rely on them to do more things about the house looking after their younger siblings, for instance.
- The older they are, the more questions they will have about what the future holds.
- Your daughters in particular will most likely have a number of questions about genetics and what their likelihood might be of getting a similar diagnosis.
- Although you may be asking them to take on a bit more of the housekeeping side of life, also allow them to feel that going out with their friends and socialising is still important, and that it's okay to carry on with their lives.
- Daughters will often tend to be more sensitive to changes in your appearance. However, if you are able to express openly how you feel about the changes in your body, this will help them adapt. If you are going to need a wig after chemotherapy, take your daughter with you and have her help you choose.

- There are excellent resources available from the doctors' and specialists' rooms you will be attending. Encourage them to have a look through information. However, constantly surfing the net may only serve to frighten them as they scan for information.

- Information they access should emphasise the treatable nature of breast cancer. They may not want endless information, so encourage them to stick with the specific sites I refer to in this book (for example, www.breastcancer.org is a very useful site).

Breaking the news

Friends and family

Another fabulous website http://www.about.com/ was a brilliant find in the course of my search for the most helpful information. I would like to pass on some of their pointers for telling friends and family.

You don't have to tell everyone

You may even feel that you should, and that's an understandable response, but you don't. Take it from one who knows — every time you have to say those four words, 'I have breast cancer,' you take another punch to your soul. I remember as if it was yesterday: each time I picked up the phone, I would immediately begin to relive the pain associated with being told myself. Each conversation makes the diagnosis more real.

Though it's hellishly difficult, it *does* start to get a little easier as you move through your list of friends and family and then on to those abroad.

It can be a lengthy process, but eventually I found that my emotions became a little more desensitised to the news with each phone call.

The first step in acknowledging cancer

I was moving into a stage that's considered to be therapeutic — for the first time, you are admitting that you have cancer. Because at the time, if you're like I was, you are probably not feeling physically ill, and there are often no apparent symptoms.

It's great if you can inform your loved ones in a way that will reassure them and prevent them from overreacting, but if this feels like too much of a strain, don't do it. Remember, the priority now is your health; you can't take on helping everybody else to feel better.

My advice for telling friends

1. There will be those you *do* want to tell yourself — your family, and your closest friends — but you will find that telling the story, from the mammogram callback to where we are now, draining and emotionally exhausting. There will be overlaps where groups of friends connect, so allow the announcement of the news to evolve.

2. Hand over the telling of the news to your support team.

3. Have it conveyed that you do want people to know, but you're still too shell-shocked to make contact, and you'll talk to them soon. Don't forget, these people will become your extended support team.

4. On the other hand, if you and your family are private people, you can still monitor to whom the news is conveyed. This way the people you love get to know, but without putting too much pressure on you.

5. Utilise email. It proved invaluable to me; it's far less exhausting than talking all the time. I used email to provide my loved ones with updates as I travelled at ever-increasing speed along the Breast Cancer Highway. This is a time when avoiding strain will become a priority.

The workplace

Oh no! What will I tell the boss?

My boss, being me, was the first to hear the news. Personally, I thought my alter ego worked through it reasonably well.

I was living alone, rebuilding my practice after a bout of depression, struggling financially — the timing couldn't have been worse, but when is a good time to be told you have breast cancer?

My recovery time was a major consideration in my choice of reconstruction. Tram flap surgery, which we'll cover later, has a longer recovery time. That's why I eventually chose silicone implants, as the procedure is less complex and you can get back to work sooner. Also, I didn't have to consider how and what to tell my employer.

Your relationship with your boss will also dictate how you approach the topic. You may never have told your employer anything personal, and so have no idea how supportive they will be. You are the best person to assess how to announce the news.

Some tips for dealing with the boss:

- If you work for a large corporation and have no close relationships with anyone in management, it's always helpful to ask friends what their experiences have been.

- This is another conversation to be prepared for. Write down some questions regarding sick leave and time off work (as you may need extra sick time, depending on your diagnosis and recommended treatments). You'll be emotional, as once again you are faced with the reality of the diagnosis and, because your livelihood is (possibly) at stake, you will be anxious.

- Take a supporter with you. Depending on the basis of your work relationships, you may want to work with Human Resources.

- Try to wait until you have more information from your medical team. If you have a personal relationship with your boss this may not apply, and you may want to go to them almost immediately. However, some knowledge of the diagnosis and predicted recovery time will help your employer make plans: whether or not you could start doing a bit of work from home, or if taking on a temp while you're recovering is an option.

- No matter how prepared you are, your boss may ask you a question that you can't answer because it's too early in the process. It is okay not to know, and to say so.

- It's a foregone conclusion that you will be emotional. What I find useful at times like these is to take a few moments, and a few breaths (see the exercises on page 67). Not too deep, as this results in hyperventilation and will increase the physical sensations of anxiety. What you *don't* want is to be so overcome that you can't continue with the conversation.

- Ask your supporter to take notes of what you need to do and what paperwork your employer may require, so that any anxiety you may have regarding leave and ongoing company medical insurance is relieved.

- Again, it's up to you whether or not your colleagues are told; if you don't wish this to happen, ask your boss to keep your conversations confidential. However, if you are a part of a close-knit team, your employer making the announcement is one less thing you have to do, and you also open up another support network.

The conversation with your employer is a high priority, as from the time you are diagnosed there will be frequent medical appointments and, depending on the intrusiveness of the procedure, you may not be able to go back to work. This also continues with the post-operative treatment regime.

If you find that your employer is not co-operative and compassionate, it might be time when you are well again to consider what sort of work environment you are involved with, as ongoing antagonism will not assist in your medium to long-term recovery. But that's hopefully much further down the track, if it applies at all.

It was my experience that everyone I told, including the checkout staff at the supermarket (when I couldn't lift my shopping bags), to taxi drivers and security X-ray operators at the airport, were all very compassionate and willing to help. So don't be too proud to ask for help when the time comes — I don't think I've come across anyone who hasn't been closely touched by some form of cancer or another.

Breathing exercises

Try doing this exercise four or five times a day if you can. It helps relieve tension, both in terms of the physical sensations (rapid heart rate, butterflies in your stomach, shortness of breath), and because the activity itself and counting the breaths distracts from the thoughts activating the anxiety.

This does not require the same level of concentration and time input as full body relaxation, so try not to dismiss this idea as too hard.

Slow breathing technique

Hold your breath and count to ten (don't make the mistake of taking a deep breath).

When you get to ten, breathe out, say the word 'relax' on an out breath.

Breathe in and out slowly in a six-second cycle. Breathe in for three seconds and out for three seconds. This will produce a breathing rate of ten breaths per minute. Breathe in a smooth and light manner.

At the end of each minute (after ten breaths), hold your breath again for ten seconds and then continue breathing in the six-second cycle.

Continue breathing in this manner until the symptoms of tension and perhaps any over-breathing have gone.

Where was I?

Oh, that's right — I was at home announcing my news, with all my buddies coming over in shifts. The rest of diagnosis day was almost like being at my own wake, and being at least 67 per cent Irish I found it fitting in an Irish sort of a way. Friends arrived with questions and tears and bottles of wine. I explained as much as I could remember and cried until I had run out of tears.

I went to bed exhausted that first night. But when I took off my bra and looked down at my bare breasts, the realisation of what was happening came a little closer.

8

The day after the diagnosis

The dawning of a new day brings a new reality. Not quite the dawning of the Age of Aquarius, but a new reality all the same. That's if you managed to get any sleep; more than a few wines at my 'pseudo wake' certainly ensured a deep slumber in my part of the world.

On waking, you will find that within a few seconds you'll be hit with the reality: *breast cancer!*

You won't feel like it, but today is the day when the process begins. Your life is about to be dominated by medical appointments and carrying around your mammography X-rays in your handbag. You will have been advised by the screening agency what needs to be done.

First stop: your doctor

Ring today, but make the appointment for a day or so ahead, allowing time for reports to be distributed among your healthcare professionals.

The first choice would be your partner/husband. I emphasise this not only because they will be the closest to you, but it's important for husbands and male partners to be included as far as possible. Because this is almost exclusively a female diagnosis, it's a situation where men tend to feel sidelined by the predominance of a female support network (post-natal depression is also very much in this category).

Your doctor (hopefully yours is as wonderful as mine)

This is also an appointment where it's wise to have one of your supporters with you.

will take you through the findings as documented in the report, gently explaining and translating for you what the medical terminology actually means. This has the benefit of demystifying what would otherwise be alien information, and the educational process will also assist in the management of your fears and anxiety.

Here is my letter. As you can see, regular mammograms provide an excellent record of changes. Microcalcifications (tiny abnormal deposits of calcium salts) can show up and not present a problem. However, an increase in number signals the need for a biopsy, and the biopsy provides the information required for a breast cancer diagnosis.

Dr Jeffrey C Fetherston
Jervois Rd Medical Centre
78 Jervois Road
Ponsonby
Auckland City

GWENDOLINE SMITH
PO Box XXXXX
Auckland Mall Centre
AUCKLAND

4th March 2009

Dear Jeffrey

Further to our telephone conversation this is to confirm that the microcalcification seen in Gwendoline's left breast on previous mammograms have increased and core biopsy of 2 areas has shown intermediate grade DCIS. There are a significant number of calcifications in this left breast and as such Gwendoline almost certainly requires a mastectomy. There are also some very faint benign appearing microcalcifications in the opposite breast and before any surgery it would be very wise to undertake some magnification views of these and/or an MRI scan.

I have explained all of this to Gwendoline today and answered her questions in relation to further investigations and surgery. Unfortunately this diagnosis is bound to put a strain on her recently established stable mood. I would be very grateful if you could refer her on to the Auckland Breast Clinic and wish her all the very best for her upcoming surgery.

With kind regards

Yours sincerely

Mr Stephen Benson
Surgeon

SB:PS

NB: This letter was dictated by Mr Benson but not sighted by him prior to mailing.

Get yourself a file, or a file box of some sort, to keep everything together so you don't get stressed looking for the documents. I got myself something in pink, which seemed fitting for the occasion.

Supporters, this is certainly something you could do, as dealing with the documents and seeing the diagnosis over and over again is initially very painful and frightening.

The wonderful thing about being required to visit your GP first is seeing a familiar face (assuming of course you have a regular doctor; if you don't, have a think about finding one, as it makes all the difference when a cataclysm like cancer impacts on your life).

When I walked into Jeffrey's office I immediately burst into tears. He put a comforting arm around my shoulders and guided me towards the chair. We looked across at each other and sighed in unison.

Your doctor will also be your reference point for choice of surgeon. You may have girlfriends who recommend their specialists to you, and that's fine. You may also have concerns about the gender of your surgeon. You may feel that for a disease of the breasts, and the subsequent reconstruction (if that is your desire), a female surgeon would be preferable. I wasn't unduly influenced by gender preference.

In fact who better, I thought, than a man — as men spend so much of their lives looking at, fondling or being sensually stimulated by female breasts — to make sure that your breasts are at their best when they've been rebuilt? No disrespect to the skills of female surgeons intended — just a thought that made me giggle at the time.

Jeffrey's recommendation was based not only on the surgeon's expertise but also on how he thought we would 'click'. In other words, a bedside manner that would suit my somewhat quirky sense of humour and the idiosyncrasies of my personality. This is important, as you're placing your trust, your life and your breasts in the hands of this person. And you're going to be spending a lot of time with him/her in the months to come.

Your GP will be networked into the system and will also know more about the route you will need to consider for funding. Some specialists work both in the private and public health domains. This may be important, depending on what insurance cover you have, and the health systems available in your country.

Once you've talked this through, you will be given a referral note. It's your job to inform the screening service which surgeon will be requiring the X-rays.

When faced with the C word, the immediate fear is of the potentially life-threatening nature of this illness. This heightened level of anxiety will focus you on the worst possible outcome. The understandable tendency to catastrophise and magnify the fear will create further anxiety and take you to places in your mind that are neither rational nor evidence-based.

At the time it may sound like they're soft-soaping you, but when the medics tell you that ...

breast cancer is one of the more treatable forms of cancer

... this is a true statement.

So I was still on my own, but not too worried as this appointment was like visiting a friend. What I recall is that I could trust what was going on in the room. The warmth of this experience was a result of a longstanding relationship with my doctor and my respect for his skills. However, this may not be the case for you. You may not feel that sense of trust. In fact, at such a time you may not even know whom, or what type of knowledge, to trust.

The last time I saw Dr Jeff I had my breasts off and my writer's cap on — I had been in so much of a daze when I went to see him the first time with the diagnosis that I went back to ask him some questions.

Gwendoline: Where does a GP fits in the process from diagnosis onwards?

Dr Jeff: By the time I get to see my patient, she will have been for the additional mammogram, had a biopsy and ultrasound. I will have been faxed the information by the surgeon, which allows for a more detailed discussion about the findings. I will then go through with her (and her supporter) the mechanics of what needs to happen next.

I will talk about the services available and explain the relationship between the private and public health sectors.

As I will be making the appointment with the surgeon direct, I start to assess the criteria for a good match, the quality of the surgeon's ability and credentials, the comfort factor and any gender preference. I provide her with choices. This direct contact with the surgeon's office also allows for the provision of information with regards to any existing health conditions, allergies, etc. that will need to be accounted for.

G: Are there any significant differences in how you approach your patient when working with a breast cancer diagnosis?

J: I always make a point in my practice of providing for extra time to talk. It tends to be a longer consultation. I like to approach my patients with a genuine empathy, as that is the essence of a general medical practice.

I don't really change the format in response to a diagnosis of breast cancer. Also, by the time I get to see them, women already have the diagnosis and they've had the callback. What is worse is when someone has had a clearance and then they get a callback that's much more difficult as the phone call announces bad news, which you then can't talk about over the phone, and they have to go through that waiting period where they don't know what the extent of the bad news is until they can make an appointment.

thanks to the lovely Dr Jeffrey Fetherston, 2009

It's true that breast cancer is one of the more treatable forms of cancer. However, what also needs to be taken into consideration is that there are many idiosyncratic differences. So treatment choices and prognostic outcomes also differ, and that is the scary bit. The not knowing. It will of course be a great temptation at this time to sit for hours in front of the computer visiting medical sites.

Information gathering

The internet: friend or foe?

In the 21st century a stupendous volume of information from all schools of thought is made available to you in under a second. It is important to address this global phenomenon, particularly in the health arena.

Be careful in your use of the internet!

Supporters, that includes you! I wrote an article many years ago entitled: 'The Internet: Friend or Foe?' My main point was that although it's an amazing tool that has changed our lives in so many ways for the better, the internet also provides information from all sources, reputable and otherwise. When I searched for 'breast cancer' via Google, 129,000,000 sites appeared for my perusal in 0.12 seconds. You will be overwhelmed enough already without drowning in this excess of information, and you won't necessarily have the knowledge base to filter it reliably.

Uninformed searching can also create additional anxiety, something you're trying to avoid at this time. In the fields of psychology and psychiatry there's a new term for the descriptor, hypochondria. It's now called health anxiety, and people presenting with this condition more often than not have a tendency to spend hours searching on the internet, diagnosing themselves and attaching their condition to the worst possible prognostic outcomes. Don't do this to yourself!

I have gone to great lengths to research the issue with as much discernment as I'm capable of. As I mentioned, if you Google 'breast cancer' you will be provided with myriad results. When you search for 'breast cancer alternative therapies' you will also be provided with countless sites in a fraction of a second. Controversy and debate about the treatment of cancer as well as its origins and causes continue to rage.

9

Some thoughts on causality

The evidence at the time of writing (in 2010) makes it clear that being a woman and over the age of 40 are the biggest indicators for breast cancer.

There is no need to feel shameful or guilty about having breast cancer. You have NOT brought this upon yourself.

While researching *Breast Support* I've observed a judgemental tone in the popular media — women's magazines in particular — that seems to suggest women are somehow to blame for suffering from this disease.

There is no hard evidence at this time to suggest that women get breast cancer because they haven't managed their lives adequately. That if they had avoided alcohol, caffeine, charred meats, dairy products, drinking from plastic water bottles, lattes, and curbed the carbs, things would be different. Apart from anything else, they'd probably be bored.

All that aside, I am not saying definitively that science will not discover significant links between cancer and diet and stress. As yet, however, that hasn't happened.

Stress and cancer: is there a link?

I have observed the shaky beginnings of the science linking stress and physical disease, such as cancer, during the course of my career. I was first introduced in the seventies to the stress-related illness research of such ground-breaking pioneers as Ivan Pavlov, Hans Selye and James Pennebaker. It was some time before academic medicine acknowledged that stress had a significant part to play in heart disease, gastrointestinal conditions (ulcers), asthma, allergies and skin conditions (psoriasis), to name but a few.

As early as 1926, Selye concluded that:

> It is not stress that harms us but 'distress', i.e. persistent stress that is not resolved through coping or adaptation, deemed distress, may lead to anxiety or withdrawal (depression) behavior.

Any strain on the system can still result in exhaustion. It does *not* equate to strength vs. weakness, or success vs. failure. It is as a result of such misconceptions that a judgemental appraisal of stress can occur.

Selye didn't say that stress caused certain illnesses, but that it could exacerbate the severity of disease and reduce resilience, impairing the process of recovery. This is very much the case with the current thinking on breast cancer.

The hard evidence now, as I have mentioned previously, comes to us via genomic medicine. This is not to say, however, that as we learn more, stress, anxiety, diet, environmental toxins and lifestyle won't come to the fore in our understanding of the causes of breast cancer. It is my opinion that the answer most likely lies in all of the above.

The best-kept secret of them all is that life balance is a matter of 'all things in moderation', and in an ideal world that's how we would all live. But in the meantime just keep on doing the best you can.

Nobody's perfect. And anyway, who gets to decide what's perfect?

Stress/strain is neither positive nor negative. It's just a part of living.

10

Treatments and therapies

Orthodox vs alternative and complementary medicine

In my research, both academic and anecdotal, a dividing line appears to be drawn between Western orthodox medicine on one hand, and (often Eastern) alternative medicine on the other. It is my observation that there are a number of reasons for the current turning away from mainstream orthodox medicine, across several different health sectors. My first experience was with psychiatry.

When one reflects on the so-called halcyon years of the sixties and seventies, the strength of the New Age movement to reject orthodox medicine is hardly surprising. Still reeling from the holocaust of benzodiazepine (Librium and Valium) addiction, people would try anything before they would consider using medication for mental illness.

> Doctors were seen as drug-company whores, ready to prescribe the latest medications for a set of new golf clubs or a week in Club Med. These sentiments are of course perfectly understandable. However I believe very strongly that the time has come to redress the balance.
>
> *Depression Explained*
> Gwendoline Smith (Exisle, 2005)

More recently, during my experience with oncology I also observed the same mistrust and cynicism, albeit far less prevalent.

In essence, I perceive it this way:

- Mainstream therapies such as surgery, radiotherapy and chemotherapy, and drug therapies such as Herceptin for HER2-positive metastatic breast cancer, do tend to be the more 'aggressive' forms of treatment.
- The ongoing battle for subsidised treatment, e.g. Herceptin, anti-depressants, and AIDS drugs, continues against the following backdrop:
Johnson & Johnson (2009) revenues: US$61.9 billion
Pfizer (2009) revenues: US$50 billion
GlaxoSmithKline (2009) revenues: US$44.64 billion

Source: http://en.wikipedia.org/wiki/List_of_pharmaceutical_companies

A hostile groundswell is no big surprise. Not a good look, and a difficult life paradox to swallow when people are suffering.

One could go on endlessly about the academic, philosophical and ethical debates on New Age alternative healing versus traditional medicine, homeopathy versus drug therapy, naturopathy versus chemotherapy and radiotherapy. But at the end of the day, when you're suffering you'll look anywhere and everywhere, and that's exactly what happens.

What still deeply concerns me, however, is that:

> A holistic approach, by definition, must acknowledge the contribution of orthodox medicine. The danger of certain schools of thought in the fields of alternative medicines is their nihilistic view of medical practice, a scepticism that rejects orthodox medicine, and in doing so interferes with treatment.

> *Depression Explained*

With an adult daughter, for instance, you may find yourself caught between the desire to honour her choices regarding a treatment option and your own opinions on what is best.

My advice when you are called on to counsel loved ones or friends on alternative treatments is to speak honestly: this is not a time to hold back your opinion. But at the same time try to avoid these discussions becoming heated, as raised voices and additional stress are of no value to anyone.

You will want to help in the most informed way that you can. So provide research, talk with others, and have friends visit that have recovered from breast cancer. Don't forget, however, that younger adults will ultimately make their own decisions and they may not turn out to be the ones you agree with.

So remember, supporters: expressing your opinions and your desire for certain treatment options for your loved ones does not guarantee that you will get your own way.

But at least you can feel that you have tried in the best way you could with what you had available to you. Besides, whatever treatment choice she makes, you will be fearful and at times frustrated and even angry. But you won't stop loving her, and that is important at this time.

Boosting the immune system

Dr Trevor Smith, in *Breast Care: Information and advice on all aspects of breast care* (The Breast Centre, 2008), provides a wonderful resource. His book is factual, accessible, considered and balanced.

His research and his experientially based knowledge of treatment options and considerations have led Dr Smith to the view that a strong immune system is vital in combating cancer. To ensure that our bodies react optimally to fight cancer, we need first of all to stop smoking, reduce stress, take exercise, get plenty of sleep and reduce alcohol intake.

Complementary treatments

This refers to all forms of therapy that make you feel better and can potentially help your recovery. Examples include yoga, meditation, acupuncture, massage therapy and pilates.

Non-prescription medications

You need to inform your doctors of any non-prescription medication as some preparations can interfere with surgery or chemotherapy.

Diet and cancer

A healthy balanced diet will ensure the body is best prepared both to fight the cancer and to cope with the stresses of treatment.

- High fibre is good. Reduce fatty food. Reduce sugar.
- Choose lots of ginger, garlic, green tea and turmeric.
- Likewise broccoli, cauliflower, cabbage and brussels sprouts.
- Eat berries, whole grains, linseeds and tomatoes.
- Also include nuts and seeds rich in essential fatty acids and selenium.

Selenium is a trace element necessary for good health. New Zealand, where I live and eat, has some of the lowest levels of selenium in the world as well as some of the highest cancer rates. Although there's no hard evidence, it is suggested that it would be a wise precaution to increase intake. This can be as simple as eating a couple of Brazil nuts daily. You may also want to discuss with your GP what trace elements are lacking in your particular region.

Dr Smith also recommends *Cooking with Foods that Fight Cancer* by R. Beliveau and D. Gingras. A Google search of these two scientists' names revealed volumes of their work along with great respect accorded by the cancer research community.

Alternative treatments

When you have cancer and the outlook is poor, it is understandable that you'll want to try virtually anything to improve the odds. Unfortunately, one is very vulnerable in this situation. Some of the therapies available are very costly and there may be little evidence of benefit. I suggest that patients discuss any of these options thoroughly with their specialist. Remember also to ask the alternative practitioner for evidence of efficacy, and check on side effects.

Last but by no means least, I want to suggest you read another book I came across: *Trick or Treatment? Alternative medicine on trial*, by Simon Singh and Edzard Ernst (Bantam, 2008). Let me tell you a little about who they are and their credentials to comment in this area. Clinicians and laypeople alike who are intolerant of alternative medicine are often deemed to be blinded by their belief in orthodox medicine, funded as it is, they maintain, by corrupt pharmaceutical companies. Or is it simply that the medical establishment is desperate to maintain its patriarchal power base?

Professor Edzard Ernst was formerly a clinical doctor; he is the world's first professor of complementary medicine. He has studied and practised homeopathy and many other alternative treatments. His research group has spent 15 years trying to work out which treatments work and which do not. Dr Simon Singh has a PhD in particle physics and has spent almost two decades as a science journalist. Like me, he is dedicated to explaining complicated scientific and medical ideas in a way that the general public can understand.

I cannot advise you for or against alternative therapies, but I can provide you with some research and then it's up to you. I am a believer in healthy eating, a balanced diet, exercise (after all, had I not been at yoga that day I could have procrastinated on my mammogram for another six months and might not have been here to tell the story).

My personal leaning is toward scientific evidence-based medicine. Hence, as soon as I was diagnosed, I was off to the surgeon, discussing surgery. My double mastectomy, along with early detection, means that I haven't required chemotherapy or radiotherapy. However, had either of those treatments been needed I would have accepted the recommendation.

Readers of my first book on depression, *Sharing the Load: What to do when someone you love is depressed* (Random House, 1996), were surprised when I declared that, if required, I would have ECT (electroconvulsive therapy) for my depression. I've seen it work for people with severe depression that won't respond to anything else. ECT has had a lot of bad press, and without doubt has been used inappropriately for the purposes of behaviour modification (as portrayed in *One Flew Over the Cuckoo's Nest*, and *Frances*, the 1982 movie about the actress Frances Farmer). However, I hope that in your part of the world as in mine, things are different now. But as I've mentioned earlier in this book, depression paralyses me and I would consider the use of ECT rather than staying that way.

Here's some advice from Simon Singh and Edzard Ernst:

- Before commencing any form of alternative therapy — acupuncture, herbal medicines, chiropractic therapy and so on — inform and consult your doctor in case it might conflict with any conventional therapies you may be undertaking.

- Don't discontinue your conventional therapies unless your doctor advises you accordingly.

- Alternative therapies can be expensive, so make sure there is evidence of efficacy.

- The estimated global spend (2008) on alternative medicines was £40 billion, making it the fastest-growing area of medical spending.

- All therapies can generate placebo effects (imagined benefits), but this alone is not enough to justify their use.

- Every treatment can carry risks, so make sure the benefits outweigh the risks.

Another piece of advice I'd like to add is to remember that the time you dedicate to the use of alternative medicines can give the breast cancer cells more opportunity to spread.

I would apply these considerations across all interventions. As Singh and Ernst point out, 'A general judgement about the wide variety of naturopathic treatments is not possible. Each naturopathic treatment must be critically assessed on its own merits.' (*Trick or Treatment*, page 379).

There are herbal medicines that work. For example, St John's wort is a good approach for mild to moderate depressive states, but won't treat a significant clinical depression; garlic works for high cholesterol; and echinacea seems to be effective for the prevention and treatment of the common cold.

But there are no herbal medicines that work for serious health conditions such as cancer, hepatitis or diabetes. My opinion? Whatever you choose to do, consult with your specialist or doctor so that you 'first do no harm'. If you don't trust his/her medical opinions, then you are with a clinician who is inappropriate for your needs.

Supporters, once again during all of these appointments it is essential to have a set of separate ears, whether you agree or not with the treatments being recommended. You need to be there to ask questions to do with efficacy and side effects.

11

The really important things to remember so far

Supporters, these points are to jog your memory as well:

1. Take someone with you, right from the initial callback. In fact, as soon as the normal routine of your mammogram is in any way disturbed. At this stage, it doesn't have to be your partner/husband. Any of the supporters will be fine.

2. Keep your thinking as philosophical as you can; this is not a personal attack.

3. Ask your support team to distribute the news for you. Email is wonderful for keeping loved ones in touch with what is happening. Get your support team to take over computer-based social networking.

4. Don't allow yourself to feel any kind of shame at the diagnosis. The stigma once attached to cancer (including breast cancer) is now utterly outdated.

5. Beware of too much Googling. Only go to websites recommended to you by people you love and trust. Be aware that information overload acts to increase anxiety.

6. Life can go on as normal. Certainly your emotional reality is very different, but that doesn't have to prevent you from doing things you enjoy.

7. Spend time with friends and family.

8. Accept all support. Even if you don't quite know what it will be as yet. Just say 'Yes'.

9. Start to formulate a roster of people who will be able to take you to appointments. Or ask your darling to take that on for you.

10. Your kissing partner should be involved as much as possible, particularly at medical appointments that will cover important diagnostic and treatment information.

11. In fact, start compiling a question list to take with you to the appointments with your surgeon, as you will be overwhelmed and will forget things.

12. Put a notepad by the phone or get a small whiteboard where you can write things down as you think of them.

13. Take up invitations to spend time talking to women who have been through what you and your family are about to go through.

14. Do things and be with people that are uplifting. Spending too much time with close family can be a little draining, as the room is often full of fear. It's true that laughter is the best medicine, and humour is an important part of your resilience.

Do as much giggling and belly laughing as possible (that's an order!).

Between appointments

While the various pieces of the diagnostic puzzle are being passed around, you will get a few days off before your appointment with the surgeon. What you decide to do with this time will of course depend very much on your personal circumstances — your family life and your work life.

I wanted to be with friends. I spent a lot of time on the phone talking to people I hadn't yet had a chance to get to. Friends organised little dinners and, because of the epidemic nature of this illness, at almost every gathering there was a woman who'd had breast cancer either recently or at some point in the past. Nearly everyone had stories of friends or family members affected, and the stories were for the most part positive with happy endings.

This is also an opportunity for you to start gathering information about the different experiences that women have had. There are a number of treatment options, but yours will of course depend on the type and extent of the cancer you have. And at this stage you won't know a great deal about that. Women who have been through the experience are also very open about showing scars and reconstructions; it's like being desensitised to what you are about to face.

The wonderful thing about sharing this information is the way it takes away the loneliness. You see the results of surgery first hand, and most women are keen to laugh and share stories about some of the more humourous aspects of this sojourn in the world of oncology. These storytelling sessions are fabulously supportive and such a good tonic.

You could see it as a way for women to get things off their chest, rather than (as in my case) getting your chest off.

You'll hear stories about the odd saline implant leak that happened while hiking in the Himalayas. You'll hear about how you can still go shopping while attached to your blood drainage systems; you'll hear about all the things you can and cannot do.

You won't be able to put on close-fitting tops with tight sleeves, and then the fabulous news: you won't be able to hang out the washing or do the vacuuming. Remember: never put off till tomorrow what your partner can do for you today!

Yes, the benefits are seemingly endless, so milk it while you still can.

12

The day you meet your surgeon

This is a very important day!

When it was time for my appointment, I was slowly but surely coming to grips with my new reality. I made sure I had my friend Dene with me. We discussed in the car what I would need help with and the questions I would need to ask. That way, if I forgot something my supporter would remember to ask.

I took in my little pink plastic folder (the one I felt was symbolically appropriate), my X-rays, doctors' letters, screening results, all the things that were necessary in the management of my care and the procedure.

I also had a letter, a list of questions and pointers, from another buddy who was also a member of the Breast Cancer Club. It went like this (you will also have your own suggestions):

My dearest friend,

I have been thinking of you on and off since we spoke and putting together a list of questions you should ask your surgeon:

1. What kind of breast cancer do you have?
2. Exactly where is it located and exactly how big is the cancer? The biopsy should have covered this.
3. This leads to the next question: what are the survival rates, and what kind of adjunct (added) treatments are recommended?

4. Is the urgency about fitting into someone's surgery lists, or is it because of the type and spread of the cancer? (Depending on the answer to this, a couple more weeks to get your head around the situation and put some arrangements in place could be very useful. This is not postponing the inevitable; it's merely giving your emotions a chance to catch up with what your brain can accept. It might also give you a chance to get some of the financial side of things sorted. It would also be an opportunity to get yourself in shape for surgery.)

5. What kind of mastectomy and reconstruction are they looking at? What are the possible side effects? (Get the support network operating for your post-surgery recovery. You won't feel like doing a lot for the first few weeks — you'll be very tired.)

7. You need to talk with the anaesthetist about what he/she is proposing, and what pain management. You may have added complications because of your other medications.

8. There is some research that suggests doing the surgery in the progesterone (female hormone) dominant part of the cycle leads to better longevity outcomes, so that's week three to four of your cycle. I did this — my surgeon didn't think it made any difference, but he was happy to accommodate my idiosyncrasies.

Can't think of anything else right now. Just dreadfully sad that you got to join the club that no one wants to be a member of ... It's a very strange feeling, I call it a loss of innocence, when you hear that diagnosis. You cross a line that you can't step back over. However, there's so much fear around cancer in our community and in our consciousness. I don't buy the whole cancer bogey monster thing; I think of it as a chronic illness that I have to manage.

On the bright side, your Mum is still alive and so am I. And I have much better tits than most of my age cohort … So make sure you get a good plastics guy.

Mastectomy on the left, lift and reduction on the right. Spaghetti straps and perky by next summer.

Much love Jen xxxxx

The meeting

Wayne Jones came out to greet me at reception and welcomed us into his consulting rooms. As with all my experiences with health professionals in this field thus far, his manner was warm, empathic and compassionate. The first step was to go through the story from the beginning, how it was discovered, any familial history, and so on. Being something of a raconteur, I of course laced my story with little anecdotes to help break the intensity of the moment.

I also presented my list of questions, and described the various medications I was on. As it turned out, pethidine as pain-relief medication wasn't recommended with my antidepressant (Aropax). Mr Jones took the list to scrutinise during our session, with reference to what would be relevant in my case.

I dressed in an outfit that I felt good in and that would also convey the sort of person I am, and how I like to present myself to the world. Funnily enough, this turned out to be helpful for the surgeon when we discussed the timing of the reconstruction.

Let me explain this. One of the biggest fears is of looking down and seeing yourself without breasts. I have spoken to other women who, like my friend Angela, took a week to look down after the dressings came off. It has taken me years to look at where my darling mother had her breast removed. It's a very difficult time.

I explained to Mr Jones that no matter how things moved ahead, I didn't want to have to face looking down for the first time at a scarred and empty chest. This is not the same for all women. Neither is breast reconstruction an option for all women; it depends on the healthcare situation, particularly within the public health system. We are fortunate in New Zealand in that most surgeons still tend to work part-time in both private and public sectors, so you can, as I did, still have your own surgeon in either healthcare environment.

In fact this was another reason that Dr Jeff suggested Wayne to me, as he was aware of his flexibility. And at the time I hadn't explored my private healthcare insurance policy.

Wayne went on to say that by the way I presented myself he could see which aspects of my appearance were important to me, and how I liked to be perceived by the world. He was very clear from the beginning that he would be attending to the reconstruction at the time of surgery.

More explanations of the X-ray results followed, and then another map of my breasts appeared. Until this time I had thought my cancer was non-invasive. But apparently not; it was in fact invasive. So with this news came more tears and a sense of impending doom. I shakily got undressed, and my darling supporter did little things like putting my clothes on the chair, instead of where I would have dropped them on the floor. You'll become aware how important the smallest of gestures are.

So back to the desk, and now the discussion of my treatment options.

The precise post-operative treatment options can't be defined at this moment, as they are dependent on what's found when you are being operated on. This is when the surgeon is able to see whether or not the cancer has moved into the lymph nodes, and if so, to what extent. The lymph nodes are tiny masses of tissue that act as little filters and immune monitors, removing the cancer cells that are trying to break through. With breast cancer, they are under the arm or in the chest.

The post-operative treatments include radiotherapy, chemotherapy and the use of medications such as tamoxifen and Herceptin. Other concepts to come to terms with included lumpectomies, single, partial or double mastectomies, silicone implants and tram flap reconstructive surgery (see pages 139-41).

As I mentioned earlier, one of the main considerations in my case was the recovery time. The more complex the procedure, the longer the recovery time, and for me when I could return to work was of the utmost importance. Also, when you are living on your own it's advantageous to minimise the time that you are totally incapacitated. However, these will be decisions that you make after discussions with your surgeon and your loved ones.

You will feel rushed, particularly when 'invasive' has been attached to the front end of the word cancer. However, this is not a decision that you will have to make on that day. Further diagnostic tests will need to be carried out to determine with more certainty what is available for you.

I had watched just enough episodes of *Nip/Tuck* and seen sufficient variations on the 'Boob Jobs Gone Wrong' theme in the tabloids and on 'reality' television shows (you know, all those reliable sources of information!) to have more than a few questions about saline versus silicone, and it is in this exchange that you discover the truth rather than the sensationalism that plasters the corridors of the popular media.

Anyway, back to Mr Jones' office. I had pretty much decided on the silicone by the time I left that day. But I had another decision to make, and that was whether or not I would need to have both breasts removed. Now clearly this is a decision that requires further histology (biological disease analysis), but is also a consideration for women thinking about the future: does having both breasts removed offer a better prognosis? I would like to emphasise that this is *not* a decision to be taken lightly! Not once in my life do I recall thinking, God, if you're there and can hear me, any chance of breast cancer so I can have a free boob job?

More on that subject later.

We not only discussed the prophylactic (preventative) benefits of a double mastectomy, but also ventured into the question of symmetry. I asked Mr Jones what would be the overall look with one silicone and one still remaining of an organic nature.

So we agreed to stay in touch, and then the referral for the MRI scan was made to confirm and clarify the mammography results. I was delighted with the personality match. So I left in a bit of a daze, but confident enough to send an email update out to the clan.

Hi everyone

Thought this would be a bit easier than calling you all. Results from today: there is a possibility that I have bilateral breast cancer, i.e. diseased in both. And have thought it through and will get a double mastectomy. The good news is that I am booked for surgery next Friday at Ascot hospital.

Another silver lining is that with a double mastectomy I get two perfectly shaped boobs. Don't know with regard lymph nodes but will cross that bridge when and if it happens.

Feeling okay, the only dark news being that if I have the cancer gene, it may be in my ovaries but again cross that bridge if I need to.

I explained to the surgeon that I am very pain sensitive and will need a lot of pain relief, but not pethidine because that conflicts with my head medication. Much to my horror have been informed that there are only small amounts of morphine prescribed. So no silver lining there!

Surgeon is fab, with a great appreciation of tits, so feel confident about the authenticity of my new ones, another benefit of a male surgeon — they've spent most of their lives contemplating the perfect breast.

In fact on my way out I said, 'If I had known life was going this way, I would have married a surgeon!'

To which he replied, 'If you had Gwendoline, you would have been divorced three times by now.'

Maybe another silver lining, although he was cute in an English public school kind of way.

Love to you all

Gwendoline xxxxxx

What comes next?

I was very excited about the surgery being brought forward, as of course I had to close down my life and my private practice. So I continued to prepare for the following week. This was able to occur because of my private medical insurance — or so I thought!

The next steps would involve MRI scans and ink radiation tests, which would occur in the week prior to the surgery.

The MRI scan preparation: this is a day you have to be prepared for; so do your supporters.

1. Again, be sure you take a supporter — preferably someone who likes to read a lot of magazines and is patient, as the wait can be long. If your supporter is middle-aged, make sure s/he has glasses (in case s/he's still pretending s/he doesn't need them). Or take a spare pair yourself — you're not going to need them where you're going.

2. Make sure you are dressed in a very practical manner. By this I mean making it easy to strip down to your knickers. Put the robe on and wander through to the room. There you will meet this large machine that looks like something out of a high-drama medical series.

13

The magnetic resonance imaging scan (MRI)

This involves the use of radio waves and a powerful magnetic field to produce images of the breast.

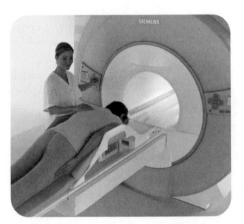

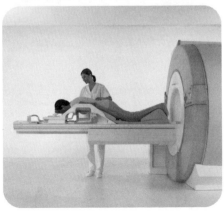

These images provide a very useful suggestion on what to wear for your MRI. The key words are practical and comfortable, and ensure you are able to take top and bottom garments off so that you can be photographed with just your knickers on. Unlike what yours truly did and paid the price of embarrassment!

MRI does not replace clinical examination, mammograms and ultrasound in routine diagnosis, but now plays an important part in providing more accurate assessments of certain situations.

Indications for MRI

These include:

1. Pre-op planning for breast conserving surgery. In some situations MRI can provide a better estimate of the size and extent of a tumour than mammography or ultrasound. This applies particularly to younger women with dense breast tissue. It can also detect other areas of cancer in both breasts.
2. Surveillance after breast cancer surgery.
3. It's not a perfect tool; although considered more sensitive for picking up breast cancer than mammography, it can also miss some cancers. That is why it is recommended only in combination with other tests.

Why breast MRI is not recommended for screening all women

Breast MRI is not recommended as a screening tool for women who are at average risk of developing breast cancer.

Yes, breast MRI has been found to be more sensitive in detecting cancers than mammograms, which does seem like an advantage. However, a major disadvantage is that breast MRI screening results in more false positives — in other words, the test finds something that initially looks suspicious but turns out not to be cancer. If breast MRI were adopted as a screening tool for everyone, many women would end up having unnecessary biopsies and other tests, not to mention the anxiety and distress.

MRI is also more expensive than mammography, and dedicated breast MRI screening equipment is not widely available. (Further information available at www.breastcancer.org.)

So why did I go for MRI screening?

My lovely surgeon Wayne Jones told me to. Wayne needed additional information to be more precise about the possible spread of the cancer. Looking at the research, MRI scans for further information are also recommended for women with a family history, as well as my diagnosis of DCIS (ductal carcinoma in situ), and the fact that I had extremely dense breasts, or unevenly dense breasts when viewed via mammograms.

But, like I said, I went because Wayne told me that was what was needed. This is why it is so important to have respect for and a good rapport with your surgeon.

The surgeon directs you through what will happen according to a specific list of procedural requirements.

This was one of those days when my desire to get on to the next bit of life — particularly if it seems guaranteed to be more fun — overtakes any remaining common sense. I had a little gathering planned that evening and, given that their days were numbered (my breasts, that is), I was keen to wear as much expensive underwear as possible.

For the MRI scan I chose undergarments totally inappropriate for the occasion, i.e. a black and red Spanish lace teddy suit. Why inappropriate? Well, as I walked in, the lady in the skirt and cashmere cardigan, who was called Dianne, asked if I'd mind just heading off into that little cubicle and undressing to my knickers.

'Of course, no problems.' I get in there and realise that there are no knickers, only a one-piece, and given that I'm here to get my bosoms jammed in a tray and head off into a tube face-down, what would this mean?

Potentially butt naked, as I think the Americans would say. I had no idea if there were one-way screens. Would anyone be looking through, would students be being trained, and would those students be the young adult children of one of my friends?

Oh no, I thought. Why can't I just take life a little bit more seriously? Why couldn't I have just been satisfied with the new jockey shorts for girls and a basic cotton sports bra? Instead of that, here I am sporting a bit of La Perla. Why? Because I still can.

I can only say in my defence that I didn't because I don't. Not only that, but I had also been hit by the stupefying realisation that I had over the years invested a great deal of hard-earned money on exceptionally beautiful underwear.

In I walked, sat down, and had things explained about the dye that would be put through and exactly how everything would work.

I turned to Dianne and said, 'This is a little embarrassing, but I don't have any knickers on. I'm planning a farewell to the girls party tonight, and I thought I'd just start the day with my party lingerie.' She smiled and promised to take care of things.

Into the room with the space capsule we went, and my dignity was maintained by a robe delicately placed over my posterior. Tucked in, boxed, tubed up, earplugs in, I was ready to go.

If you get anxious in enclosed spaces you may want to mention this to your doctor and perhaps take a mild tranquilliser beforehand.

It does take some time, and you are very closed in. The machine is also surprisingly noisy, though you are provided with ear plugs. It's still a bit like being at a party in a shed with a tin roof, with house music and 700 kids doing E. Just as you think you've established a rhythm to get in tune with, it changes.

Tips for this appointment:

1. You do not necessarily need a support person as you will be able to drive. There's no cutting or prodding or bleeding involved. However, it is nice to have company while you're waiting to enter another phase of the unknown.

2. All jokes aside, wear sensible underwear.

3. You can go back to work after this procedure, but you are not always able to specify how long you will be — you may have to wait for your turn.

4. You will need to stick to the allocated appointment time as there is such a demand for the use of MRI technology. These tests *must* be completed before surgery can occur, so arrange to have a supporter pick up children from school, etc.

5. I would suggest clearing your afternoon as it is difficult to work to your exact schedule, and this is the priority. You don't need to introduce time-related stress into the equation.

14

Light relief

So it's over, and that's it for the day.

Although you're having lots of tests you still don't feel sick, as it were. So with another weekend up my sleeve I decided to do two things, neither of which may work for you but are worth considering all the same.

I was about to face something fearful and unknown. I was about to lose a part of me that I had been gifted by Mother Nature. 'The Girls', as they'd come to be called, a very voluptuous D cup, had always provided me with something of a fifties hourglass figure. I was never a Twiggy, and even as a feminist in the seventies I could never quite manage to burn my bra and float free and unshackled under my many kaftans. But now the Girls were going, and I was damned if they were going to leave without a celebration and acknowledgement of their contribution to my life.

I received a cake with 'Get Well Soon' from my Leo birthday twin Zoe, flowers, food — and a bottle of wine, aptly labelled 'Nipple Hill', from my buddy Toni (if you look very closely you can see the mammary-shaped mountain). Almost Freudian, I thought.

Even farewell cards to the Girls. All these little gestures from distant supporters are really appreciated, and they begin to turn the tears into laughter.

Gwendoline,

Even though we didn't know them well, we will miss them. They shall be remembered.

Craig & Mel & Ali

A Farewell to the Girls' party

Hi there,

This bravado and narcissism are a tribute. In keeping with my resilient sense of humour, I thought you would appreciate this farewell testimonial to a decent pair. Love you all ... am in for surgery as you know on Friday. Insurance company atrocious and insisting on another biopsy tomorrow as not prepared to take MRI evidence as a diagnosis — my luck continues, but I will not be beaten ... well, not without giving participant permission. No offence taken I hope.

Emails continued to arrive, many with mature and touching boob innuendos. This of course may all seem very silly. But 'This is my party, and I'll do what I want to.' Why? you may ask. This is how I see it: when your friends show up and emails from those who are absent begin to arrive, everything is like food for your courage and your soul. And the value of the laughter? Priceless.

1. Hi Gwendoline,

    Gosh, so, so sorry to hear your news, can't believe it ... If there is anything we can do, please don't hesitate to ask ... I'm always around (got no job) and would be happy to help with anything, cleaning, shopping, driving ... Your before shots are great, you're such an amazing lady and we love ya and hope that all goes as well as possible on Friday!

Enjoy the morphine and looking forward to seeing you as soon as ... take care and lots of love.

Natalie and Nicky x x x x x x x x x x x x x x x x x x x x x x x x x x x x x

2. BUGGER! I never did get a feel of them!

Thinking of you all the way, and admire your bravado and narcissism ... may it continue. Love to you my lovely,

Roy xxx

3. Hi darling girl, Thanks for being so kind to your friends in the way you have broken this huge news to us! Roy and I have been slowly absorbing what it means. I hate responding by email but at least you will get this before Christmas, given the speed at which I now write & send snail mail.

So this is just expressing my love and concern, and very best wishes for the process of surgery, and of course for everything around that.

Please don't reply, I expect that you will need all your time & energy right now to deal with the anxieties of everyone around you — and I acknowledge that you have decided to continue to entertain us, in your customary wry way!

You are a strong and brave woman. I'll see you when I'm over some time in the next few months. Good luck, old pal.

Lots of love, Linda xx

4. Now you lassies, you're a bunch of wee larrikins. So make sure there's nae funny business. Aye, and ye're not to drink too much!

Grandmother Mary xxx

No one can convince me that wasn't worthwhile!

So there is my little indulgence, but you're allowed to indulge at a moment like this — and to indulge in your femininity, because breast cancer does put that under threat, as much as we may perhaps believe it shouldn't.

15

Breasts, bosoms, sexuality, sensuality and erogenous zones

They may have been designed for breastfeeding, but our breasts are also an important part of our appearance, of our sexual being. Nipples may not be the centre of everything erogenous for all women, but breasts are definitely a part of how we define our sexuality and how we have fun erotically.

It seems to me that the impact of the crisis we are faced with is closely connected to the age we are when it occurs. Close to 50, and recently single, how was I going to find a new boyfriend without my hallmark 36 D cups? I know I make light of the question, but it's real and it was distressing.

Women over the age of 45 or 50 make up the most significant age cohort for breast cancer. Although it was frightening, and having both my breasts removed was a terrible decision to be faced with, I could only imagine what it must be like to be faced with that very same decision in your twenties or thirties. What it would be like for younger women, perhaps with a new love, not having yet started a family, about to get married? What would the trauma be like at the other end of the continuum?

To address in significant detail the many differing issues for younger women would be a book in itself. However, for younger women reading *Breast Support*, I will include links to some of the websites I've discovered. You can blog and chat and read, watch videos and feel connected with your sisters faced with the same fears, the same sense of isolation, that you must be feeling right now.

First, here are some of the facts.

Young women and breast cancer

Young women CAN and DO get breast cancer. While breast cancer in young women accounts for a small percentage of all breast cancer cases, the impact of this disease is widespread: many young women and their doctors are unaware that they are at risk of breast cancer.

- There is no effective breast cancer screening tool for women 40 and under.
- Young women are often diagnosed at a later stage than their older counterparts.
- There is very little research focused on issues unique to this younger population, such as fertility, pregnancy, genetic predisposition, the impact of hormonal status on the effectiveness of treatment, psycho-social and long-term survivorship issues, and the higher mortality rates for young women.
- Young women diagnosed with breast cancer often feel isolated and have little contact with peers who can relate to what they are experiencing.
- As the incidence of breast cancer in young women is much lower than in older women, the young are under-represented in many research studies.

What is different about breast cancer in younger women?

There are a number of significant differences:

- Diagnosing breast cancer in younger women (under 40) is more difficult because their breast tissue is generally denser than that in older women. By the time a lump in a younger woman's breast can be felt, the cancer is often advanced.

- In addition, breast cancer in younger women may be aggressive and less likely to respond to treatment. Women who are diagnosed with breast cancer at a younger age are more likely to have a mutated (altered) BRCA1 or BRCA2 gene.

- Delays in diagnosing breast cancer also are a problem. Many younger women who have breast cancer ignore the warning signs — such as a breast lump or unusual discharge — because they believe they are too young to get breast cancer.

- As a result there is a tendency to assume a lump is a harmless cyst or other growth. Some healthcare providers also dismiss breast lumps in young women as cysts and adopt a 'wait and see' approach.

Fertility issues in young women with breast cancer

At a time when more young women are surviving breast cancer and delaying childbirth, it is important to take their needs and wishes about their future fertility into consideration when deciding on treatment. Although survival remains the most important priority for most women, many are also concerned about being able to make choices concerning their fertility and potential to become pregnant.

The use of chemotherapy and hormonal treatments in young women can have significant implications for their fertility. Such treatments can stop the ovaries producing eggs, sometimes temporarily but in some cases permanently, thus leading to early menopause. Options to preserve fertility include freezing eggs or embryos, and also freezing ovarian tissue for transplant at a later date, although this is a new and, to date, little-used technique.

Because of rising breast cancer survival rates and the trend to delay pregnancy until later in life, childless women increasingly experience fertility dilemmas.

For further information, contact: Mary Rice

mary@mrcommunication.org ECCO the European CanCer Organisation

The impact of breast cancer on sexuality, body image and intimate relationships

L. R. Schover of the Center for Sexual Function, Cleveland Clinic Foundation, Ohio, has this to say:

> For women, breast cancer remains a common and dreaded experience. It is normal for a diagnosis of breast cancer to evoke grief, anger and intense fear. Most women, however, face this crisis and master it without developing major psychiatric disorders or severe sexual dysfunction.

The options of breast conservation and reconstruction give women a new sense of control over their treatment, and are quite successful in helping women feel comfortable with their bodies again. However, the effectiveness of breast conservation and reconstruction in preventing or ameliorating sexual problems after breast cancer diagnosis is less clear.

Any impact these options have on sexuality is subtle and may relate more to a woman's feelings about her desirability than to how often she has sex, her lovemaking practices, or how much she enjoys sex.

Among sexually active women, greater body image problems were associated with mastectomy and possible reconstruction, hair loss from chemotherapy, concern with weight gain or loss, poorer mental health, lower self-esteem, and partner's difficulty understanding one's feelings.

The Young Survival Coalition exists to help young women with the disease and to enable them to share their experiences. I think you will get a lot out of their website: www.youngsurvival.org.

Because I'm that much older, it was different for me in some ways. My mother Bette was diagnosed even later in life; she chose not to have reconstruction because she was in her late sixties, and my darling father Alan was suffering from Parkinson's disease. Most of us are uncomfortable with the notion of our parents having sex; Bette informed me that she didn't look into breast reconstruction because they were no longer 'sexually active' (but as far as I'm concerned, they were never sexually active apart from the purpose of procreation!).

In my role as a clinician, I've worked with women whose partners have left them because they couldn't face what was happening. However, I have also come across many men who are not remotely concerned with such superficial issues and are only concerned that they don't lose their darling.

I also heard about a young woman who cancelled her wedding and dissolved her relationship because she couldn't deal with the ramifications/implications of having no breasts. However, it is my belief that true love is about the whole person; it's about loving the soul of your sexy best friend, with or without her mammary glands.

But girls, it's a hard one, and I dedicate this chapter to you and hope you make it.

'A Big Pink Kiss from Me'

On the subject of body image, I want to take some time in the following chapter to discuss the issue of breast cancer and mental health issues. Not just because I understand the issues to do with 'psycho-oncology' but also because I am a manic depressive as well as a psychologist *and* a woman who's had breast cancer.

16

Bipopsy, bipolar, biopsy: breast cancer and depression

An unusual chapter heading I know, but one that came out of the 'mouths of babes', so to speak. I'm referring to my mother Bette's almost childlike innocence on certain subjects, particularly evident after a couple of glasses of an especially lovely bottle of New Zealand sauvignon blanc.

We were at my home one evening, not too long after I had been through another flare-up of my manic-depressive illness.

Bette looked across at me as I topped up her glass and said, 'Now, about this bipopsy you've got.'

To which I replied, 'Bi-what?'

'This bipopsy condition you've just been through. Was it your childhood? Did your father and I do something wrong? What is it?'

Of course I realised this was Bette's malapropism for 'bipolar'. 'No darling, it was nothing you did. Bipolar disorder, or good old-fashioned manic depression as I prefer to call it, is genetic. No different from being born with blue or green eyes, or asthma, or a Roman nose. Oh, and by the way that term you've got confused is *bipolar*.'

Bette gave a sigh of relief and took a sip of her wine (did I mention she was a sprightly 80-year-old?). And it was on that very evening I came up with the concept for this chapter.

Quite a few years back, I was working with a young woman in her thirties (I'll call her Theresa) who had been through an experience of breast

"Don't worry love she's just a bi-polar bear."

cancer with complications I can't recall in detail. The outcome though was that she was thrown into early menopause, which is often the case.

She went through major surgery, and yet it wasn't too long before she was back in corporate uniform and leading her sales team into battle. Then the mood swings started, and eventually these developed into a full-blown manic episode, followed — in the expected course of the illness — by severe depression.

We met in my role as a psychologist. The impact of the bipolar disorder threw Theresa off her horse again and into the swamp of a major depression, once more taking her out of the workplace and her busy, fulfilled life.

I'll never forget the day she said, weeping as she spoke, 'You know Gwendoline, dealing with cancer is a walk in the park compared with this horror story.'

I remember thinking that sounded a little extreme. After all, the C word was one of the most terrifying words in the English language, so I was surprised when she told me of her experience. And I'd already had my first manic-depressive episode (in 1994); perhaps, as they say is the case with childbirth, I'd forgotten the pain.

So life went on. And then again in 2008, as the result of a situation far too complex for this book (and I've already described it on my website: www.depressionexplained.com), I was visited once again by the mood-disorder gremlins. I was unable to work for most of that year and had to be hospitalised.

Now that *was* the worst experience of my entire life — and I haven't exactly spent my time wrapped in cotton wool. It was akin to living on the set of *One Flew Over the Cuckoo's Nest* without having fun and getting into trouble with Jack Nicholson. I still managed to get into plenty of trouble, but there was no Jack to hang out with.

Like Skuld, a valkyrie (battle goddess) of late 12th and early 13th century Norse mythology, I desperately tried to get back on my horse. I identify with the notion of strength, of fighting my way through and overcoming the battles in life. And of carrying with pride the scars of those battles.

However, the struggle to remount and ride on defeated me. I was diagnosed with another major depression. Being a fighter, I tend to expect myself to triumph through sheer bloody-mindedness and determination. I'm always trying to put on a brave face, a bit of lipstick, and wait for my laughter and lightness of being to return. But I couldn't, it wasn't possible! I was paralysed by the depression.

I think you'll agree that this photograph by a friend of mine, David Shields, depicts superbly what I felt like (www.davidkshields.com). David asked me to pose for this shot for a depression awareness campaign.

This was taken a few weeks before I got my callback for the second mammogram. It explains better than words can my difficulty in getting out of bed to make the appointment.

By the time I was about to go in for surgery, however, my new medication — prescribed by my wonderful psychiatrist Dr Ian Goodwin — was working; my depression was responding well to the antidepressants.

So now when I reflect on Theresa's comment, I understand and endorse her sentiments. In fact, in this *New Idea* article (4 October 2010) for Breast Cancer Awareness Month, I was quoted as saying:

> Having had severe depression and breast cancer, depression is far worse. With breast cancer I was in pain but I wasn't depressed, so I could still function. Without minimising breast cancer cases where women are facing death, this reconstructive surgery has been a walk in the park compared to a depressive illness — because you can still laugh.

At last you get to meet my mother Bette!

I want to take a moment to emphasise the profound difference between physical and psychic pain. With physical pain you can see what's wrong with you — you have bandages and evidence of an illness. Blood is as tangible as it gets.

That's not the case with depression. Depression is as insidious as it is invisible.

I was aware that in the case of breast cancer, people around me were very willing to offer help in any way they could. Whereas with depression, many people are just not sure what to do or say; they tend to want to avoid you. This is probably because of a lack of understanding, and perhaps their ambivalent beliefs about the true nature of depression. Not that I'm complaining; I understand perhaps more than most people do the truth behind this observation.

So this is an account of what it's like for me, having lived with both conditions. I happen to have manic depression (bipolar disorder), and then I was diagnosed with cancer. This is not an uncommon occurrence, but it is far from the norm. Such statistics are difficult to collect.

A major fear my loved ones held for me was best articulated by my friend Dene: 'When you told me you had breast cancer, after the initial shock I started to think, My God, how will she handle this, how will she cope with something this big with her bipolar?'

But I did.

If you have a pre-existing mood disorder, stay close to your doctor or psychiatrist. Here are some further points to consider:

I would include within this range: bipolar disorder, depression, diagnosed anxiety disorders and post-natal depression. These are all stress-sensitive conditions, and a breast cancer diagnosis imposes a lot of strain, emotionally and physiologically.

Hormonal changes are closely related to mood fluctuations. As I mentioned earlier, treatments for breast cancer such as chemotherapy or radiation can throw you into early menopause.

Obviously, this can be psychologically traumatic in younger women, and especially if they are planning a family.

Coping with hot flushes and additional mood swings at such an emotional time is an added complication.

The medication for your mood-related disorder also needs to be discussed and listed for the anaesthesiologist as part of your pre-operative assessment.

This matter also needs to be considered in the choice of post-operative pain relief.

Cause and effect

There is now increasing research into identifying any cause-and-effect relationship between cancer and depression. I have focused on the research that specifically refers to breast cancer. Before we go on, however, here is a checklist (from the World Health Organisation) that may help you to identify the presence of any symptoms of depression.

Persistent experience of any of the following may indicate that you should talk to your doctor about depression:

- Loss of interest in all activities once enjoyed.
- Changes in weight or appetite (either significant weight gain or weight loss.)
- Changes in sleeping patterns (restless sleep, unable to sleep, early morning wakening, sleeping too much, feeling more depressed in the morning.)
- Fatigue or loss of energy.
- Feeling hopeless or worthless. Loss of self-confidence.

- Irrational thinking (beliefs not based on reality, preoccupation with physical disease, constant feelings of inappropriate guilt.)
- Inability to concentrate, remember things or make decisions.
- Ongoing thoughts of death or suicide (wishing to die, or attempts at suicide).
- Loss of sexual drive.
- Feelings of sadness or irritability.
- Restlessness or decreased activity, boredom.

To avoid confusing the issue any more than necessary, I need to point out that the following factors should be considered before rushing to the conclusion that there's a mood disorder in the picture. I gleaned the following information from a CNS (Central Nervous System) forum conducted by the Lundbeck Institute (www.cnsforum.com), where a number of specialists spoke on the subject.

Keynote speaker Professor David Spiegel emphasised that:

- Depression complicates patients' efforts to cope with the illness and adhere to the medical treatment. Many cancer patients do not suffer depression but there are those who do.
- This is often overlooked, as the symptoms of depression are easily misattributed to the cancer and its treatment.
- Pervasive sadness and hopelessness can be explained as a reaction to a poor prognosis, sleep disturbance to disease-related anxiety and poor appetite to chemotherapy side-effects.
- Some studies have commented on the bi-directional relationship between cancer and depression. What they mean by that, is that the more rapid progression and increased symptoms of cancer are associated with

more severe depression, and depression and cancer existing together can result in increased functional impairment and a poorer quality of life over the course of the illness.

- The good news is that the prevalence of depression in cancer patients has been lowering in the past two decades, reflecting improvements in treatment, including less mutilating surgical interventions (e.g. lumpectomy vs mastectomy for breast cancer).

Wow, that was a serious few pages. If I wasn't writing at 4.30 am it would be time for a celebratory glass of champagne. Mind you, what's the time over there in Paris, Rome, New York, Copenhagen, anywhere?

Supporters, I have a few notes for you:

1. Looking in from the outside, you may also notice changes in physical appearance and a lack of interest in what she wears. Now, of course, in the initial stages of post-operative recovery, pain will dictate clothing choice. However, without the presence of depressive symptoms, she will still want to look her best, even in the ugly hospital pyjamas — a bit of lippie and a quick squirt of the expensive perfume you will have bought for her overnight bag.

2. Expressions of pain and discomfort may be evident — a little 'ouch', or 'Oh f@#k' while readjusting the pillows or having to move. However, if it appears that even talking is an effort, and there is little or no expression, this could be a symptom of depression.

3. Ask your loved one how she feels emotionally: is she experiencing sadness and grief at what has happened; whether it's after the initial diagnosis, or post-mastectomy, there will be some grief. Grief does not necessarily become depression, but if it persists for longer than three or four weeks, it may be time to talk to her doctor or oncologist.

Depression risk for partners of breast cancer patients

Supporters, here is a big wake-up call for you guys and girls.

Browsing through the www.webmd.com/depression site, I came across the following research. These findings relate to male partners/husbands. However, in keeping with my approach I would like to suggest that similar statistics would apply to lesbian partners — in fact, I believe it is something any close loved ones affected by the breast cancer diagnosis need to be aware of, particularly where the prognosis may not be good.

Researcher Christoffer Johansen, MD, PhD, and his colleagues at Denmark's Institute of Cancer Epidemiology (http://www.cancer.dk/epi+research/) followed more than a million men enrolled in a nationwide Danish health registry for 13 years.

Those with partners diagnosed with breast cancer during this period were almost 40 per cent more likely to be hospitalised for depression, bipolar disorder, or another mood disorder, than men whose partners did not have breast cancer. Dr Johansen also observed that the partners of women with breast cancer may be more at risk because their emotional response to what is happening can often be overlooked.

Risk factors and percentages also increased incrementally among the partners of women whose breast cancer advanced after the initial treatment, and the risk was higher again for men whose partners died of the disease.

So don't forget to look at that depression checklist for any symptoms you may be experiencing or may notice in your children. Powerlessness is known to be one of the most significant psychological contributors to a reactive depression, and you will be feeling powerless at times. Besides, you can't effectively support if you're not well.

Just like a breast cancer diagnosis, depressive illness does not discriminate or make choices between bad and nice people.

So supporters, look after yourself. There is a burden attached to caring for someone you love. It places a great strain on everyone.

17

How to get off the worry roundabout

My life has been full of terrible misfortunes most of which never happened.

Michel de Montaigne
(French philosopher and writer, 1533–1592)

Speaking of mood, I'd like to introduce you to a condition we in the trade refer to as Generalised Anxiety Disorder (GAD), more commonly known as 'worry'. Yes, we have a diagnostic classification for worry. Why? Because it's a debilitating condition, previously misunderstood as merely a quirky thing that some people spend a lot of time doing.

Most people experience anxiety over certain things, and a diagnosis of breast cancer would certainly be considered one of those things. However, there is a difference between appropriate levels of concern and intense ongoing worry that has the potential to result in collapse of our physiological system.

Clinicians understand more and more these days that long-term untreated anxiety (or worry) is one of the primary pathways to depression. Here is a list of the criteria for GAD from the DSM-IV (the psychiatric diagnostic bible we use in this part of the world) for anyone experiencing at least six months of 'excessive anxiety and worry', and:

1. Who has difficulty in controlling the worry — experiencing a struggle to regain control, relax, or cope with the worry.
2. Who has felt the presence on most days over the previous six months or more of three of the following:
   - Being wound-up, tense or restless
   - Becoming easily fatigued or worn out
   - Concentration problems
   - Irritability
   - Significant tension in muscles
   - Difficulty with sleep.
3. And for whom the symptoms cause significant distress or problems functioning in daily life.

Don't misunderstand me. I'm not saying that all of you out there who are worried have GAD. I am merely quoting the extreme case to illustrate what chronic worry is capable of doing.

You can imagine how this sort of strain on the system ultimately results in an impairment of functioning and people becoming sick. Supporters, you need to be aware of this. And you girls too — it doesn't help to keep you 'match-fit' for the operation or post-operative recovery if your sleep is disturbed, and you are tense and irritable.

Girls and supporters alike, take note: sleep is the brain's food, and it's important that all of you are getting plenty of refreshing and nourishing sleep.

There are now a number of softer, non-dependency producing medications that can be used to aid sleeping. Talk to your doctor about a homeopathic (sub-therapeutic) dose for sleep and worry. You could also ask at your local pharmacy about alternatives.

Don't worry, be happy (yeah, right!)

The first thing to appreciate about worry is that there's no point at all in telling a worrier to stop worrying. Let me demonstrate to you why.

Here we go. While I'm talking to you, I don't want you to think about camels, or any pictures you have ever seen of camels. I want you to focus on what I'm saying and while I'm talking to you, I don't want you to think about camels. Just concentrate on me and the pearls of wisdom I am giving out and while doing so there is to be no thinking about, visualising or remembering any images you have ever seen of camels. That includes *National Geographic* covers, cushion covers, travel brochures, camels in or out of the zoo, camels sauntering past a pyramid. Nothing, just focus on what I'm explaining to you.

Right, I think I've got that point across — you can't trick the brain in that way. This is why I have great difficulty with the New Age school of positive thinking. The assumption is that if you tell yourself to stop worrying and just feel at one with the universe, all will be well in your world. Again: yeah, right!

I couldn't resist a quick nostalgia visit to youtube.com and smiled as I watched Bobby McFerrin and Robin Williams on the 'Don't Worry, Be Happy' clip. However, when you look at the lyrics a little closer the main message is that worrying doesn't fix anything; action plans and collaboration with your loved ones are what will help you towards a solution.

'… In every life we have some trouble …

When you worry you make it double, don't worry, be happy …

In your life expect some trouble, but when you worry you make
it double, don't worry, be happy...'

Bobby McFerrin (1988)

The difference between worry and concern

Worry as a thinking process is very circular:

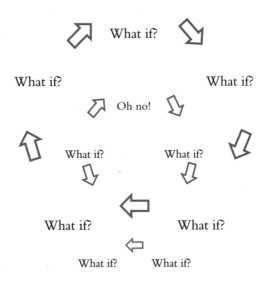

There is no beginning or end, no movement towards a solution, just endless going round in circles. One of the principal psychological themes is the tendency to create anxiety by underestimating your ability to cope and overestimating the risks, thus anticipating the worst possible outcomes.

What triggers worry is those two magical words, 'what if', which I call the 'mantra of the worrier'.

However, there are reasons why people continue to worry and are not prepared to give it up. There's a lot of mythology attached to worrying it's like a superstitious belief system: if a worrier stops worrying, they believe that something bad will happen.

One of my favourite anecdotes concerns a mother who says, 'Someone in this family has to worry. God knows what would happen if I didn't worry, the whole family would fall apart. It's not that I want to do the worrying, but given that your father refuses to worry, I have to!'

And if something bad *does* happen, the worrier has further evidence, perceptually speaking, that there was and always will be a need to worry. But of course in reality worrying is a thought process and, last time I looked, thinking wasn't able to move matter or control what occurs in the world. You might be planning a wedding, worrying constantly about whether it's going to rain on the day, but no amount of worry will influence the weather.

Concern, on the other hand, has specific destinations in mind: time frames, solutions, action plans.

For instance, *concern* can aid you in:

- Planning to minimise the impact of, or hopefully avoid, the feared situation occurring.
- Putting steps into place, and action plans for if and when it does.
- Making lists of time frames and who can help, and what needs to be prepared.
- Putting time aside for the necessary housekeeping if you are concerned about what may happen financially after a poor prognosis.

- Planning a funeral. It may seem 'silly', or unnecessarily dramatic to want to, but if it provides you with a sense of completion, why not?

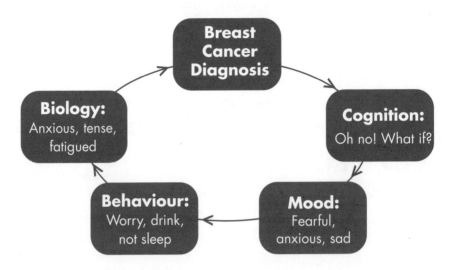

A breast cancer diagnosis is a harsh reality. You could go round and round this cycle, yet no matter how much you worry it won't cure the cancer. And if you're not a doctor (yes, doctors get cancer too), your only information will come from your overactive imagination, or as a result of spending hours on the internet fearing the worst.

Yes, breast cancer can be a life-threatening illness; it's also a very curable form of cancer. So focus on as many practical things that need to be done, leading up to and after the operation, as you can.

It may not really be possible for you as a lay person to discriminate between valid, helpful information, and its opposite. That is why it's so important to trust — not idealise, but trust — your surgeon and your other medical specialists. I had great respect for my surgeon, Wayne. He would answer any questions I presented him with, would give me options — for instance, regarding reconstruction and implants — so I never really bothered to research those things. I didn't want to look at a whole lot of pictures of tumours (you'll note the absence of such images in *Breast Support* — I'd rather look at an art book).

Worry behaviour

I also want to draw your attention to outward signs of worry, because concern can mimic these patterns when the news is fresh. It is only to be expected that you will be highly distressed when you begin meeting with your specialists and they are unable to tell you the extent of the cancer and how many lymph nodes are involved.

However, try to be mindful of where the children are in the house. They can't help but be aware of the sighing, they see the tears, the pacing, the shoulders slumped.

Not only do they see all this; they also notice that other adults around them appear to be engaged in some form of it. Imagine, say, a six-year-old boy: his older sister twirls and twirls her hair around her finger endlessly, biting her nails in between. Their mother rubs her brow over and over, in between sighs and cups of tea. If their father has a tendency to worry too, he might be sitting on his own drinking, unapproachable and grumpy.

When children witness the behavioural aspects of worry, they start to believe it's important to worry because it's what grown-ups do, so the little boy is quiet and withdraws into himself. Children learn that the world is a dangerous place, full of potential disasters, and that these are to be addressed in part by engaging in worrying.

The most important people in their lives worry, so it must be the right thing to do.

Then hopefully a doting grandmother, a woman of great wisdom, like my darling Lindsay, pours a glass of vino and a few glasses of juice before stating authoritatively:

'Now let's all just wait before we start to worry, shall we!'

This homegrown wisdom reminds us that nothing bad has happened; it's your worry-haunted imagination that is creating the difficulty at this point in time.

Technically known as 'anticipatory anxiety', this is the state in which you act as though you can predict the future and see only the worst possible outcome.

Helpful vs unhelpful

We'll concentrate now on the *content* of the thinking, and how that thinking may be working against you — what we in the industry call 'thinking that isn't helpful'.

There are excellent Cognitive Behavioural Therapy books to help with the management of worry, and I'll mention them at the end of the chapter.

Once again, considering your limited time and the speed at which everything is pulling you along the Breast Cancer Highway, I'll give you a few 'band-aid' tips to get you by in the meantime.

A few strategies

These are for you as well, supporters.

Here is a little template. You may want to copy it on a card and carry it around with you, referring to it when you feel yourself getting anxious and ruminating on good old 'what if'. The little prompt card provides you with an exit path from the roundabout.

Exit Path

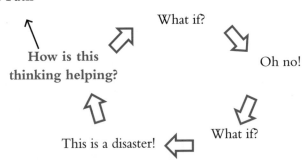

How is this thinking helping me?
Look at the card for 15 seconds
no less — each time you get anxious, or three or four times a day.

To complete this chapter I would like to introduce you more formally to the wonderful word 'helpful'. It reminds me of this symbol.

It's recognised globally as a symbol of people helping people. Only terrorists show no respect for it, because of their fanatical belief systems.

The word 'helpful' isn't about making judgements; it's not based on shoulds or shouldn'ts, and neither does it make statements about what's normal or abnormal. So next time you find yourself on the 'worry roundabout', ask yourself:

How is this thinking helping me?

On the subject of 'shoulds'

At all times during this ordeal you want your thinking to remain, as far as possible, rational and helpful to your wellbeing and that of your family. Once your thinking becomes irrational (in other words, no longer based on fact, reality or what's true), you are more likely to experience unpleasant emotional and physical side effects.

For instance, you may tell yourself that there *shouldn't be cancer* and, even if we acknowledge its existence, that *nice people shouldn't get it*, but in reality of course cancer knows no bounds. Cancer isn't going to respond to a 'should'!

Should is a word that puts a great deal of pressure on how you are thinking:

'I shouldn't; he should; the children shouldn't have to; I must make sure...'.

All these imperatives place a lot of demands on you. So when you become aware of *shoulds/musts/have to's* going round and round in your head, ask yourself: 'How is this thinking helping me?' (Remember 15 seconds!)

So give this a try. You will find that when you look at your thinking and challenge its irrationality, you'll experience a shift in the levels of your distress. This wonderful stuff works; I see it working every day.

Another commonly used cognitive technique is the Worry decision map (opposite). You may find it useful to either tear this page out, or make a copy and stick it on your fridge where you'll see it every day.

Distractions can include the breathing exercise (see page 67), yoga, meditation, even just going for a walk. They can all contribute to your physical and psychological wellbeing.

Worry delay strategies

Here is a technique that will help keep your mind clear during the day if you're still at work or busy running your family life. We often hang on to worry, concerned that we'll forget something important that needs to be done. Have a notebook with you and write it down; this allows you to let go of the thought.

If your thinking is focused more on the cyclical type of worry discussed earlier, try saying to yourself, I'm not going to worry about that now; I'll worry about that later in the day. Allocate 10–20 minutes a day of

Worry decision map

The Worry decision map is a structured way of solving the worry problem. It is a way of asking yourself a branching series of questions that help to let the worry drop.

Question 1: What am I worrying about?

Question 2: Is there anything I can do about this?

No → Stop worrying and distract yourself.

Yes → Work out what you could do, or how to find out what to do. Make a list.

Question 3: Is there anything I can do right now?

Yes, I could do:
.... → DO IT NOW → Stop worrying and distract yourself.

No → Plan what you could do, and when → Stop worrying and distract yourself.

uninterrupted time when you can write down everything you've been concerned about. You delay the worry, knowing that you will attend to those thoughts later that day. This has a twofold benefit: clearing your mind in the here and now; and formulating a plan for the concerns that require action to be taken and may involve assistance from others.

Remember too:

- It might never happen.
- It could be worse.
- Don't make a mountain out of a molehill.
- There will be a solution.

In the words of the Dalai Lama:

> If there is a solution to a problem, there is no need to worry, and if there is no solution, there is no need to worry.

And in the words of Gwendoline Smith:

> If all else fails take a pill (I'm not joking).

Here is some useful reading for worriers:

- *Six Thinking Hats*, Edward De Bono, Penguin Books, 1985
- *Overcoming Worry*, K. Meares & M. Freeston, Constable & Robinson, 2008
- *Manage Your Mind*, G. Butler & T. Hope, Oxford University Press, 1995

Remember though that there's a lot of reading in those books. I'd recommend making a few appointments with a cognitive psychologist who can take you through the treatment strategies for self-confessed worriers even prior to the breast cancer diagnosis.

18

Back on the Breast Cancer Highway

Surgical appointment number two

At this stage, Mr Jones explained to me the results of the MRI scan. He also expressed concern that, although the MRI had shown irregularities in my right breast, to satisfy the insurers I would have to have another biopsy as well as the standard imaging tests. It was then that he introduced me to the possibility that if there were no definitive signs of cancer in the right breast, *my insurance company might refuse to pay.*

They could argue that the removal of the right breast was a preventative choice, or an even harsher interpretation that I was merely trying to get a free boob job on the right. I was disgusted at this suggestion, and horrified at the possibility of no funding, as by now I had started to prepare my life for going into surgery and not being able to work. I agreed to the second biopsy, which was scheduled to occur two days before the surgery was booked.

Make sure you have a supporter with you for this second appointment, as this will most likely be (as it was for me) the time when you'll start to discuss in more detail your:

Treatment and reconstructive options

At this point it would be too cumbersome to go into the detail of all the possible alternatives, especially as your experience and options will be different from mine. Your circumstances will be unique to you, and limited, of course, to what is available where you live.

Annabel at work in Malaysia.

It has come to my attention while writing this book that breast cancer rates are on the rise throughout the world, but treatment options are often more limited and less sophisticated than they are in North America, Northern Europe, Australia and New Zealand.

Searching through treatment options available in Malaysia, for instance, I came across this daunting statement:

> Trained counselors to advise on post-surgery care, exercises and diet. Services range from buying silicon external prostheses, to helping you make your own.
>
> Kuala Lumpur ref: www.radiologymalaysia.org

Annabel Mackenzie, the sister of my dear friend Fiona (another birthday twin, who accompanied me to the medical imaging appointment) wrote to me about her work in Asia:

> I work for a company called Amanita (the name came from a combination of two Malay words meaning 'peaceful woman'). It was actually started by an Irish woman married to a Malaysian. After getting breast cancer she wanted to do something for the women in Malaysia. The situation there was that women were not being offered much support after breast cancer, and prostheses were virtually impossible to find. Women who couldn't afford to purchase from overseas resorted to stuffing bras with towels, handkerchiefs, stones and coins — I've seen it all! And the doctors and nurses also were not educated sufficiently regarding breast cancer aftercare to be able to advise.
>
> It has been the most rewarding aspect of my job visiting these rural government hospitals — some days I have fitted up to 40 women and each one of these women has a story to tell. Never in their lives would they imagine owning such a lovely bra and a prosthesis, which costs more than their monthly income! Every two or three months I fly to the east coast of Malaysia with two huge suitcases of prostheses and bras to do fittings over there, which I love.
>
> The women are all from the villages, many suffering from sore backs, shoulders and lymphoedema, so you can imagine how happy they are to get a prosthesis. Of course I initially have to teach them how to wear their bras properly as many of them survive without bras! Anyway the stories can go on and on as I must have fitted hundreds of women over the past few years.
>
> Next week I am off to a small hospital in the North where I understand there are 200–300 women who need prostheses —

not sure how we will organise that, but will soon find out when I go there. Our website has actually generated us business from neighbouring countries such as India, Thailand, Indonesia and the Philippines — all countries like Malaysia where the incidence of breast cancer is rising, but there is very little government support like we have in NZ.

One of the first things we did was organise a special course for breast care nurses every year. We got this funded by different organisations here and Professor Kate White and Jane Gregson came up from Australia to conduct these courses, which were attended by nurses from all over the country. This is the only course that is offered to breast care nurses in the country and to date we have educated 100 nurses. Many of them have gone ahead and started support groups in their own hospitals and organised us to visit their hospitals to fit their women with prostheses and mastectomy bras. Most of these women are from very low-income families, so Amanita has worked with local organisations to fund these women.

Hope to meet you soon.

Annabel

I just love these stories, and during the many hours I spent, kind of procrastinating, but officially searching Google images, I was touched by and amazed at the groundswell of women from all walks of life, all ages, and from all over the globe, getting together to help one other. Whether it's for cancer research or, at a much more basic level, to help fund prosthetic bras… Go Girls!

I consider myself very fortunate to live in New Zealand where we do have choices. The following information is based on this understanding. I do emphasise that this is a very brief outline, as your options will be dictated by the type of breast cancer you have, the stage of development, whether it has been detected early or is at an advanced stage, and — as I have discovered — by where you live and how much money you have.

Again I refer to what I consider to be my bible — *Breast Care* by Dr Trevor Smith.

I was introduced to this book by another darling friend of mine, Marilyn (also a member of the the BCC — and, I would like to add, looking fabulous in the most gorgeous wig I've ever seen).

Because this book was published in 2008 by a New Zealand-based breast surgeon, the information is relevant and up to date. However, the same range of treatment options may not apply to all women in all regions throughout the world. Nevertheless, I would like to refer to it as a source for the information on treatment options; readers in other parts of the world will hopefully be able to access similar resource material specific to where they live, through breast clinics, breast cancer organisations and foundations.

The most accurate information about the possible future behaviour of the cancer is obtained from the pathology report (the report on tests that find the cause of disease). The results describing size, features and lymph-node activity can only be known after surgery; the initial operation not only attempts to remove the cancer, but also to stage the disease.

Hence, when you are going in for surgery there is still a significant element of the unknown. Assessment technology, in the developed world, becomes more and more sophisticated. However, once the surgeon goes in to operate, the histology (the microscopic tissue study) provides the most accurate information of all. This does not mean that the prognostic (predictive) information you have been given is of no significant value — it's just that this is the defining moment.

You will consult your surgeon about what your treatment options are and what combinations of treatment apply. I consider myself to have been very fortunate in that I had a double mastectomy, but with no radiation or chemotherapy required.

Other women I know had other combinations: one girlfriend had a lumpectomy; some had radiotherapy and a breast reduction; another had a lumpectomy, radiotherapy and chemotherapy. My mother had a single mastectomy with ongoing hormonal treatment (Tamoxifen).

Because of the many possible combinations of treatment, depending on the type and spread of your cancer, you need to consider the following:

A few pointers:
- You need to have a surgeon that you respect, trust and can develop a good rapport with, because he/she will be the best source of information for your individual requirements.
- You will need to discuss:
  - the extent of the surgery — partial/full mastectomy,
  - the need for axillary (armpit) surgery,
  - the time and place of the reconstruction, dependent of course on whether or not you want a reconstruction, if that option is available, and if/when it is possible depending on your healthcare facility. You may choose, if given the option, to have the reconstruction when your other cancer treatment is completed.
- It's okay to seek a second opinion. Your surgeon won't be offended by this request (or shouldn't be; if yours is, you may want to consider

another specialist). Ego, in my opinion, has no place in medicine if it impacts on the patient. In fact, the specialists I've interviewed encourage this process. Although you may feel, as I did, as if there's an incredible urgency to make these decisions, a few days won't make a great difference with regard to the cancer's progression; Dr Trevor Smith makes the comment that the cancer won't change significantly even over a period of two to three weeks. So there's no call to feel rushed; you need to feel comfortable with your surgeon and your treatment recommendations.

- Ask questions. There is no such thing as a wrong question. The more questions you can remember to ask, the more it helps your consultant understand you.

- It's very important that one of your support team is at this appointment to provide that extra pair of ears — belonging, I might add, to someone whose state of shock will be milder than yours.

- Try not to be overly influenced by bad-news stories you may have heard; people have a tendency to recall the most graphic details of cancer horror tales. As I have said many times, there is very little likelihood that your cancer will be like that. Stay with the good news and avoid the rest — they only serve to heighten your fears.

Once I'd made the decision to have a double mastectomy, it was time to decide what type of surgery. Because this is another set of decisions, take your time. If your principal supporter is your darling, you can discuss the options jointly. However, it's ultimately your decision and will be based on the considerations that your surgeon will go through with you.

And the options are…

Tram flap (The French champagne of breast reconstruction options):

> This is what I perceived to be the more 'organic' option, using flesh from your stomach to reconstruct the breasts (so you get a

tummy tuck at the same time — see what I mean about the endless benefits). But I decided against this option for the following reasons: flap procedures require four to five hours in theatre and about five to six days in hospital. The recovery time and getting back to your daily routine and exercise also takes longer.

Living on my own and being self-employed ruled this out for me. However, it may work for you; the advantages are that it avoids the need for an implant and additional surgery during the implant procedure. I spoke with Jill, another BCC member, while writing *Breast Support*. She'd chosen to have a tram flap and was delighted with the result.

Certainly, comparing Jill's boobs with my 'never-to-sag' teardrop silicone breasts, hers feel more natural, and of course move in rhythm with her own flesh. With the silicone, although they soften with time, there's a sense of having something attached to your chest that you can feel isn't you.

In fact, these days — almost a year later — I could swear they move slightly to the side when I lie down. Wayne assures me this is not just my imagination.

Latissimus dorsi flap with an implant:

Another one I didn't consider and can't remember quite why — could have been that I would never have been able to pronounce latissimus, particularly after a few wines while showing off the 'New Girls' to the girls.

Basically what it means is that one of the back muscles is used to provide additional tissue to cover the implant. This method is designed to provide a more natural 'droop' to the breast. It seemed to me that, given I was going to spend the rest of my life not drooping, my breasts immune to gravity, I'd give the 'droop guarantee' a swerve. But the literature considers this particular flap to be one of the most durable and reliable options available.

Something to think about.

Implant:

A bag filled with saline or silicone gel that can be inserted under the chest wall muscle at the time of the mastectomy. This suited me; as I mentioned, I didn't want a more complicated larger flap procedure. They do tend to have a bit of a plastic feel, but the initial implants are only for the purposes of tissue expansion. The ones that replace them, as I am finding, do seem to meld with time and a bit of gentle massage (hopefully by your darling; it's not as much fun doing it yourself).

The pathology report

Now this is a very important document and, although I outline the content below, I understand very little of the technicalities. However, you will have this explained to you by your specialist team, as it determines post-operative treatment. So I just thought I would provide you with a synopsis that you could use as a guide at some stage, if you wish.

This report will become available after the surgery, and will provide the following information:

Type: Ductal or lobular cancer

Size: In mm

Grade: There are three grades. Grade One cells are the best behaved and Grade Three the most 'troublesome/aggressive' cells.

Lymphovascular invasion: Have the cells moved into the blood and lymph vessels in the tissue?

Hormone receptor status: There are small parts of the cancer cell that bind strongly to the female hormones oestrogen and progesterone. These hormones can stimulate the growth of some cancers. There are a number of drugs available that can block this action, which may be useful in treating the cancer.

There are two types of receptor, an oestrogen receptor (positive/negative) and a progesterone receptor (positive/negative).

HER 2 (human epidermal growth factor) — also far too technical for me to explain — is another molecule that can stimulate the growth of some cancers. It has a special receptor on the cell surface that can be tested for. Herceptin is the drug that can block this receptor and may be useful in treating some cancers.

Decisions about treatment

Making decisions about treatment

Your treatment and management plan will usually involve a combination of treatments.

The lump:
- Local treatment
- Surgery
- Radiotherapy

The lymph nodes:
- Regional treatment
- Surgery
- Radiotherapy

More extensive spread
- Systemic treatment
- Chemotherapy
- Hormonal therapy

To return to my own consultation, I found it most amusing to see Mr Jones take from the shelf above his desk a small vinyl kit bag, white with pink piping (which I thought rather appropriate), full of breast implants. There they were — all different shapes and sizes and textures. The Rolls-Royce of the implant world was the new teardrop silicone implant. Worth a small fortune of course, but guaranteed to provide that *slight* droop and the flatness at the top to impart a more 'natural' shape and density.

I've always been a girl with champagne tastes, so the teardrops were the ones I had my eyes on.

Then comes sizing: this is an unusual exercise, as you're still sitting there with the breasts Mother Nature gave you, measuring up with various-sized plastic discs. Which you, your companion and the surgeon get to make comments and have a giggle about. You can go larger, or you can go smaller; I decided to stick to a similar sizing, worried that if I went for a Paris Hilton cleavage with Pamela Anderson cup capacity, it might affect my intelligence quotient.

You will find that, with each appointment, you are slightly better equipped to see the lighter side. Although it still seems surreal, you are adjusting with each day and the fear is slowly replaced by a growing adaptability. As I've mentioned before, humour is a very important (and scientifically proven) component of resiliency, and to see your surgeon rummaging through a bag full of false breasts mulling over which size suits you best definitely has its comical side.

Size agreed upon, we left and I set about preparing for another round of pre-operative tests. However, just before we get to that, I'd like to present you with another educational experience.

19

Insurance

Another corporate misnomer

You may have noticed a number of slightly scathing references to medical insurance cover scattered through the text. I shall now explain this. First, I'd like to refer to the good old dictionary and remind us all of the actual definition of the product we spend so much money on each year.

Insurance (noun): Financial protection against loss or harm. Means of protection.

Now I don't know about you, but to me losing a breast would seem to fit that category. And, yes, I was covered — but only for the *one* breast, a fact I was unaware of until the eleventh hour. At which time I started to panic. I became very distressed. Hence my choice of the word 'misnomer'.

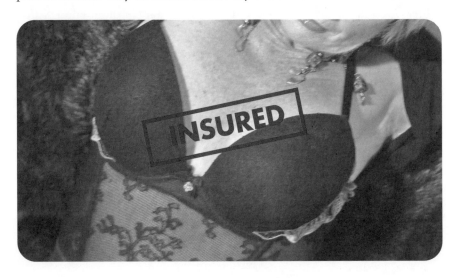

My VIP cover also provided for expenses up to NZ$75,000, or the actual surgical, hospital and anaesthetist fees, whichever was the lesser amount. It seemed to me that amount would comfortably cover all costs, and in fact when I collated them it would have done.

I could have chosen to go through the public health system, as the surgeons working in the breast cancer area in New Zealand do for the most part provide their services for both public and private sectors. Other women (members of the BCC) had told me that they had been perfectly happy with the service the public health system had provided, and this was also my mother's experience. She had also received home help and a certain degree of aftercare at home with changing dressings and so on.

The deciding factor for me, however, was the wait. When it comes to the C word sitting there on the same piece of paper as the adjective *invasive*, I was keen to be operated on as soon as possible. So I looked at the availability of beds and the surgeon's ability to book theatre time, both of which are more flexible in the private sector. Looking back, I would perhaps be prepared to acknowledge that I over-reacted regarding time frames. However, in fairness to myself, I was frightened and I wanted to have the operation, to recover, and to get back to work.

It would never have occurred to me in a million years that only one breast would be covered. I know I've advised people often enough that universal justice is a myth. But this had nothing to do with fate, or luck; this had to do with paying my premium — in fact, paying the VIP premium — for surgical cover and getting the insurance cover required. A no-brainer, I would have thought. Wouldn't you?

I was reminded of the old Chinese saying: 'Good things come in pairs.'

It takes two to tango. It takes two to kiss.
A couple is two people sharing lives.
Parents come in twos. A friendship takes two.
You can stand on your own two feet,
Look with your very own set of eyes,
And feel with your pair of hands
That other wonderful fact of nature:
Yes. Breasts come in twos.

That piece of poetic common sense, written by yours truly at a somewhat enraged and melancholic moment, testifies to what I would consider a very rudimentary grasp of human anatomy — breasts, arms, legs, eyes, ears and testicles all come in sets of two. Equally obvious, surely, that a high-premium medical cover would in fact remove any financial pressure at such a time.

But oh no, no such luck!

So let me just take you through a little bit of this horrendous discovery. On that fateful day when I had been told that I had DCIS (ductal carcinoma in situ), Wayne informed me immediately that I would have to have a full mastectomy of the left breast. I had observed, through watching various documentaries and breast cancer stories on television over the years, the phenomenon of younger women opting for a double mastectomy, even prior to a diagnosis, if there was a significant incidence of breast cancer in the genetic stream of their family.

I had always found that to be quite an extreme response, but then I'd never been faced with that decision-making process. Although my mother and three of her sisters had had breast cancer, Mum wasn't diagnosed until she was in her sixties, and a later-in-life diagnosis of that kind is seen as a function of age rather than anything necessarily to do with genetics. I did (as I've mentioned earlier) begin regular mammograms at this time, but 40 was the age when it became advisable to do so.

A couple of days after my diagnosis, as I became ever so slightly more adjusted to the news, I began to consider the possibility of a double mastectomy. Initially my loved ones were perturbed and encouraged me not to be too hasty. The more members of the BCC I spoke to, however, along with input from my ongoing medical appointments, especially with Wayne, the more it seemed that this difficult decision was also the wisest.

Let me list the evidence I was weighing up:

1. 03/03/2009: Diagnosed DUCT CARCINOMA IN SITU AND FOCI SUGGESTING INVASIVE DUCT CARCINOMA.
2. 04/03/2009: Report to GP on intermediate grade DCIS: Gwendoline almost certainly requires a mastectomy. Some faint benign microcalcifications in the opposite breast. Before surgery would be wise to undertake further tests.
3. 04/03/2009: Radiologist's report. Words like lobulated lesions, multi-clustered microcalcifications, more foci suggesting invasion, indeterminate to suspicious features and additional magnification views recommended.

I'm sure you're getting the picture. I didn't really know what the words meant, and was still struggling to take it in; all I could absorb were the verbs that were suggesting cancer cells on the move. Wayne had also explained to me that there was a 20–50 per cent chance of cancer developing in the right breast in the future, even if the second biopsy did not reveal anything at this time. I didn't need the knowledge of statistics I'd gained at university to tell me that 20–50 per cent was significant.

By this stage, I'd decided to go for the double mastectomy. I considered myself to be acting prophylactically. Now prophylaxis is an interesting word from the medical world: it means 'preventative measure'. The word comes from the Greek for an advance guard, an apt term for a measure taken to fend off a disease or other unwanted circumstance. What perfect sense, I thought — not imagining for one minute there would be any debate.

That wouldn't have been just unfair; it would have been cruel. When it happened, I felt for the first time that I was being victimised and made to struggle and suffer, and for what? Policy wording?

As events started to unfold for the worst, I found myself yelling down the phone as I was pleading for help and understanding, 'I bet your chief medical officer would have a different take on it if his f#@*ng testicles were involved!'

Irrational, and scientifically speaking probably a bad analogy as well as sexist, I know. But what can I say? I'd been quite reasonable until then. This couldn't be real. I had insured with the company that was *not* for profit, but for you and me!

Even from an accounting perspective, I couldn't make sense of this stance. Let me give you an example that illustrates the absurdity. Mother Bette was staying with me for a few days (post-op), and the invoices started to arrive. When I saw the amount of the shortfall, I started to cry. Where was the money going to come from? Then the tears stopped, and I just felt pissed off!

'Listen to this Mum. They'll only pay for half the anaesthetic! What the f@#k was my other breast going to do, wait in the car park?'

As you've gathered by now, I was outraged, morally, philosophically, ethically — along with the fear I was feeling of not being able to pay for the surgery on my right breast.

So this is a totally unnecessary part of the procedure that I will fight for other women not to have to be exposed to, and hopefully it's not something you are going through as you read this section of *Breast Support*.

I have subsequently researched and spoken to insurers who market an insurance product specifically for cancer. I know I repeatedly said that I wasn't going to get breast cancer, it couldn't possibly happen to me, and so on. But it did, and as I've become better versed in the research and the statistics, I've learnt that being a woman and over the age of 40, as diagnostic indicators go, doesn't exactly narrow the field.

Endangered species!

So have a think about taking out cover for your daughters,
because one never knows, and one can also never predict
how the underwriting of insurance policies with
regards to breast surgery and reconstruction
will unfold in the years to come.

The second biopsy

I took a loved one with me of course, as I knew from the first biopsy it
would be painful, and this time I was also distressed about being put through
this additional testing because of an insurance company's policy.

> Wear something like jeans and a shirt so you can undress to the waist,
> and make sure the top is comfortable and easy to put on over the
> dressing later.

The second biopsy was a lot more intrusive than the first. Again, I tried not to look down — from where I was placed, the needles looked like satay skewers heading into my flesh. And, unlike the knife in the magic trick where the blade disappears into the handle, the needle buries its full length into your flesh.

A few words of comfort here though: the local anaesthetic works very effectively and, as has been the case throughout, the staff explain everything and try to make you as comfortable as possible.

Because the wonderful radiologist was trying so hard to find the results that would provide evidence of the abnormalities shown by the MRI scan, the inserts were deep and a blood vessel was burst. Not that I minded, but in the morning when I got into the shower to prepare myself for the ink testing session (the next pre-operative procedure), my dressing was soaked in blood and I started to feel the profound nature of the fear I had spent so much time hiding from.

The second biopsy in a nutshell:
1. Wear comfortable, loose-fitting clothing.
2. You must have a supporter to drive you home (thanks Sandra, you were a real trooper, even though we did get lost on the way back ...)
3. Take some pain relief tablets in your bag; it will hurt when the local anaesthetic wears off.
4. Don't look at what's happening unless you really need to — it's intrusive, and involves blood.

But there was no time to waste, and I continued on my way to the following day's appointment. Yes, it was time for my introduction to the world of nuclear medicine.

20

Lymphoscintigraphy (or nuclear medicine)

Otherwise known as 'Sentinel Node Mapping'. I know the term 'nuclear medicine' has a slightly spooky connotation. However, the radiation doses are comparable to those of X-ray examinations. The technology uses radioactive tracers, to which there are no known reactions, and the tests are exceptionally safe and well-tolerated.

Let's take this from the beginning, so you and your support team are well prepared. Fiona (my previously mentioned birthday twin) drove me to this appointment. You can drive if you wish, but I was in agony from the previous day's second biopsy and, as I've said before, it's better overall to have a supporter with you for company.

In this instance, supporters, you can plan to do a drop off and pick-up. These things can take time. Although most appointments are usually about an hour, on some occasions pictures are delayed, which means the appointment could take two hours or more.

At New Zealand Medical Imaging they're happy for you to have company throughout the procedure, but to be honest it's a bit like watching paint dry.

What does the scan involve, and why?

TENDER JUICY BEEF
What's your cut?

Chuck · Shoulder · Rib · Breast · Loin · Rump · Thigh · Round

As crazy as this cowgirl image may look, it's actually the easiest (and the cheekiest) way I can find to explain what this procedure is about. On a serious note, the reality is that cancers can spread either by blood routes or by lymphatic routes to the lymph nodes.

So this fabulous piece of technology creates a visual map of this activity, which is scanned and reproduced on film that you'll take along with you to surgery. You will also leave with lines drawn in waterproof felt pen, in my case by another compassionate and skilled practitioner, Dr David Newbury. These dotted lines on your skin are to help guide the surgeon to the location of the sentinel lymph node, helping him/her locate and remove the node faster and (hopefully) via a smaller incision.

So when you get home, you do look a bit like one of those pictures at the butcher shop — cut here for rump steak, over here for eye fillet and up a little bit and to the right for spare ribs.

Okay, enough of the meat metaphor. I'll just outline for you and your support team what to expect and, as always, what to wear.

1. After a warm welcome and a form to fill out, you'll be taken into a small office and made comfortable on a recliner bed/chair arrangement.

2. Another occasion to be wearing jeans or something comfortable; you will of course be taking your top off (you'll be used to this by now).

3. You'll be given one of those robes — not really much of a fashion statement, but they do the trick.

4. Then a *very, very small, very, very slightly* radioactive pharmaceutical is injected near the site of the primary malignancy. This stings, and when I say stings, I mean it *f#@*ng stings*!

5. This tracer then travels along a few lymphatic channels, heading to accumulate in the nodes, so that the nodes can then be visualised using a gamma camera and reproduced on film.

6. While the tracer is tracing, have a book (preferably this one) or a trashy magazine with you, as you will have to sit for a while. I took the opportunity to start making notes for *Breast Support*, having an early suspicion that another book was being conceived.

7. Then you change rooms, and get to lie on another fantastic piece of technology. (I hope the medical technology in your country is as wonderful as we have here in New Zealand.)

I love this image with the toys. I remember thinking, How cute, then remembering that they were there for our sick children.

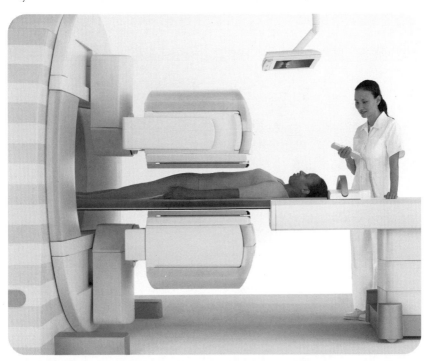

You'll be lying more like this. The technologist will move you and the camera slightly for the best shot.

The scan takes about 30–40 minutes. It's not distressing in any way, and as you can see from the illustration, the feeling of enclosure you may have experienced with the MRI scan does not apply.

You won't need to take any medication with you for pain relief. It won't really alleviate the stinging, and once that passes there's no further discomfort. On the subject of the stinging, David said just before the very teeny-weeny injection of the radioactive pharmaceutical, 'Gwendoline, you can swear if you feel the need.'

That's an odd thing to say, I thought — just prior to opening my mouth and yelling 'F#@K!' in a far from teeny-weeny manner.

He told me about a woman of mature years (that means older than me), elegant stature and great composure, whose reply to his comment had been, 'No, that won't be necessary. I never swear,' followed almost immediately by, 'Well, maybe just this once. Ow, shit!'

Don't forget to take the images to the hospital the following day. Supporters, make sure this happens.

21

Preparing for hospital

The night before

Well girls, here we are. I think you'll agree it's been very much a fast-tracked trip down the Breast Cancer Highway. All of a sudden it's the day before, and of course you're still quite mobile and probably not really feeling that sick — maybe anxious about tomorrow, but that's totally understandable.

I expect you will be doing something different from what I did on this particular evening. I was living on my own, and really didn't want to be by myself. So I went to my girlfriend Fiona's place, and there I met Paula for the first time (I was to interview her later about how she told her children). Anyway, there were the three of us, and Paula was amusing me — and easing my anxiety — with stories of shopping trips with no hair, struggling with her drainage bags, while Fiona poured the odd sauvignon blanc, which also helped with the anxiety. Wanting to be match-fit for the following day, I didn't stay late but the company was important to me that evening.

The other great benefit came after I said to the girls, 'Well, I'd better get home and pack my bags.'

Paula said, 'Now Gwendoline, make sure you have a kimono-type top, or something with very loose sleeves, as you'll be leaving with drainage bags and you're not going to be able to tuck them inside a sweat shirt, let alone a pink cashmere cardigan.'

What an amazing tip that turned out to be (though it never would have occurred to me to wear a pink cashmere cardigan!). Seriously though, I probably would have just taken a loose sweat shirt, which wouldn't have worked. These days, depending on your choice of surgery, you are only in for a couple of nights and then you're off home, which is what most people prefer. So there's a strong likelihood that you'll be attached to some sort of apparatus on the way out of hospital. I've decided not to let you see the picture; I've been making an effort not to show you too much stuff that isn't that nice to look at, but take it from me:

You will most likely have a Jackson-Pratt (JP) drain. It's there for a whole lot of good reasons, keeping unwanted fluids away from the surgical site. It also provides a way of measuring progress.

Your discharge from hospital will also be linked to how well all of this is going. A nurse will explain how to do everything before you leave. You will be given a chart to keep records, and so on. Also on this subject, when it comes to showering, Wayne later suggested tying a ribbon round your neck to keep all those tubes out of the way. Something I didn't think of then, so had to rely on Bette to hold them for me — all terribly awkward, but great to have my mum there to help.

That's enough of that; you'll be fine, but I just wanted to let you know that it's important to take a top with large sleeves!

The overnight bag and other pre-hospital tips

1. You will have been given a list of what to take. I can't remember if I took my pyjamas or not, because the hospital robes have little ties in all the right places to move things about, to check on dressings, the Jackson-

Pratt and so on. I did take a robe or top just for a bit of glamour for visitors.

2. Take a little bit of perfume and a basic face kit if you want to freshen up a little for visitors. Don't feel obliged to buy make-up the day before, because if you never wear it it's not necessary to start now.

3. Take sunglasses regardless of the weather, as putting mascara on is going to be difficult; you won't want to be moving your arms any more than you have to.

4. You may want to take a book, but the probability of feeling like reading anything apart from trashy gossip magazines is not that high.

5. Take your cellphone if you have one. If you can text, it's a good way of communicating with the outside world without having to talk or ask for the ward telephone.

6. Also you can say to friends, 'Send a text and I can let you know if I'm up for visitors.' This also allows you to co-ordinate when they come. Nothing worse than having them all turn up at once — you get exhausted, they all politely leave and then you're bored for the rest of the day watching daytime television.

7. Apart from perhaps your kissing partner and your children, you should discourage other visitors on that first day. You'll be 'stoned' — legally, so it's okay — and you'll only have a certain amount of energy for people, which you'll want to save for your nearest and dearest.

8. Another helpful tip from a BCC member: flowers are lovely, but when you get home, particularly if you live alone, you're not going to be able to lift that vase and the water will get really stinky.

9. Gourmet food and French champagne, on the other hand, can sit quietly being admired until the time is right. Also, by the time you feel like a glass of champers, you won't be having to pop the cork.

The trip to hospital

Here again, this is a matter of personal choice. Admission time is usually quite early, with nil by mouth instructions from the day before. My girls offered to take me to the hospital, and it wasn't that I was being unnecessarily self-effacing, I just prefer to take that sort of trip on my own. I see it as a bit like taking a taxi to the airport; you can only wave goodbye so many times, and there are only so many cheeks you can kiss. Particularly given that you'll be back in two days.

However, your family may not want you to do that. You decide.

I decided to chat to my taxi driver. He was from Bangladesh. By the time we got to the destination, Shaffik was going to do a couple of prayers to Allah for me. Why not? I thought.

And what to wear

I'm going to describe to you *what* I was wearing and, more important, *why* I chose such extravagant apparel to go for surgery. Then it's up to you to decide.

Your decision will of course be weather-dependent. However, if it's slightly chilly (like it is down here in April), wear as many garments with sleeves as you can and your favourite bra. I went for a pair of jeans, for warmth a carrot-orange Christian La Croix jacket with narrow sleeves, over a favourite top with clinging sleeves, over a delicately adorned grey satin padded bra.

The reasoning behind all this? This is the last time in a while you will be wearing anything with clinging sleeves, and that bra may never fit again (don't forget, this is the time to change cup size if that's an option for you).

And don't forget that medical imaging photography. Get it together, supporters: it's D-Day.

I checked in. Reception was just like going to a hotel for the weekend. Then you get escorted to the ward and it's not so much like a hotel any more. There was a little bit of a wait while the theatre was being prepared and the surgeons were scrubbing up.

My next step was to be introduced to the 'Stocking Butler', a little piece of equipment that makes putting on stockings a breeze. These particular stockings don't require a suspender belt as they're compression stockings. Hope you haven't already slipped one in your bag, but who cares? It's not like they take up a lot of room. These stockings are not to be laughed at — they have an essential role to play. They're for preventing the formation of deep vein clots that can result in pulmonary complications and death.

Pleased I didn't know that those sorts of considerations were going on behind the scenes, I was, by this stage, rather looking forward to my pre-op medication.

I'm not quite sure how the next bit happened, but on all the medical soaps I've ever watched on television, the patient is wheeled in on the bed to the accompaniment of comforting words from the nurse. Not in my case. I ended up walking into theatre to see Wayne in his blue scrubs and the anaesthesiologist, both sporting a pair of gumboots.

Exactly how messy is this floor going to get? I thought. What *was* cool was being able to ask what sort of music they were going to play. I was on the set of *Nip/Tuck* and about to cruise away on a cloud of modern-day anaesthetics.

So that was it.
Goodbye Girls.

Couple of nights in hospital, visitors coming and going, hardly any of which I can remember. In fact when my girlfriend Janet turned up she had to introduce herself. Oh dear, must have been leaning on that morphine pump by mistake.

On that subject, don't be shy. If you feel any pain, just ask. Squeaky wheels are the ones that get oiled.

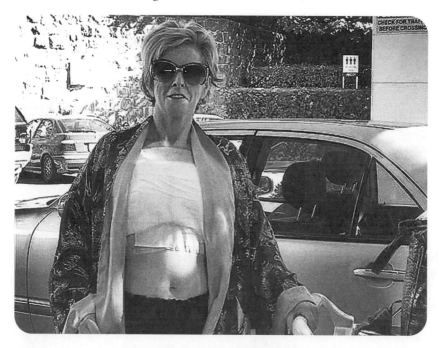

Thanks for the kimono tip, Paula.

On the way home

Now, this is not the most flattering photo of me but what it does illustrate is how happy I was when leaving the hospital — I didn't even make an effort to hold in my stomach while the photo was being taken. In fact, with the post-operative medication, I don't think I would have cared if you could see wrinkles or grey hair.

See how effective that kimono is, not a blood bag in sight!

The lovely Verna was there, with her rather spacious, not to mention

luxurious, Mercedes. So there I was heading home to mother Bette —
there's no one quite like your mother when you're feeling poorly; she seems
to know just what you need without even asking. And you don't have to
hold your stomach in when she helps you into the shower. Particularly if
you have drainage bags.

She was pleased to see me, as was my little spoodle Gerry, who even
seemed to know not to jump on me. Who says dogs can't think? Well, they
can't, but they look as if they can — it must be all that extra-sensory
perception they have.

22

Back at home: the convalescence

Your needs and requirements at this stage are very practical in nature, and dependent on the finely tuned engine of your supporters. This chapter includes a list of the most incredibly helpful things your supporters can do as a backup to your now quite fragile darling.

(This is also a way of saying a huge heartfelt 'thank-you' to my own support team. You were everything a girl could have hoped for.)

'I love you lot.'

Wisdom from my experienced support team

Sandy: The only thing I would say is that after surgery make sure friends help with lifting shopping, and walking the dog. Small things really, and making sure that if depression sets in, to ensure there is an abundance of favourite foods on hand to tempt even the fussiest or depressed mate into eating a few calories to lessen the weight loss. Also check on her regularly and know that when she doesn't want you to come over, don't take it personally as she will need a bit of space. Hope that is helpful.

My absent girlfriend Jane: The first feeling when told the news is surreal, and is this true — surely not? Being away, you imagine her as she was the last time you saw her — healthy, without a care in the world.

The second thought is, I need to get on a plane and go and help, but as soon as that thought hits, you realise that you have enormous responsibilities as well as flights, accommodation and appointments booked for the next decade and you can't leave!

Then guilt sets in.

As guilt goes you begin to feel like a shitty friend who is helpless to help, and you just generally are left with a whole lot of worry about the person. When I came home to see you, after the op, the reality of the situation set in, again as you still have this funny part of your brain where you think it's not really happening nor that bad.

Then you see it and realise that isn't in fact true.

Leaving to return to your regular life and leaving the person behind is hard, although at least you can be practical at that point. The twins have gone, and therefore one assumes so is the immediate danger and now the healing begins.

The feelings you go through may be selfish, but you genuinely and desperately want to be there to do something.

If this isn't a possibility, regular contact is the key, to help you understand how she is and obviously offer her support even if it is simply being there at the other end of the phone battling with time zones.

Coming home to see you was great as it puts everything into perspective, not to mention at that point you've spoken to others, who of course know someone who has been affected and can tell you what they felt and saw.

Hope all of that waffle helps!

And Jane is right; it's great having long telephone calls as you're lying on the couch. Make sure you have a cordless phone, as you won't want to be endlessly having to get up to answer calls. You don't have to answer every single call — you'll be needing to rest during the day, as the general anaesthetic alone is exhausting for a while.

Help is never far away

Meals on wheels

There happen to be a lot of foodies among my support team members. The lovely Kathryn would just make a bit extra of anything she was cooking, pop it into a container and drop food parcels off for me. You see, you won't be able to lift pots and pans, and neither are you going to be chopping vegetables. Some of the girls would come over, cook and stay for dinner, while the less domesticated team members would bring takeaway meals and watch telly with me. As I was writing this section, it occurred to me it's only about a month since I threw out Sylvia's frozen lasagne, 18 months after the expiry date and I'm not even living in the same house!

The neighbours

Once my mother had left and I was on my own, I began to notice how we take for granted our ability to attend to so many day-to-day chores.

Taking out the rubbish is one of them. I'd told Jason, a neighbour, that

I was going into hospital and asked if he'd mind keeping an eye on the house. Then one day after I got home we were chatting on the street and I asked him if he'd mind wheeling the bin out for me. 'Not a problem,' he said. 'And don't be shy if you need anything else done.'

You just need to ask.

Housekeeping

You're not going to be able to lift piles of dry washing, let alone wet. Neither will you be hanging washing out on the line. Then there's changing the sheets on the bed — that's out! (I've never seen my bed so well made as when Beverly did her hospital corners.) Washing the floors and vacuuming — also out! Driving to the supermarket — no! Carrying bags of groceries — definitely not!

I think you're getting the picture. So when anyone asks if they can help, just say yes. You can let them know later what you need, when it becomes apparent to you. Clearly, this is not going to go on forever. In fact, I was surprised at how rapid my recovery was.

A good time to take a break away is when you're a little bit more mobile, but still off work. I went down to a beautiful beach house in the Coromandel to stay with two of my dearest friends, Mark and Diana. It was in their little boatshed, staring out at the water and listening to the soothing voice of Mercedes Sosa, that I started writing this book. Peaceful music is good for the soul; watching too much of what's going on in the world on the TV news can become agitating.

For my birthday that year, another Leo twin, 'My John', treated me to a trip to Bali, as he was in Australia when I was diagnosed. So John and Brett, two of my dearest gay boyfriends, and I took off to Bali. Fabulous. I also got to do some work on the book; I could actually see myself in floating outfits, being a writer in a South Pacific paradise.

Getting your strength back

A bit of gentle exercise is helpful in getting your upper-body strength back. One of my other girlfriends, Dinah (bless her little cottons), gifted me a voucher for 10 'Pink Pilates' sessions. The Breast Cancer Foundation in New Zealand subsidises payments, which is wonderful. Here's a shot of me doing Pilates. This fantastic photograph was taken by a very gifted young photographer, Damien Nikora.

Pilates is great for getting full movement back across your shoulders, rotating your arms, that sort of thing. Yoga is also excellent for the same purpose. I made it back to Marilyn's yoga class, which if you recall prompted me into having my mammogram all those pages ago.

There are a few things I don't find too comfortable and therefore don't do. Lying flat on my stomach is one of them, as I tend to feel like I'm lying on an inner tube. Those moments, however, do get the yoga class giggling, which I love. I guess I also feel that by being very open about my mastectomy, I allow people to feel relaxed and ask the odd question.

And I get to be there, laughing, joking and just getting on with life.

Moving right along

So here I am almost two years later — and my mother's here too, 20 years later, and Jennifer, after 11 years. We're still here and happy, like so many other women around the world. It didn't take me too long to get back to work; I started doing a bit of part-time psychology work within about five weeks.

I still had medical appointments for follow-up and dressing changes. In fact, the day my dressings were taken off, Wayne was able to pump up my saline/silicone tissue-expanding temporary implants. During the surgery, little things called portals are put in place to enable access to the implants via a large syringe for the purpose of the 'pump up'.

This is in no way painful. In fact, it was hilarious: you lie down on the bed flat-chested, and there in front of your eyes you grow boobs the size of Pamela Anderson's.

I had to have those deflated eventually, as I kept bumping into them trying to reverse the car. Last December (2010) I had my Rolls-Royce of the implant world put in — my very own teardrop silicones. That was another major piece of surgery, but I was up and about with virtually no pain after about two or three days and off on holiday.

I had become so used to not have any nipples I was actually a bit apprehensive about seeing the ones Wayne created during that last surgery. He used the ancient art of origami — yes, paper-folding art for nipple creation.

I guess I could have got some of these:

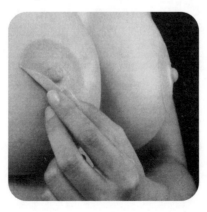

However, I didn't know they existed and, looking back, no nipples was the least of my worries. Amazing how adaptable we are. But they do look as if they could be quite good — a question of personal choice, I think.

My last visit was about a month ago now. I received a clearance, which was pretty fabulous! I also got a couple of shots of a very sophisticated version of a dermal filler, the stuff the cosmetic medicine industry uses to get rid of those deep wrinkles around your mouth. In fact, I did take the opportunity to suggest to Wayne that if there was any left in the vial… but no such luck.

Next year, I go in for my nipple tattooing session. This is where they tattoo on the pink circles that used to be there. You may still have yours, depending on where and how the surgery was performed. I've had a great deal of fun teasing my new boyfriend Murray about what I might like to get instead of just plain old fleshy pink circles.

Maybe a couple of frangipanis along these lines, so next time I'm in Bali I don't have to wear a top.

Just kidding! I can't imagine Murray, or my surgeon Wayne, finding this hugely entertaining.

Sitting at an intersection on the Breast Cancer Highway

I have thought long and hard about the role this book would play in your life. Initially, I was tempted to research further on chemotherapy, radiotherapy and Herceptin, and all the other possible treatment options. However, *Breast Support* is not a textbook, and I'm not equipped to comment in the way I'd like to do — and have done so far in this book — on treatments I haven't experienced.

So for you girls who need to continue on the highway, this is where we part. By now you will have your medical team established, and you will be able to continue discussing with them what comes next, just as I hope I have encouraged you to do. Although there will be similarities in our experiences, in some ways each woman's experience of breast cancer is unique, and your treatment will therefore be tailored to your requirements.

A wonderful woman friend of mine, Marilyn, was diagnosed and became a club member while I was convalescing at the beach. Well, sort of convalescing: I didn't mention earlier that while I was down there, I got an infected root canal and had to be rushed off to an emergency dentist — the infection was on the move toward my breast. Panic! Back to Wayne, huge doses of antibiotics, and by the skin of my teeth (literally and metaphorically), I didn't have to go back into hospital.

The moral of that story is to try to avoid possible sources of infection. Even where colds and flu viruses are concerned, keep away from anyone who may pass something on to you. If one of the children is sick, maybe they could stay with their grandparents, depending on what the problem is. In any case, check in with your family doctor.

Now, where was I? That's right — Marilyn. She and I sat down with a dictaphone one afternoon. It was the first time I'd seen her since her op, but she was looking fine. A testimonial to yoga, her flexibility and full arm movement came back very quickly. She was part-way through her chemotherapy, and we talked about the sophistication of the new treatments. There are pills for the nausea, and they can pinpoint to within a day when you can expect to lose your hair.

Also, I was made aware of the research into preventing hair loss during chemotherapy. I found a site which, rather than advertising products, deals with researching the options www.hairloss-research.org/UpdateChemo10-07.html

This site presents information on the following: the Cold Cap System, Thymuskin and Alopestatin (a new form of antibiotic). I would ask your oncologist about the evidence, and whether or not one of these treatment approaches would be suitable for you. I am unable to offer an opinion on this area as I didn't know they existed, and didn't end up having chemotherapy.

Although I've just said I'm not equipped to comment on other forms of treatment, I did get a couple of fabulous tips from Marilyn:

- Start getting your hair cut shorter and shorter before the significant hair loss starts. This way, when the time arrives, you won't be waking up next to great clumps of hair on your pillow (let's try to avoid any more emotional trauma than is already occurring). I would also like to add that the wigs these days are quite the fashion statement. So experiment, treat yourself, get a new look.

- Marilyn's other great suggestion was that you ask your male surgeon as he's going through the surgical options: 'Is that what you'd recommend if I was your wife/mother/sister?' With a female surgeon, I guess the question would go, ' … if you were making the decision for yourself?' There are many ways of asking for reassurance about the decisions that are being made — this is a whole new world. So don't hesitate. It's not intrusive; it's just people talking to each other.

Cheers for that, Marilyn.

23

A final word

Girls, you are going to be a different shape when all this is over. After surgery you will need a post-surgical bra, one that hooks up at the front, as you won't be reaching around your back for a while. Come to think of it, being able to fasten a bra at the front was great, even though the bra itself was totally unattractive.

Depending on what type of surgery you're having, you may be advised against purchasing bras with wire inserts. There are some lingerie stores that have a female staff member to assist with these early fittings. Again, I'm reminded of women in other parts of the world who don't have the opportunity to make these choices, and feel saddened. Then I remember the women, like Annabel, who are taking prosthetic bras to those less fortunate, and feel hopeful.

When I returned to the land of mainstream underwear, I remember feeling quite unattractive and for the first time really stared at my scars in a different way. I wanted to get out of the changing room and rush home to the comfort of the old unattractive surgical bra. I didn't, because my darling was there supporting me, and admiring the new — smaller — black and white lace I'd found (which I now wear with great satisfaction, and am back to not even noticing). This is an important part of your return to womanhood, femininity and your sensual being.

Well girls, that's it from me. If you are travelling further down the highway…

May the Pink Force be with you!

Gwendoline Smith, fellow member of the BCC

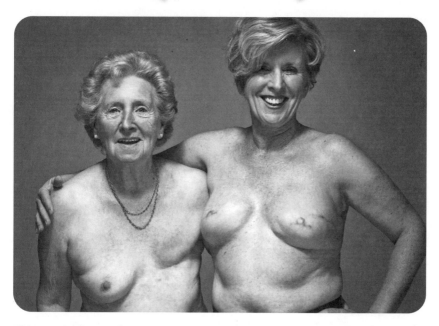

This portrait of my mother Bette and me is a favourite, not just because it shows the closeness between us, but also to illustrate, very powerfully, the genetics of breast cancer. (Not bad for an 81-one year old — that's Bette, not me.)

Epilogue

You first met Murray's hands on the front cover of this book. Here they are again. This image portrays hope. We met when all I had to show were scars and tissue expanders and we are still together to celebrate my silicone teardrops. (Thanks again to my gifted surgeon Wayne.)

So perhaps it's true that 'love is blind' or, more importantly, that 'breasts alone do not the woman make'.

Further reading

Books

R. Beliveau and D. Gingras, *Cooking with Foods that Fight Cancer*, Allen & Unwin 2008.

G. Butler & T. Hope, *Manage Your Mind*, Oxford University Press, 1995.

Edward De Bono, *Six Thinking Hats*, Penguin Books, 1985.

Susan Love, *Dr Susan Love's Breast Book*, fourth edition, Da Capo Press, 2005.

K. Meares & M. Freeston, *Overcoming Worry*, Constable & Robinson, 2008

Marc Silver, *Breast Cancer Husband*, Rodale, 2004.

Simon Singh and Edzard Ernst, *Trick or Treatment? Alternative medicine on trial*, Bantam, 2008.

Gwendoline Smith, *Depression Explained*, Exisle, 2005.

Dr Trevor Smith, in *Breast Care: Information and advice on all aspects of breast care*, The Breast Centre, 2008.

Websites

General

Breastcancer.org provides up-to-date information on breast cancer and seeks to help women with the disease: www.breastcancer.org

The National LGBT Cancer Network advocates for and seeks to improve the lives of lesbians, gay, bisexual and transgendered people: www.cancer-network.org

Men Against Breast Cancer (MABC) provides support and educates men on being effective caregivers to women with breast cancer: www.menagainstbreastcancer.org

The European CanCer Organisation (ECCO) shares information among oncology professionals and the general public: www.ecco-org.eu

CNSforum is the website of the Lundbeck Institute, which provides information for healthcare professionals in psychiatry and neurology: www.cnsforum.com

For information on hair loss: www.hairloss-research.org/UpdateChemo10-07.html

For more information on pharmaceutical companies:
http://en.wikipedia.org/wiki/List_of_pharmaceutical_companies

For more information on depression: www.webmd.com/depression

For further information on the work of the College of Radiology in Malaysia:
www.radiologymalaysia.org

Australia

The National Breast & Ovarian Cancer Centre (NBOCC) focuses on education:
http://www.nbocc.org.au

The National Breast Cancer Foundation (NBCF) raises funds for research:
http://www.nbcf.org.au

The McGrath Foundation raises funds and manages breast care nurses for women with the disease: http://www.mcgrathfoundation.com.au

Breast Cancer Network Australia (BCNA): http://www.bcna.org.au

New Zealand

The New Zealand Breast Cancer Foundation (NZBCF) is dedicated to fund-raising, education and support for women with breast cancer: www.nzbcf.org.nz

The Breast Cancer Research Trust (BCRT) raises funds and promotes research into the disease: www.breastcancercure.org.nz

The Breast Cancer Aotearoa Coalition (BCAC) provides information and support for women with breast cancer: www.breastcancer.org.nz

BreastScreen Aotearoa is a free national breast-screening programme for women aged 45-69: www.nsu.govt.nz

Photographer Damien Nikora's unique collection of portraits of women with breast cancer: www.portraitsofstrength.com

And finally, if you want to know more about me and my work:
www.thinkingexplained.com

Index

Also by Gwendoline Smith

DEPRESSION EXPLAINED

How you can help when someone you love is depressed?

Depression is a common disorder, but it is surrounded by ignorance, fear and prejudice. As a clinical psychologist, Gwendoline Smith has worked with many depressed people, but it wasn't until she suffered depression herself that she fully appreciated how these factors can prevent effective treatment. In *Depression Explained* she faces these issues and combines personal experience, clinical information and commonsense advice for all those who have to deal with depression, including childhood and adolescent depression, post-natal depression and depression in the elderly. She defines depression and explains how to recognise it, outlines the role of the psychiatrist, describes the various medications and therapies available, discusses the place of natural therapies, offers advice to the carer, and throughout the book includes the experiences of many families and the lessons they have to offer.

'Highly recommended — to comprehend what a depressed relative
may be experiencing and the type of help they require.'
Graham D. Burrows, Professor of Psychiatry,
University of Melbourne.

www.exislepublishing.com

Also from Exisle

THE INFERTILITY HANDBOOK

The complete resource for couples longing to have a baby

Angela I. Hutchins

This book is the essential reference for couples diagnosed with infertility. Here they will find options, answers and, above all, hope. Areas covered include: understanding your reproductive cycle, the causes of infertility in both men and women, assisted reproductive technologies (IVF and FET), complementary and alternative therapies, the emotional aspects of experiencing infertility, adoption and surrogacy, and legal considerations. Throughout, experts in various fields provide additional insight into the many aspects of infertility, while comprehensive reference and resource sections list organisations, books, websites and products that will assist couples on their journey towards parenthood.

Angela I. Hutchins experienced a miscarriage, failed IVF cycles and unsuccessful FET (frozen embryo transfer) procedures before traditional Chinese medicine proved to be her solution. She is now the mother of two children.

www.exislepublishing.com

For further information on this book:

www.breastsupport.com.au

www.breastsupport.co.nz